PSYCHIC SLEUTHS

PSYCHIC SLEUTHS

ESP AND SENSATIONAL CASES

EDITED BY JOE NICKELL

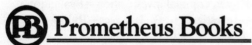

Prometheus Books
59 John Glenn Drive
Buffalo, New York 14228-2197

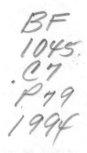

Published 1994 by Prometheus Books

98 97 96 95 94   5 4 3 2 1

Library of Congress Cataloging-in-Publication Data

Psychic sleuths : ESP and the sensational cases / edited by Joe Nickell.
    p.   cm.
    Includes bibliographical references and index.
    ISBN 0-87975-880-5
    1. Parapsychology in criminal investigation—Evaluation.
2. Parapsychology—Investigation. 3. Psychics—Rating of. I. Nickell, Joe.
BF1045.C7P79   1994
133.8—dc20   93-43069
                                                                   CIP

Printed in the United States of America on acid-free paper.

Contents

5

List of Contributors

James E. Alcock, Ph.D., is professor of psychology at Glendon College, York University, Toronto. A Fellow and member of the Executive Council of the Committee for the Scientific Investigation of Claims of the Paranormal, he is also author of *Parapsychology: Science or Magic?* (1981) and *Science and Supernature* (1990).

Michael R. Dennett is an investigative writer who lives in the Pacific Northwest not far from Seattle. He has written many articles for the *Skeptical Inquirer* (the journal of the Committee for the Scientific Investigation of Claims of the Paranormal), covering such topics as firewalking, Bigfoot, UFOs, and the Bermuda Triangle. His work has also appeared in *Frontiers of Science, Caveat Emptor,* and *Omni* magazines.

Kenneth L. Feder, Ph.D., is a professor of anthropology at Central Connecticut University. An archaeologist, researcher, and writer, he has authored a number of articles on pseudoscience and archaeology, including one in the *Skeptical Inquirer* that focused on the claims of self-proclaimed psychics that they can help discover and interpret ancient archaeological sites with their paranormal skills. His recent book is *Frauds, Myths, and Mysteries: Science and Pseudoscience in Archaeology* (1990).

Henry Gordon is a professional magician, journalist, author, lecturer, and broadcaster. Formerly of Montreal, he taught a course titled "An Objective Inquiry into Psychic Phenomena" at McGill University, and he also wrote feature articles for the *Montreal Star* and the *Montreal Gazette.* He subsequently moved to Toronto where he became a columnist for the *Toronto Sun* and later the *Toronto Sunday Star.* His books include

ExtraSensory Deception (1987, 1988), *It's Magic* (1988), *Channeling into the New Age* (1988), and *Henry Gordon's World of Magic* (1989).

Jim Lippard, a doctoral candidate in philosophy at the University of Arizona, founded the Phoenix Skeptics in 1986 and was its executive director until 1988. He was also the editor of *The Arizona Skeptic* from 1991-1993. He has written on paranormal and fringe science topics for various magazines and journals, including *The Arizona Skeptic, Creation/ Evolution, Skeptic,* and the *Journal of Scientific Exploration,* and he has been a regular contributor to electronic discussions of these topics on the Internet, Usenet, and GEnie.

Ward Lucas is a television anchorman and investigative reporter for KUSA-TV in Denver, Colorado. A member of the Professional Private Investigators Association of Colorado, he has reported on numerous "paranormal" subjects, including psychic detectives, Gypsy mind readers, and psychic confidence rings. Also a member of the Psychic Entertainers Association, over the past decade he has become a popular speaker on the national circuit, often lecturing on mentalism, psychic phenomena, and Gypsy Magick.

Joe Nickell, Ph.D., a former professional magician and investigator for an international detective agency, teaches technical writing at the University of Kentucky. An investigative writer whose articles have appeared in numerous magazines and journals, including *Law Enforcement Technology* and *The Journal of Police Science and Administration,* he is also author of several books featuring his investigations of paranormal claims. These include *Secrets of the Supernatural* (1988) and *Mysterious Realms* (1992), both written with forensic analyst John F. Fischer.

Michael Alan Park, Ph.D., is a professor of anthropology at Central Connecticut State University where he has been on the faculty since 1973 teaching courses in general, physical, and forensic anthropology, and human ecology. He is the author or co-author of three anthropology texts and of numerous technical and popular articles and essays, many of them concerning the nature and importance of science and scientific inquiry. He has also written an article for the *Skeptical Inquirer* on palmistry.

Stephen Peterson has a bachelor's degree in journalism from the University of Kentucky; is a former news editor of the *Georgetown News & Times,* Georgetown, Kentucky; and is currently a staff writer for the *Woodford Sun* in Versailles, Kentucky. He is also treasurer of the Kentucky Association of Science Educators and Skeptics (KASES) and co-editor of its quarterly newsletter, *KASES FILE.*

Gary P. Posner, M.D., an internist in Tampa, Florida, is founder of the Tampa Bay Skeptics and an investigator of paranormal claims, including those of psychic detectives. He is also the national coordinator of a "Skeptics Service" for his fellow members of Mensa and a Scientific and Technical Consultant to the Committee for the Scientific Investigation of Claims of the Paranormal.

Lee Roger Taylor, Jr., who received a Fulbright Scholarship in 1987, is an associate professor of English and Astronomy at Western Wyoming Community College, Rock Springs, Wyoming. In addition to his scholarly work, he also writes a weekly film and video review column for the *Casper Star Tribune,* Casper, Wyoming.

1

Introduction

Joe Nickell

Professional crime solvers achieve success the hard way: searching on hands and knees for trace evidence, interviewing countless witnesses, maintaining surveillance for days or weeks on end, conducting crime reconstructions and related experiments, searching records endlessly, and so on and on. But if a growing number of self-styled "psychic detectives" and their enthusiastic supporters are to be believed, there is a much easier approach.[1]

While the exact nature of the approach is difficult to characterize, it appears there are various alleged techniques that may be subsumed under the term " 'New Age' methods"—i.e., methods that supposedly have an occult or paranormal basis.[2]

In ancient times those who would seek the missing or attempt to uncover crime had recourse to oracles or to various other forms of divination. After "witching" or "dowsing" became popular in the sixteenth century, that form of divination was soon applied to detection. For example, in 1692, after the robbery-murder of a wine merchant and his wife, French dowser Jacques Aymar supposedly used his divining rod to track and identify a trio of culprits.[3]

Through the nineteenth century it was typical for "sensitive" persons to receive information regarding crimes in their dreams. For instance, in 1828, ten months after an English village girl, Maria Marten, supposedly ran off to get married but was subsequently not heard from, the girl's stepmother reputedly dreamed of her death and place of burial.[4]

11

Again, during the heyday of Spiritualism, some séance mediums claimed to solve crimes through contact with the spirit world. Such reportedly transpired in the case of a ten-year-old English schoolgirl named Mona Tinsley, who left school one afternoon in 1937 but never reached her home at Newark-on-Trent. Subsequently, a medium named Estelle Roberts claimed to have made communication with Mona, who was dead, and who—via the medium—led police first to the house of a suspect where she had been strangled and then to a nearby river where her body had been dumped.[5]

Today, both Bill Ward and Dorothy Allison claim they see visions as if they are on a television screen, but, interestingly enough, both also reportedly "combine astrology with their psychic efforts."[6] Some other psychic claimants use psychometry,[7] i.e., divination in which an object provides clues to its owner by occult means. Yet again, it is claimed that some psychic sleuths have used telepathy, or mind-reading, to solve such crimes as homicides.[8]

Self-proclaimed psychic Greta Alexander employs a hodge-podge of techniques. Like the late Dutch psychic Peter Hurkos, who reportedly received his psychic powers after a fall from a ladder,[9] Alexander claims to have gained the gift of second sight after allegedly being struck by lightning during the birth of her fifth child,[10] and now, just as Hurkos frequently had clairvoyant visions,[11] Alexander regularly tunes in to psychic "flashes."[12] She also claims she is aided by two spirit guides, named Raoul and Isaiah. As well, according to the *Chicago Tribune,* she owns an astrology and numerology chart business (computerized for her by an electronics buff), operates an "inspirational" 900-number message line, provides (as her "bread and butter") palm readings (charging $40 per half-hour session), and even sells fortune cookies.[13]

At face value, at least, this disparity of approach—especially given that some of the techniques used smack of sheer pseudoscience—does not inspire confidence in so-called "psychic" detection. Neither does the fact that under properly controlled test conditions the alleged psychics' powers invariably desert them.

For example, the seventeenth-century dowsing sleuth Aymar, mentioned earlier, was extensively tested in Paris with embarrassing results. Reports folklorist Andrew Lang: "He fell into every trap that was set for him; detected thieves who were innocent, failed to detect the guilty, and invented absurd excuses; alleging for example, that the [dowsing] rod would not indicate a murderer who had confessed, or who was drunk when he committed his crime."[14]

In 1991, British "police psychic" Nella Jones consented to tests of her alleged ability to "psychometrize" possible murder weapons. The tests were conducted for Granada Television by famed magician and psychic investigator James Randi. Alas, the results did not indicate that Ms. Jones possessed any psychic ability.[15]

More extensive, controlled experiments of the alleged abilities of psychics to divine evidence about crimes were reported in the *Journal of Police Science and Administration*.[16] Conducted by Martin Reiser, Director of Behavioral Services for the Los Angeles Police Department, and three colleagues, the study involved twelve alleged psychics examining evidence from each of four crimes—two that had been solved and two that remained unsolved. Each psychic made responses to each crime, supposedly based on his or her psychic impressions. Of the total number of responses produced, approximately half were discarded as unverifiable, and the rest were checked against known information about the crime, victims, and, for the solved crimes, the perpetrators. The result was that the alleged psychics scored no better than estimated chance levels, prompting the researchers to conclude "that the usefulness of psychics as an aid in criminal investigation has not been validated."[17] (See Appendix A.)

Psychic defenders Arthur Lyons and Marcello Truzzi, in their book *The Blue Sense: Psychic Detectives and Crime,* are critical of the Reiser study.[18] They are doubtful that "this group of alleged psychics is truly a representative sample from what may be the universe of genuine psychics," although the subjects were selected by an advocate of the police use of prominent psychics in the Los Angeles area. Reiser responded to several other criticisms made by Lyons and Truzzi by pointing out that the hypothesis being tested was much more specific than "can psychics produce accurate information about crimes?"[19]; rather, the study was designed to see whether psychics were able to reveal specified information about crimes, victims, and criminals that would enable the crimes to be solved.

Moreover, the Lyons and Truzzi criticisms were somewhat dampened by a follow-up study conducted by Nels Klyver and Martin Reiser, which essentially replicated the earlier study but which also added two control groups: one consisting of eleven college students, the other of twelve homicide detectives.[20] Although the difference between any of the three groups was not statistically significant, the psychics—while producing about ten times as much information as the students or detectives—actually provided fewer accurate statements than did the students. (See Appendix B.)

Undaunted, Lyons and Truzzi suggest "that proponents might argue that comparing these particular psychics to students and detectives and finding no differences may simply indicate that the students and detectives have more psychic ability than we usually assume."[21] Actually, if one adopts that argument, then the fact that psychics provided ten times as much information as students yet yielded fewer correct statements (in absolute number, not percentages), suggests that students are actually more psychic than psychics themselves![22] In any case, none of the subjects in the study produced the type of specific information—e.g., names, addresses, or license plate numbers—that would have been helpful in solving the crimes.

How, then, is it that psychics are widely perceived as helping police solve crimes? Defenders of psychics suggest that they really do have exotic "powers" but that these are not very amenable to the strictures of the laboratory, especially when the examiners may be skeptics who give off "negative vibrations"; neither should they be expected to turn their power on and off on command. Such objections frequently serve as excuses for the many psychics who adamantly refuse to undergo rigid testing. Actually, the psychics' own actions would often seem to belie the excuses: they often demonstrate a willingness to "read" multiple articles, maps, etc., frequently under the skeptical gaze of analytically minded detectives.

In contrast to the defenders of psychics, those skeptical of their alleged powers argue that frequently there are mundane explanations for the touted successes. Here are some of the possibilities.

First, some famous cases of successful psychic crime solving never actually transpired. For example, Peter Hurkos, "the man with the radar brain," claimed to have solved the case of a priest murdered in Amsterdam, his success supposedly earning him a letter of commendation from the pope. Skeptical investigators, however, soon learned that no such murder had ever taken place![23]

Second, psychics may use ordinary means of obtaining information which they then present as having been psychically obtained. Take Hurkos again, for instance. He was once arrested for impersonating an FBI agent, and in his possession were various guns and a collection of police gadgets— the type of paraphernalia, said one critic, that was "ideal equipment for putting up the front necessary to obtain information about police matters."[24]

Again, as with police, well-known psychics may be the beneficiaries of tips provided by informants. The psychic, anxious to maintain his or her reputation, may be less likely to admit receiving an anonymous telephone call than to pretend the information was the result of a clairvoyant "flash." Yet again, the media may be a source of information for an alert and determined "psychic."

And there are even more subtle methods of obtaining information. A shrewd psychic may glean clues from unwitting police officials by employing the clever technique of fortune-tellers called "cold reading." This is a procedure by which the psychic provides accurate information about a matter that is known to the client but apparently unknown to the alleged clairvoyant.[25] The psychic begins with whatever few facts may already be known, or with some vague generalizations. As she begins to narrate apparent psychic impressions, she watches the client's reactions. Eye movements, facial expressions, and other bodily mannerisms can provide the cues that tell the psychic whether to pursue that line of reasoning or abandon it. Sometimes a client may, unaware, be gently nodding his head, and may even blurt out valuable information. (In this case, after a suitable interval, the psychic reader usually feeds the information back to the client in such a way as to make the client think it has been mystically divined.) Or the client may be frankly smirking, promoting the alleged sensitive to make a 180-degree change in approach. States psychology professor Ray Hyman, a psychic investigator who is himself an expert practitioner of the art of cold reading: "Invariably, the client leaves the reader without realizing that everything he has been told is simply what he himself has unwittingly revealed to the reader."[26] Of course, cold reading does not necessarily have to be a conscious deception; all of us frequently take advantage of subtle cues without even being aware of the fact.

A third potential explanation for psychics' apparent successes is faulty recollection of what was actually said. The fallibility of memory is well known. People tend to remember what accords with their expectations and beliefs better than what conflicts with them, and as time passes their memories of what they observed can shift toward their preconceptions.[27] Therefore, one who is critical of psychic claims will be more likely to remember erroneous statements, while one who is favorably disposed will remember accurate statements.

Fourth is the fact that psychics tend to deal in vague generalities. Rather than provide concrete, specific, individual statements that can easily be tested, they tend to speak in stream-of-consciousness style, giving their impressions of an event. For example:

> I get a man, black. I hear screaming, screaming. I'm running up stairs and down. My head . . . someone bounces my head on the wall or floor. I see trees—a park? In the city, but green. Did this person live there? What does the number "2" mean? I get a bad, bloody taste in my mouth. The names "John" or "Joseph" or something like that. I am running on the street like a crazy. This is a *very* serious crime.[28]

Fifth, psychics frequently benefit from after-the-fact interpretations. For example, the statement, "I see water and the number seven," would be a safe offering in almost any case. After all the facts are in, it will be unusual if there is not some stream or body of water or water tower or other source that cannot somehow be associated with the case; perhaps the criminal once worked as a lifeguard at a swimming pool. As to the number seven, that can later be associated with a distance, the number of people in a search party, part of a license plate number, or any of countless other possible interpretations.

Sixth, there are social and psychological factors that may influence people to accept the accuracy of information—even though it may come from such dubious sources as palm readers or astrologers. While he was a college student, Ray Hyman (now a University of Oregon psychology professor) worked as a palm reader and was convinced of its accuracy until, at a friend's suggestion, he began giving palm readings which were the opposite of what he saw in his clients' palms. Yet his customers were just as convinced of his accuracy as before.[29] Similar experiments with astrological readings, in which false charts are substituted for real ones, show no effect on the perceived accuracy of a reading.[30]

Despite these valid alternate explanations and the failure of psychic detectives to succeed at scientific tests, the popular literature and news media generally take a less-than-skeptical look at the subject. Among the few book-length treatments is Fred Archer's *Crime and the Psychic World,* published in 1969 and billed as "the first book of its kind—an extraordinary collection of anecdotes in which a psychic has been instrumental in solving or preventing crime."[31] It is indeed a collection of anecdotes and—lacking documentation—is scarcely deserving of serious consideration.

The same may be said of Colin Wilson's *The Psychic Detectives* (1984),[32] which provides only a bibliography for documentation and contains much silliness. For example, glossing over Peter Hurkos' dubious claims and outright falsifications, but crediting his blow-on-the-head tale about acquiring psychic powers, Wilson states: "Yet Hurkos' success or failure in any particular case is hardly a matter of central importance. What makes him, from our point of view, one of the most significant figures in the history of psychical research is the accidental way he acquired his powers."[33]

In its treatment of Hurkos, as in many other respects, the book by Lyons and Truzzi, *The Blue Sense: Psychic Detectives and Crime* (1991), is a much more respectable effort.[34] Thoroughly documented, it goes far in trying to be fair to both sides in the controversy over the merits of psychic detection.

But the authors seem overly desirous of defending psychics and of promoting the concept of a "blue sense" (i.e., a "sixth sense," but renamed "after the common color of police uniforms"[35]). For example, they state:

Even a psychic scoundrel like Peter Hurkos, who frequently lied about his successes, sometimes seems to have produced hits that we find difficult to dismiss.[36]

Again, they say:

Discounting fabrications and confabulations by psychics and their biographers, media distortions, and cases of outright fraud, there remains a considerable body of documented cases in which psychic sleuths have scored impressive and seemingly inexplicable successes.[37]

Such a stance has provoked a response from psychologist Robert A. Baker, who reviewed the book for *Skeptical Inquirer,* the journal of the Committee for the Scientific Investigation of Claims of the Paranormal (CSICOP).[38] He writes:

It is very clear that the nation's psychic detectives have, at last, acquired their champions. Although at times they pose as pseudo-skeptics, Lyons and Truzzi are clearly out to convince all comers that "the blue sense" exists and that in certain heads at certain times it is valid.[39]

He continues:

In summing up their book Lyons and Truzzi modestly claim they never intended to supply any final answers but only to evaluate the arguments and point out directions for future research. Again, they make the point that the case for a "blue sense" remains not proved, but *nonproof* does not constitute *disproof.* Most psychologists would take exception to their next statement, that "intuition remains a largely mysterious and perhaps even transcendent capacity." Recent studies in cognitive science have shown clearly that a considerable amount of information processing, memorization, and learning takes place automatically at unconscious levels in the central nervous system. (See Jeremy Campbell, *The Improbable Machine,* Simon & Schuster, 1989.) What we call "intuition" is probably nothing more than the conscious mind's dim awareness that the unconscious has already solved the problem and is trying to provide the answer. We now know that we *know* much more than we think we know. When this information wells up from below and crosses the threshold of awareness we call it a "hunch" or an "intuition." It is in no way "a transcendent human capacity."[40]

To the authors' warning that it is a mistake to theorize before one has data, Dr. Baker replies: "An even greater error, however, is to base our theories on faulty, erroneous, or misleading data." He adds:

What we have for the most part are case reports from either the psy-chics themselves or those they have persuaded. Such data are unsound, soft, and flawed. Controlled laboratory studies have failed to support such a sense. In sum, there can be but one conclusion: the evidence for a "blue sense" is not one whit stronger or better than the evidence we had around the turn of the century for the ability of mediums to converse with the dead. Those who wish to believe it *will*, those who choose not to *won't*.[41]

And so the controversy continues. I have long felt the need for an in-depth, skeptical look at the phenomenon of psychic detection. Although years ago Paul Kurtz, chairman of CSICOP, had asked me to investigate psychic detectives, I had declined on the grounds that there were simply too many claimants and cases for one person to investigate effectively.

However, after the airing of a prime-time ABC television program, "Psychic Detectives"[42] (for which Truzzi was a consultant), CSICOP's Philip J. Klass was concerned about the impression left by the program. Despite token caveats, the program was essentially a sustained promotion of the idea that psychic detectives are directly responsible for solving numerous crimes. A subsequent editorial in *KASES File,* the journal of the Kentucky Association of Science Educators and Skeptics (KASES), concluded: "Prime time presentations like this do little to promote the cause of science over superstition."[43]

Finally, I decided that the best way to approach the subject of psychic detectives was to create a "task force" in which several experienced, tough-minded investigators were each assigned to a well-known psychic claimant (those featured on the TV program represented a starting point) and given a year to examine the claims. Their reports were to be written in chapter form, and the noted psychologist James E. Alcock, author of *Parapsychology: Science or Magic* (1981) and *Science and Supernature* (1990), agreed to write an afterword that assessed the findings. This book is the result.

It should be mentioned that while this task force was generally guided by the objectives of CSICOP, which urge that claims not be rejected on *a priori* grounds, but rather that they be examined objectively and carefully, it is not in fact a CSICOP project, and the views expressed do not constitute an endorsement by CSICOP. Moreover, since each investigator worked independently, the responsibility for any statements contained in the various reports is necessarily that of the individual authors and not that of CSICOP or the other authors, either singly or collectively.

With these stipulations in mind, we turn now to the investigative reports that delve into this controversial subject. It is hoped that the reader will find the reports illuminating as well as fascinating.

NOTES

1. I am grateful to Jim Lippard for his contributions to this introduction.

2. Deirdre Martin and Mark Levine, "Psychics & Law Enforcement Agencies," *Law Enforcement Technology* (September 1990): 58.

3. Colin Wilson, *The Psychic Detectives* (1984; reprint San Francisco: Mercury House, 1985), pp. 59–61. For a discussion of dowsing, see Joe Nickell with John F. Fischer, *Secrets of the Supernatural* (Buffalo, N.Y.: Prometheus Books, 1988), p. 90.

4. Fred Archer, *Crime and the Psychic World* (New York: William Morrow, 1969), pp. 47–49.

5. Ibid., pp. 25–27.

6. Arthur Lyons and Marcello Truzzi, *The Blue Sense: Psychic Detectives and Crime* (New York: The Mysterious Press, 1991), p. 67.

7. Ibid.

8. Archer, *Crime and the Psychic World,* pp. 36–46; Wilson, *The Psychic Detectives,* pp. 147–52.

9. Lyons and Truzzi, *The Blue Sense,* p. 108.

10. Ibid., p. 1.

11. Ibid., pp. 108–112.

12. Wes Smith, "Seeing Things," *Chicago Tribune* (June 9, 1991).

13. Ibid.

14. Andrew Lang, "The Divining Rod," *Cornhill Magazine* 47 (January 1883): 89; cited in Lyons and Truzzi, *The Blue Sense,* p. 17.

15. James Randi, *James Randi: Psychic Investigator* (London: Boxtree Limited, 1991), pp. 89–92.

16. Martin Reiser, Louise Ludwig, Susan Saxe, and Clare Wagner, "An Evaluation of the Use of Psychics in the Investigation of Major Crimes," *Journal of Police Science and Administration* 7, no. 1 (1979): 18–25; see Appendix A.

17. Ibid., 24.

18. Lyons and Truzzi, *The Blue Sense,* pp. 52–53.

19. Martin Reiser, personal communication to Jim Lippard, November 5, 1991.

20. Nels Klyver and Martin Reiser, "A Comparison of Psychics, Detectives, and Students in the Investigation of Major Crimes," in Martin Reiser, *Police Psychology: Collected Papers* (Los Angeles: Lehi Publishing Co., 1982), pp. 260–67; see Appendix B.

21. Lyons and Truzzi, *The Blue Sense,* p. 53.

22. I am indebted to Jim Lippard for this observation.

23. Joe Nickell, "Psychic Detective: Peter Hurkos," in *Wonder-workers! How They Perform the Impossible* (Buffalo, N.Y.: Prometheus Books, 1991), p. 89.

24. James Randi, *Film Flam!* (Buffalo, N.Y.: Prometheus Books, 1987), p. 272.

25. For a thorough discussion of cold reading (though not one specifical-

ly oriented to psychic detectives), see Ray Hyman, " 'Cold Reading' : How to Convince Strangers That You Know All about Them," *The Zetetic* (now *Skeptical Inquirer*) 1, no. 2 (Spring/Summer 1977): 18–37.

26. Hyman, " 'Cold Reading,' " p. 22.

27. See, for example, Elizabeth Loftus, *Eyewitness Testimony* (Cambridge, Mass.: Harvard University Press, 1979), pp. 36–51; Geoffrey Dean, "Does Astrology Need to Be True? Part 2: The Answer Is No," *Skeptical Inquirer* 11, no. 3 (Spring 1987): 259–62.

28. Reiser et al., "An Evaluation of the Use of Psychics," p. 19.

29. Hyman, " 'Cold Reading,' " p. 27.

30. Geoffrey Dean, "Does Astrology Need to Be True? Part 1: A Look at the Real Thing," *Skeptical Inquirer* 11, no. 2 (Winter 1986–87): 179–83.

31. Archer, *Crime and the Psychic World*, pp. 47–49.

32. Wilson, *The Psychic Detectives*, pp. 59–61; Nickell and Fischer, *Secrets of the Supernatural*, p. 90.

33. Wilson, *The Psychic Detectives*, p. 202.

34. Lyons and Truzzi, *The Blue Sense*, p. 67.

35. Ibid., p. 11.

36. Ibid., p. 135.

37. Ibid., p. 150.

38. Robert A. Baker, "Black Noses and Blue Nonsense," *Skeptical Inquirer* 16, no. 1 (Fall 1991): 67–71.

39. Ibid., p. 69.

40. Ibid., p. 70.

41. Ibid.

42. "Psychic Detectives," ABC television special, December 21, 1989.

43. "Private Dorks," *KASES File* (Winter/Spring 1990): 1.

2

"The Man with the Radar Brain":
Peter Hurkos

Henry Gordon

I am what parapsychologists refer to as a psychic. I am sensitive to people
and events that concern them, in much the same way as a plant is sensitive
to light, except that I respond immediately and directly to the thought
waves thrown off by the subconscious mind, whereas a plant responds
only gradually to the influence of light.[1]

He was born Pieter van der Hurk on May 21, 1911, in the Dutch town
of Dordrecht—and would eventually be known as Peter Hurkos, probably
one of the most famous of "psychic detectives," those human bloodhounds
who claim to reveal the whereabouts of victims of violent crime and the
perpetrators of those crimes. I do not use the term "bloodhounds" depre-
catingly. Hurkos himself made that comparison when he stated (in his
autobiographical book, *Psychic*) that, similar to a bloodhound, he could
not get "vibrations" from clothing that had been laundered or cleaned.

His father was a house painter in Holland, and Pieter followed in
his dad's footsteps. During World War II he was painting the exterior
of the Nazi barracks in The Hague when the accident occurred which
was to change his life. As Hurkos related it, he became a psychic, but
he did it the hard way: he fell 30 feet from a ladder onto his head. Shortly
after that he began to see the light. This event probably set an example,
at a later date, for another psychic who credited a car accident for her

21

conversion to new insights, and still another who was hit by lightning. It isn't easy to acquire these revelatory responses!

> When I shake hands with a stranger, I know all about him: his character, his private life, even the house in which he lives. For in simply touching his hand I receive a series of images like those thrown on a screen by a motion picture projector. . . . This phenomenon is known scientifically as psychometry, which Webster defines as a "divination of a fact concerning an object and its owner through contact with or proximity to the object."[2]

Hurkos also claimed to possess the full gamut of ESP gifts: telepathy, precognition, clairvoyance, etc. But it was in the field of psychometry that he became renowned.

In 1947, now an honest-to-goodness, card-carrying psychic sleuth, Hurkos took on his first case. A miner in Limburg, in the Netherlands, had been murdered. According to his autobiography, Hurkos, while holding the victim's coat, told police who committed the crime, and even helped locate the murder weapon. There is no known confirmation of the psychic's claim by the Limburg police department. The police did reveal, however, that the weapon was found in a different location than Hurkos pinpointed; also the man he had named had already been detained before Hurkos saw his image on his personal picture screen, and Hurkos was probably aware of that fact.

This bending of the truth seemed to set the stage for the balance of Hurkos' career—with his claiming to have solved a variety of cases, while later investigations revealed the falsity of these claims.

In 1950, when the theft of the Stone of Scone from Westminster Abbey was a major news story in the United Kingdom, and was carried by news wires around the world, Hurkos cashed in. He hurried to London, where he drew a map pinpointing the spot where the Stone would be recovered. Scotland Yard issued a statement:

> We are not seeing Mr. Hurkos. We did not ask him to come to London. We have not sought his assistance. He is only one of the telepathists, clairvoyants and water-diviners, etc. who have offered us information, all of which has been tested and sifted.[3]

Through routine investigation the police eventually found the Stone and returned it to its place in the Abbey. Hurkos' claim? "I knew the Stone was there . . . but I did not find the Stone." Yet he had accomplished his mission. The public was not aware of all the details, but they had been informed that Hurkos was involved, and that the Stone had been found. That, for many, was enough. His fame was beginning to spread.

If nothing else, Peter Hurkos was a master at garnering publicity. In 1952, while in Spain, he made the sensational statement that he visualized Hitler had been traveling through that country recently, disguised as a monk. "Hitler is alive," he told Spanish journalists, "I will stake my life and reputation on it." The wire services pounced on this world-shaking pronouncement and circulated it widely.

Andrija Puharich, neurologist and parapsychologist, brought Peter Hurkos to the United States in 1956. In 1957 he became involved in a case concerning the disappearance of the young daughter of the prominent businessman, William Henry Belk, from their estate in North Carolina. Hurkos claimed to have received a vision of the youngster lying in water near the Belk boathouse. And indeed, the body was found in that location.

It would seem that, having visited the estate and seen the boathouse, the psychic could have made a good logical guess, but such was his growing reputation that the mystical explanation was seen as the reason for this "hit." Oddly enough, after recovering from the trauma caused by his daughter's death, Belk was very upset by Hurkos' revelation. If he could see into the future, as the mystic always claimed, why had he not warned the family of the impending tragedy? Which of course brings up the oft-posed question: if a psychic can visualize what lies ahead, can he or she change the event that has been prophesied?[4]

In 1964 Peter Hurkos became involved in his most famous case, in which he claimed to have uncovered the identity of the notorious Boston Strangler. What he never revealed in his later publicity was that he had targeted the wrong man.

For more than a year a rapist-murderer had terrorized the Boston area. John S. Bottomly, assistant attorney general of Massachusetts, brought Hurkos in on the case. He put on a masterful performance for the officials involved with the case. Grasping some of the materials that had been used to strangle the victims, the seer asked for a map of the city of Boston. After suitable concentration he marked an area where he said the perpetrator would be located. He was later handed a letter which the police had received, and asked for his opinion of the letter writer. Once again came the concentration and intellectual nodding; then Hurkos made the flat statement that the writer was indeed the Boston Strangler.

After the man he had fingered was detained, and proven innocent, the real culprit was eventually arrested—without any psychic contributions. Albert DeSalvo confessed to the crimes and was proven guilty. This, as usual, did not deter Hurkos from claiming credit in his later publicity releases for helping to solve the case.

Although Hurkos claimed to have assisted the authorities on many occasions, he did actually have a run-in with the law shortly after the Strangler episode.

In February 1964 he was arrested in New York by the FBI and temporarily jailed.[5] It seems that in the previous December a gas station jockey in Wisconsin had noticed some firearms in Hurkos' car trunk while servicing the vehicle. Asked about this, Hurkos allegedly told the attendant that he was an FBI agent. This was reported, hence the eventual arrest. Fortunately for Hurkos, the judge who tried the case acquitted him.

Somewhat negatively, this generated more publicity for Hurkos, with the February 11, 1964, *New York Daily News* headlining: "Psychic Sleuth Failed to See FBI on His Trail."

It is really difficult to refute the claims of a so-called psychic even when they are patently false, unless one has the time and the opportunity to investigate these claims for their validity. This is particularly exasperating when these claims are made on a television talk show, and are often tacitly reported by the host of the program.

This has happened to me several times while participating on the panel of one of these shows. One particular case is quite revealing. It happened on a program called "The Brian Gazzard Show" in Montreal a few years ago. My "opponent" was Earl Curley, a well-known psychic from Ottawa, and we got into some rather heated arguments on the program.

Curley resented being called a psychic. Intuition, he said, was his bag. And he was not a prophet, he protested; he just forecast future events. In any case, one of the major claims he made on this show was that he had been called in by the FBI to help solve the multiple child murders in Atlanta, a news story that circled the globe. And furthermore, he stated that he had supplied the FBI with a composite drawing and a profile of the unknown killer, strongly implying that, as a result of his input, Wayne Williams (the convicted killer) was apprehended a few days later.

Obviously there was no way I could challenge this claim on that particular television program. Many thousands of viewers were no doubt impressed by Curley's statements. My only recourse would come at a later date, when I called the FBI Press Information Office in Washington. And what did they have to say? "Mr. Earl Curley contacted our Atlanta office (voluntarily) in 1980 and 1981. He sent in some kind of writeup of what he thought the subject would look like, and he sent in some kind of drawing. However, there was no impact on the case as a result of what he sent in." Case closed.

There was, to my mind, a rather humorous conclusion to this little episode. The previous three paragraphs were first published in my weekly column in the *Toronto Sunday Star*. They were later reproduced in my book, *ExtraSensory Deception*.[6] A short time after the book came on the market I received a telephone call from Ottawa. It was Earl Curley. He had just read my book. I half expected to receive a diatribe because of what I had written about him. Instead, he congratulated me on the book and said how pleased he was to see that I had written about him.

You might think I was surprised by this approach. But not really. You see, many times I have crossed swords with occultniks on TV shows, and after the program they would shake hands with me and suggest that we go on tour together and make a few bucks—a reminder of the old maxim: "I don't care what you write about me, just spell my name right."

When Peter Hurkos became a popular guest on television talk shows, the public was finally able to witness the renowned psychic in action, making predictions and demonstrating his special brand of psychometry. No doubt a great many viewers were suitably impressed, but not the informed skeptics, who found it easy to spot the dubious techniques he used to exploit the gullible.

His reputation, at one point in time, was so established in the public imagination, that I, a skeptic, was inclined to wonder if perhaps this man had some peculiar gift that could not be explained. I hasten to point out that this was long before I had gotten deep into research on these so-called psychics, research which revealed the lack of validity of their wild and unsubstantiated claims.

However, my illusions about Mr. Hurkos were completely shattered one far-ago evening when I was watching a Canadian television network program which featured him as the guest. This was my first direct exposure to some of his methods. He was handed a sealed, opaque envelope containing a photograph and asked if he could identify the picture without opening the envelope. He merely brushed the envelope with his fingers, concentrated deeply, spoke the usual mumbo-jumbo of the mystic, and proceeded to identify the photo. The host of the program then opened the envelope, took out the picture, and in hushed, semi-religious tones, declared that the psychic was indeed correct. Loud applause from the studio audience, and a self-satisfied look of accomplishment on Hurkos' face.

To put it bluntly, I was not impressed. If the psychic had revealed the envelope's contents without touching it, that would have been another matter. But to me, a professional magician who had been practicing "mentalism" for many years, Hurkos' method was as transparent as the envelope he was holding. (Just conceal a small sponge or piece of cloth soaked in alcohol or cleaning fluid in your hand, and brush it over a piece of paper. It will immediately render that paper temporarily transparent, revealing anything immediately behind it. Through miracles such as these are psychics born.)

In the early 1980s Hurkos seemed to have vanished from the scene. No longer did the media carry his name in association with various crime-busting events. The television talk shows seemed to be flourishing without his contributions. Where was Peter Hurkos? Becoming concerned, in one of my columns I offered to attempt to locate him, if only someone would supply me with a piece of his clothing. But my generous offer was completely ignored.

Then, one day in the fall of 1987, when the TV networks were going gung-ho featuring the stars of the New Age movement, there was Hurkos being showcased on the "Geraldo Rivera Show." With him on the panel were purveyor of the paranormal Keith Harary and Hurkos' old friend and booster Andrija Puharich. Hurkos' wife, billed as his assistant, sat beside him during the program.

A stack of personal articles belonging to members of the studio audience was piled up in front of the seer. At one point Hurkos picked up a lady's shoe and asked for the owner to identify herself. (I immediately wondered why he could not do that himself.) A young lady in the audience stood up. Hurkos stated several personal facts about her. Wrong. Then he got a "hit." "Go to a dentist; you have a toothache." The woman was stunned. "That's right, I do."

How could the great man have known this, unless he was really psychic? Here's a hint: a woman sitting next to the subject stood up and said, "It's true, my friend told me she had a toothache." Have you ever wondered how some psychics, mentalists, or faith healers seem to magically know certain facts about members of a studio or theater audience? Not too difficult. They usually have an assistant or two mixing with the audience before showtime, eavesdropping on casual conversations, picking up tidbits of information, later passing these morsels on to the performer. This is just one of many methods used to secure information.

Hurkos was later handed a sealed envelope containing a drawing made by an audience member. He handled it for a moment, but it was obvious to me he was not applying anything to the envelope's surface. He then announced it contained the drawing of a house. Wrong again: It was a sketch of a pair of lips. Hurkos was not even close.

But to this observer, miscalling the drawing was not the point. What followed was more revealing: The woman who had submitted the envelope said that, yes, she had originally sketched a house, but then had changed her mind and removed it. What does this tell us? One of the standard methods of "psychically" knowing the contents of a sealed envelope is to have an assistant secretly observe how the drawing is made in the first place. Obviously, in this case, the assistant did his/her job well, but didn't follow up on the switch. Oh, the hazards of being a psychic!

Later Dr. Puharich was introduced as being the father of the New Age movement—a tribute which he accepted with due modesty. He then made the startling announcement that Peter Hurkos was the chief psychic adviser to the U.S. Navy, and had been for 25 years—a statement that the U.S. Navy did not hasten to validate, and which was never proven.

> I can predict with almost perfect accuracy the outcome of sporting events. I have done this in tests on numerous occasions. Then why do I not use my gift for gambling? The reason is that I believe this gift was given to me by God to use for good, not to use to take advantage of people. I don't gamble, and I never shall. I prefer to use my powers honestly.[7]

This statement, in its reference as to why a psychic will not cash in on his or her insights to make big bucks at the gaming tables or the horse races, is quoted almost by rote by every psychic who is asked that natural question. Hurkos was, of course, no exception. When you consider the vast number of altruistic soothsayers who have permeated our society, it's a wonder this world is not a better place.

There are two attitudes that can be assumed regarding the activities of so-called psychic sleuths like Peter Hurkos. The first would be the humorous approach, showing the absurdity of the claims, and, of course, revealing the natural explanations for these claims.

My prime choice for the master of the really humorous approach would be my favorite iconoclast-philosopher, Woody Allen. In his book, *Without Feathers*,[8] he covers the subject of clairvoyance in typical Allenish style. He refers to the noted Greek psychic, Achille Londos, who realized he had strange powers at the age of ten, when he found that by concentrating he could make his father's false teeth jump out of his mouth. In 1964 he helped the police find the Dusseldorf Strangler, a fiend who always left a Baked Alaska on the chest of his victims. Just by sniffing a handkerchief he led police to the culprit, a handyman at a school for deaf turkeys, who confessed he was the strangler and asked if he could please have his handkerchief back.

With all deference to the humorous approach, I would submit that there's a troublesome and harmful side to the psychic sleuth situation. When police departments take the clairvoyants seriously, and follow up their "clues," they waste many valuable man-hours that could be used more efficiently—not to mention a good number of taxpayer dollars. And let's not forget the often harmful effects of all this on the families of victims, who have been fed false hopes by the boastings and predictions of the psychics.

> . . . My feelings are far more developed than those of the average man: so far developed, in fact, that after hundreds of hours of testing, scientific authorities have come to agree that the psychic gift I possess truly exists and is genuine.[9]

Who are these scientific authorities? Where were these tests undertaken? To my knowledge, no results of any tests of Peter Hurkos have ever been published in any scientific journal.

He claimed to have been tested in Antwerp, Belgium, by Dr. René Dellaert, a psychologist at the University of Louvain. Dellaert, he said, measured his brain waves with an electroencephalograph, which showed brain-pattern fluctuations when Hurkos distinguished between photographs of people who were dead and those who were still alive. There is no published record of these tests.[10]

The mystic also claimed to have been tested by J. B. Rhine, the father of ESP experimentation, at Duke University. Rhine issued a statement in answer to this claim: "Hurkos has not been investigated at the Duke laboratory and is not known to have given any such performances as those claimed in any university laboratory."[11] In any case, Rhine, while sympathetic to ESP, was still scientifically minded; therefore, he probably had little respect for any of Hurkos' claims. The psychic had for years been performing as a mentalist in theaters,[12] and Rhine would see no reason why a true possessor of ESP powers degrade himself in that manner.

In 1965 Hurkos' psychic abilities were tested by Professor Charles Tart, a noted parapsychologist who has experimented and written extensively on the subject. Tart found no evidence that his subject had any ESP capabilities. To be refuted by Charles Tart, who apparently has strong beliefs in the validity of ESP, was indeed a refutation of Hurkos' psychic claims.[13]

Dr. Puharich ran tests on Hurkos for several years. There is no way these tests can be evaluated because of the lack of scientifically graded data on them. Like every other so-called psychic detective before and after Peter Hurkos, these claims do not stand up to scrutiny.

His appearance on the "Geraldo Rivera Show" was the last I saw or heard of Peter Hurkos until the announcement of his death in 1988. And even there Hurkos got it wrong: many years ago he had predicted that he would die on November 17, 1961.

NOTES

1. Pieter van der Hurk and V. John Burggraf, *Psychic: The Story of Peter Hurkos* (New York: Bobbs Merrill, 1961), p. 5.

2. Ibid., p. 6.

3. Milbourne Christopher, *Mediums, Mystics & the Occult* (New York: Thomas Y. Crowell Company, 1975), p. 68.

4. Ibid.

5. Ibid., p. 73.

6. Henry Gordon, *ExtraSensory Deception* (Buffalo, N.Y.: Prometheus Books, 1987; Toronto: Macmillan of Canada, 1988), pp. 33, 34, 86, 87, 88.

7. Van der Hurk and Burggraf, *Psychic: The Story of Peter Hurkos*, pp. 202–203.

8. Woody Allen, *Without Feathers* (New York: Ballantine Books, 1972), p. 16.

9. Van der Hurk and Burggraf, *Psychic: The Story of Peter Hurkos*, p. 6.

10. Arthur Lyons and Marcello Truzzi, *The Blue Sense* (New York: The Mysterious Press, 1991), p. 115.

11. Ibid.

12. Christopher, *Mediums, Psychics & the Occult*, p. 69.

13. James Randi, *Flim-Flam!: The Truth about Unicorns, Parapsychology, and Other Delusions* (Buffalo, N.Y.: Prometheus Books, 1982), p. 273.

3

The Mozart of Psychics: Gerard Croiset

Stephen Peterson

If it were possible to validate the claims of "psychic detectives" strictly by the number of claims attributed to one individual, there would be no need for this chapter. Taken as a whole, few psychics of any kind, perhaps only Edgar Cayce, were as prolific and enduring as Gerard Croiset, the Dutch seer whose career as a psychic detective/healer spanned four and a half decades, until his death in 1980.

In the course of this remarkable career, Croiset is said to have performed literally thousands of paranormal feats: ". . . solved many of the century's most puzzling crimes, found scores of lost objects and hundreds of missing persons . . . performed hundreds of paranormal healings and occasionally demonstrated extraordinary powers of precognition by correctly foretelling future events."[1]

It is difficult not to compare Croiset's story with the lore of Sherlock Holmes, a fictional consulting detective called in when the police are at a loss in solving a particularly difficult crime. Croiset has ". . . helped the police of a dozen countries to the solution of murder, arson, theft and other crimes."[2] Though the address of No. 21 Willem de Zwygerlan Street, Utrecht, Holland, may lack the romance of Holmes's 221B Baker Street digs, it is difficult to see how Holmes, with his vast but normal powers, could outdo Croiset with his paranormal methods while hard on the heels of a baffling mystery.

With this kind of fat résumé, Croiset must surely pass our "Claim

Volume As Proof" standard with flying colors. But, of course, there is no threshold number of claims that can validate paranormal powers in Croiset or anyone else. The claims must stand or fall on the evidence.

THE MIRACLE DOCTOR

Born on March 10, 1909, in Laren, Holland, Croiset had a childhood that was by all accounts a troubled one. With an actor father who was also apparently something of a rake, and a mother who ultimately was unable to care for him and his brother, Croiset spent much of his childhood with several sets of foster parents, all of whom, it is said, ill-used him.[3]

In any case, Croiset supposedly manifested clairvoyant powers at an early age, though they did little to help him through a restless young adulthood. He went from job to job, and a grocery store he started in Eschede with funding from his in-laws failed. After this failure, a dejected Croiset began to consider the possibilities of his psychic powers, and soon began to build a local reputation as a healer and seer. People began to consult him about their problems, and soon he had a brisk psychic healing practice in Eschede which would eventually make him wealthy. But Croiset seldom took money for any "psychic detection" work.[4]

Had Croiset's career remained at this level, it would have resembled any of a huge number of similar stories of local seers making good. But a talk given by Professor Wilhelm H. C. Tenhaeff, a lecturer in parapsychology, at the University of Utrecht in December 1945, was to be a pivotal point in Croiset's—and ultimately Tenhaeff's—career.

One cannot discuss Croiset from this point on without also discussing Tenhaeff. From 1945 on, their lives are so intertwined that they may almost be viewed as a single phenomenon.

For Croiset's part, his powers were "scientifically" validated by Tenhaeff, who tested Croiset's abilities and in subsequent research papers endorsed Croiset's powers as genuine. He also kept "case histories" and became, for all intents and purposes, Croiset's "Watson."

Croiset attached himself to Tenhaeff in a student-mentor relationship which was to last about eight years. They died almost exactly a year apart: Croiset in 1980, Tenhaeff in 1981.

Tenhaeff can arguably be said to have benefitted from his association with Croiset because:

At this point, despite his reputation, Tenhaeff was only a free-lance lecturer at Utrecht State University (an unsalaried position) and had financially survived mainly from the small royalties from his books. In large part as a result of the widespread publicity he and Croiset attracted, in 1951 the 57-year-old parapsychologist was officially appointed a teacher at the university, and in 1958 he was given a full professorship. . . . Tenhaeff was also appointed director of the university's new Parapsychology Institute.[5]

Besides a boost in reputation and professional stature, Tenhaeff was rewarded in other ways. As it turns out, his salary at the university, albeit a small one, was paid not by the university itself but by the Dutch Society of Spiritual Healers, which Croiset headed.[6]

Norma Lee Browning, a journalist, tells an interesting and instructive tale of a personal visit to Croiset's manse in Utrecht. She describes him as "lean and muscular with reddish brown hair and flinty blue eyes" and apparently quite busy with a large number of patients on the premises. Seated in a room with about 50 other people—mostly women, she tells us—she watched the good "doctor" perform:

> Croiset did a toe-whirl and snapped his finger at the woman in a gesture that apparently meant "Who's next?" A plumpish, pale-faced woman came forward and squeezed into the chair [at the center of the room]. With his eyes closed and his head tilted upward, as though in prayer, Croiset began massaging the woman's temples, then her neck and shoulders, then her hips and thighs, and on down to her ankles.
>
> My lady interpreter leaned over and whispered, "Polio. Very bad. She's much better now."
>
> "What's the doctor's name again?" I asked, just to make sure.
>
> "Dr. Croiset," she whispered. "He's wonderful."
>
> By this time Croiset had the lady out of the chair and on her feet. He did a quick crescendo up her spine as though it were a piano keyboard, fingered a grand finale on her neck, gave her a little pat on the posterior, then waved his arm in an arc and snapped his fingers again. Next! He spent two minutes per patient.[7]

An example, perhaps, of the paternalistic zeitgeist of the age. Certainly, one can draw no conclusions as to the benefit of such ministrations, still less any powers Croiset may have possessed.

THE CHAIR EXPERIMENTS

As the validity of Croiset's claimed abilities rests on Tenhaeff's tests, it is on this work we will initially focus.

Working at times with Professor Hans Bender, a German parapsy-chological counterpart, Tenhaeff devised a set of protocols known as "chair experiments" which were designed to ". . . fit Croiset's gifts."[8]

These peculiar tests went like this: Croiset would consider empty numbered seats in a lecture hall and describe the people—and events in their lives—who would later occupy them. Croiset would have no way of knowing beforehand who would sit in a particular seat as the predicting would be done before the hall was booked. These impressions would be recorded and, later, the persons who eventually occupied the seats would be interviewed. Croiset's impressions would then be compared with the testimony of the occupant. When the two matched, it was considered a "hit," a valid instance of precognition.

Over the years, hundreds of similar tests were conducted all over Europe and have been cited by Croiset supporters as convincing evidence of Croiset's paranormal abilities.

But they have also been criticized as inadequately controlled and prone to error. Besides a number of complete test failures, there are tests whose success is called into question by the test protocols. In at least one instance, *participants in the experiment were given mimeograph copies of Croiset's impressions,* and were told, "Please read these carefully . . . if any of these points apply to you, state so in the space to the right of each point."[9] This was typical of the types of controls applied to the "chair experiments," whose designers were more troubled with the inability to keep Croiset's ". . . long-distance telepathy, psychokinesis or other form of extrasensory perception"[10] from influencing the test than with the probability that subjective validation might be behind the purported "hits."

This latter explanation seems to fit the facts better than does any appeal to supernormal abilities. The extant literature on "cold reading" techniques discussed in the introduction bears this out, as Croiset did nothing that could not be duplicated by an accomplished "mentalist" of today.

THE PSYCHIC DETECTIVE AT WORK

But even assuming Croiset did have paranormal abilities, just how good a "psychic detective" was he? Certainly, Croiset gained an international reputation as a seer, largely through Tenhaeff's tireless promotion, and through the writings of American journalist Jack Harrison Pollack, who wrote and published two highly favorable articles and, eventually, an authorized biography, *Croiset The Clairvoyant,* about the psychic detec-tive.[11] So authorized was the biography that Pollack ". . . thank[ed]

Tenhaeff for having 'indefatiguably double-checked the facts in my manuscript,' "[12] a task most biographers and journalists would surely take upon themselves and not leave to an interested party. But Pollack's chronicling methods aside, he recounts seventy cases in which Croiset displays his powers and leaves little doubt that Croiset is a genuine phenomenon.

From then on, the careers of Croiset and Tenhaeff became international in scope. Croiset met with and was tested by parapsychologists all over Europe, though he declined twice to be tested by Duke University's J. B. Rhine, and began consulting on a number of mysteries in various countries. Over the years that followed, Tenhaeff claimed to have amassed a vast, meticulously documented dossier on Croiset's cases, a case file that mysteriously failed to turn up following Tenhaeff's death.

Not being tied to normal methods of police work, Croiset had his own style of solving baffling mysteries. Rather than accumulate evidence on a particular case, Croiset rather ". . . prefer[red] to be given no more than the barest amount of information on the matter in hand, so that [he could] remain detached. Croiset even prefer[red] to be consulted by telephone to eliminate outside influences as much as possible."[13] It is here, in the lack of examination of the minutiae of the evidence, that Croiset departs from the Holmesian model—a critical distinction.

Archer (1969) recounts a typical Croiset case thus:

> . . . [T]he parents of a missing boy telephoned [Croiset] from a distance of 90 miles. The police had been trying to trace their son for two days without success.
>
> Croiset told the parents not to worry. The boy was alive and well; he had taken his bicycle and gone off in search of adventure. His idea was to reach the sea and get on a boat. He had taken the road to Valkenburg, Croiset thought, and was trying to enter Belgium. But he would be home again in a couple of days.
>
> Despite this assurance the parents were on the phone again next day. The boy was in Belgium, Croiset said, and would reach home on Tuesday.
>
> First thing Tuesday morning they made a third call. Croiset again assured them that their son would be home later in the day.
>
> Just an hour later the police called to tell them that their son had been found near Dinant in Belgium. He was home before nightfall, explaining that he had cycled to the Belgian coast by the route Croiset had given them.[14]

Archer also tells us of the case of a young woman who was attacked by a hammer-wielding assailant who struck her twice in the head. The woman somehow disarmed her attacker, who then fled. No less a person than the mayor of Wierden called Croiset into the case. Croiset told him the attacker was tall, dark, thirty to thirty-five years old with a deformed ear and wearing a ring with a blue stone. Croiset further elaborated that the man was not the owner of the hammer. The police indeed suspected a man of this description but unfortunately could not find sufficient evidence to arrest him. He was later arrested on another charge, and afterwards confessed to the attack.[15]

Given the detail Croiset apparently has at his command, these are powerfully convincing cases, if the reported facts are true. But such anecdotal cases are difficult or impossible to verify when faced with a body of work spanning four decades and, by one estimate, comprising over 20,000 cases.[16] This is especially true given that "the practical achievements of Gerard Croiset . . . share most of the features of 'spontaneous cases.' Such cases typically occur under uncontrolled conditions and are by their very nature unrepeatable. This means the only evidence we have usually consists of whatever witnesses are able to remember or care to report."[17]

EXAMINING THE EVIDENCE

Croiset's acclaim was by no means universal. In Holland especially, skeptics leveled telling criticisms at Croiset and his claims. Lyons and Truzzi (1991) write:

> In 1958, Dr. Filippus Brink published his critical study of several psychic detectives he investigated, one of whom was Croiset. Whereas Pollack and Tenhaeff described Croiset as never "fishing" for information from his clients, Brink reports he heard Croiset do little else. . . . And in 1960, a Dutch police journal carried an article by Utrecht's police commissioner that catalogued many of Croiset's psychic goof-ups, including a December 1951 case of a missing 14-year-old. Croiset told his parents the boy drowned. . . . The boy was found alive and well a few days later, hiding in a haystack.[18]

This is hardly a ringing endorsement from a grateful law enforcement community. But because these criticisms were virtually unknown outside of Holland—most were written in Dutch and not subsequently translated— they did not weigh against Croiset's ponderous international reputation.

Unsurprisingly, perhaps, the names of these critics appear nowhere in Pollack's biography.

Yet even writer Colin Wilson, certainly no skeptic about psychic phenomena, found his one close-up experience with Croiset somewhat troubling. In the course of a BBC interview, Croiset claimed to have solved a mysterious 1967 Glasgow, Scotland, murder to the extent that the victim's body had been found because of his efforts. When Wilson pointed out to Croiset that no body had in fact been discovered, Croiset vehemently disagreed. Wilson elaborates:

> What surprised me most was that Croiset insisted that he *had* solved the McAdam case, and that [the victim's] body had been found because of his instructions. I assured him that this was untrue, and he assured me . . . that I was wrong. I decided not to press the point.[19]

HOEBENS' CRITIQUE

The most devastating critique of Croiset in the more modern literature comes from the late Dutch investigative journalist Piet Hein Hoebens. Reviewing a number of Croiset's more celebrated cases, Hoebens uncovered some remarkable inconsistencies between what was claimed by Croiset and Tenhaeff and what actually happened, and has shown what can only be described as patently fraudulent claims made by the seer and his mentor.

One classic case Hoebens examines is one of a missing boy, ten-year-old Dirk Zwenne of Velsen. According to Pollack's version of the events, the boy disappeared on Saturday, August 29, 1953, while out playing. After his parents had called in the police to search for the boy, a search that lasted for two days and was unsuccessful, the following Monday (August 31) the boy's uncle contacted Croiset on the advice of the Haarlem police superintendent. The psychic immediately said that the boy had drowned. Pollack quotes Croiset:

> I see a small harbor, a small raft and a little sailboat. The boy is playing on the raft. He slipped and fell into the water. As he fell, his head struck the sailboat and he received an injury on the left side of his head. I am very sorry. There was a strong current in the harbor. The boy's body will be found in a few days in another small harbor which is connected to the first harbor.

Five days later, Pollack tells us, the boy's body did turn up, wound and all, in a harbor, and a sailboat and raft discovered in an adjoining harbor. By all appearances, Pollack's account gives Croiset a solid hit, every detail having been foreseen.

But Hoebens points out that Pollack's summary account in no way corresponds with a letter written by the uncle and published two years after the fact in *Tijdschrift voor Parapsychologie* (vol. 23, no. 1/2, 1955), a Dutch parapsychological journal. The short but critical dialogue between the uncle and Croiset is instructive:

Croiset: You must look near a gasholder.
Uncle: A gasholder?
Croiset: Yes. It might be a tank or a boiler or something like that. I see a road and a small ditch. I also see a small bridge and a small water. Do I speak to the boy's father?
Uncle: No, you are speaking to an uncle.
Croiset: All right, I can speak freely. The child has drowned. He is dead. I also see a jetty and a rowing boat or something like that. That's where the body must be.
Uncle: Could it be the North Sea canal?
Croiset: No, that is too broad. I don't see much water.
Uncle: Then where is it?
Croiset: I don't know Velsen, but you have to look near that gasholder or tank. It is to the right of it. To know for sure I ought to come to Velsen. Call me again if that's necessary.

From this firsthand account of the initial conversation between the uncle and Croiset, we find very little to correspond with Pollack's version of events. There is no mention of a sailboat, no mention of a raft, no head injury, and while there is mention of a jetty, a wall built to protect a harbor, there is no mention of a second harbor.

On the other hand, a gasholder (tank or boiler), a road, a ditch and a bridge were among Croiset's initial impressions, yet they do not appear in the Pollack version. And, as Hoebens says, the vague description of roads, ditches, rowboats, small bodies of water and bridges could apply to any number of locations in Holland.[20]

On Tuesday, police learned from one of the missing boy's friends that Dirk had mentioned finding a "nice raft." Later that day, in a phone conversation with the uncle, Croiset suddenly began getting impressions of a raft.

The police decided to drag a harbor on the North Sea canal (really a recess, Hoebens says) that day, though Croiset specifically had said the canal was out of the question, but they found nothing.

The next day, Wednesday, Croiset came personally to Velsen in the company of Tenhaeff at the request of the uncle. Hoebens writes:

> The psychic was taken to the small harbor, and there he started to get "strong emotions." He stated that the boy had been playing with his raft, had lost his balance, and had bumped his head on a hard object. . . . The clairvoyant was taken to a second small harbor that also forms part of the North Sea canal. *There, however, he felt "no emotions."* [Hoebens' italics][21]

Furthermore, Croiset said the body would not be found before Monday or Tuesday of the next week. But the next morning, Thursday, at the entrance to the second small harbor, where Croiset felt "no emotions," the boy's body was found in the canal. Though there were bruises on the boy's head, they were not in the location indicated by Croiset.

All in all, it is a case that, on a closer examination of the facts, does not hold together. It is certainly not the same set of events described by Pollock and, through him, Tenhaeff, yet it was presented by the professor as one of Croiset's strongest performances.

Time and again, Hoebens' inquiry turned up cases of questionable reporting in the Croiset literature. In at least one instance, Tenhaeff praises Croiset's solution to a murder case in which, it turns out, no such crime ever happened.[22]

In fact, Hoebens tells us that Dutch police officer Filippus Brink, who conducted a number of experiments on psychics (including Croiset) and made inquiries of various police agencies in Holland and elsewhere in the 1950s for a doctoral thesis, reported negative experimental findings and found no evidence whatsoever that psychic detectives had ever been of use to police investigations.

> The results of Brink's police department inquiries were hardly . . . comforting to the proponents of paranornal detection. With very few exceptions, all Dutch and foreign authorities stated that psychics had never been successful in furthering any police investigations. . . . The exceptions concerned highly ambiguous successes.
> Brink recently told me: I dare say that, barring an occasional lucky guess, no clairvoyant has ever been able to solve a police case by paranormal means in the Netherlands." My recent inquiries to a number of Dutch police departments suggest that little has changed since Brink's 1958 publication.

And so a pattern forms. Croiset's most celebrated cases begin to fall apart upon close scrutiny. An inquiry into the case of the young woman and her hammer-wielding assailant conducted by C. E. M. Hansel revealed that police denied that any assistance had come from Croiset.

While it is possible to attribute some or most of these discrepancies to sloppy reporting or a slight fudging of the facts, however innocent, it is more difficult to reconcile at least one case where, according to Hoebens, Tenhaeff is caught outright in a falsification of the facts.

The case, as written by Tenhaeff, involved a 1979 search for an arsonist who had been operating for months in the Woudrichem area and had so far not been apprehended. State Police Commander Eekhof reportedly called Croiset in to assist in the investigation. Shortly before Croiset's death, Tenhaeff visited Eekhof to follow up on the case and determine the extent to which Croiset had helped in the case.

> Tenhaeff wrote: "Everything Commander Eekhof told us was videotaped. The tapes are protocolled and the protocol was checked and signed by Mr. Eekhof."
> According to Tenhaeff, Croiset was consulted at a moment when all official attempts to identify the perpetrator had proven fruitless. Croiset described the arsonist. . . . Eekhof allegedly "was shocked" by the clairvoyant's statements, "for Croiset's description fitted a quartermaster in his own police group."[24]

The quartermaster was in fact arrested in 1980 and charged with the crimes.

To determine the veracity of Tenhaeff's version of events in the case, Hoebens contacted Eekhof and had him read Tenhaeff's report, which appeared in the German monthly *Esotera*. Eekhof said the report contained "outright falsehoods,"[25] among which we may count the following: Croiset never mentioned many of the "impressions" of the culprit described by Tenhaeff, and many that were mentioned were well off the mark; a person identified by Croiset in a photograph was not in fact the quartermaster; Eekhof was not shocked by Croiset's description because it did not particularly fit anyone he knew and did not lead him to suspect the quartermaster; and the consultation took place two years earlier than Tenhaeff had reported.[26]

Again, we have a large discrepancy between what Tenhaeff reports and how other principals in a case remember events. Before his death, Tenhaeff was given the opportunity by Hoebens to respond to the commander's charges, but refused comment.

CONCLUSION

Gerard Croiset's celebrated career as a paragnost is unique in the modern era in that no other psychic detective can quite match his reputation or the long period of success he enjoyed. Nor do others have the patronage of a university professor who labors tirelessly to enhance their reputations. Few have the luxury of a lucrative sideline to make their psychic detection efforts almost a philanthropic enterprise.

However, an extensive review of Croiset's work as a psychic detective reveals little evidence to support the claims made by Professor Tenhaeff in his behalf. Indeed, there is sufficient disagreement over what occurred during Croiset's participation in a number of psychic detection cases to cast doubt on the genuineness—or at least the effectiveness—of Croiset's purported powers.

Croiset has been called the Mozart of Psychic Detectives, and perhaps this is true, but there is enough dissonance in the songs of this psychic to make that description a questionable one.

NOTES

1. Arthur Lyons and Marcello Truzzi, *The Blue Sense* (New York: The Mysterious Press, 1991), p. 93.

2. Fred Archer, *Crime and the Psychic World* (New York: William Morrow and Company, 1969), p. 157.

3. Colin Wilson, *The Psychic Detectives* (San Francisco: Mercury House, 1985), p. 203.

4. Lyons and Truzzi, *The Blue Sense*, p. 95.

5. Ibid., p. 97.

6. W. Clement Stone and Norma Lee Browning, *The Other Side of the Mind* (New York: Paperback Library, 1967), p. 97.

7. Ibid., p. 98.

8. Martin Ebon, *Prophecy In Our Time* (New York: New American Library, 1968), p. 68.

9. Ibid., p. 73.

10. Ibid.

11. Lyons and Truzzi, *The Blue Sense*, p. 95.

12. Ibid., p. 96.

13. Archer, *Crime and the Psychic World*, p. 161.

14. Ibid., p. 162.

15. Ibid., p. 163.

16. Lyons and Truzzi, *The Blue Sense*, p. 97.

17. Piet Hein Hoebens, "Gerard Croiset: Investigation of the Mozart of 'Psychic Sleuths'—Part 1," *Skeptical Inquirer* 6, no. 1 (Fall 1981): 18.

18. Lyons and Truzzi, *The Blue Sense*, p. 97.

19. Wilson, *The Psychic Detectives*, p. 207.

20. Hoebens, "Gerard Croiset," p. 21.

21. Ibid.

22. Piet Hein Hoebens, "Croiset and Professor Tenhaeff: Discrepancies in Claims of Clairvoyance," *Skeptical Inquirer* 6, no. 2 (Winter 1981): 34.

23. Ibid.

24. Ibid., p. 35.

25. Ibid., p. 36.

26. Ibid.

4

America's Most Famous Psychic Sleuth: Dorothy Allison

Michael R. Dennett

Detective Richard Serafin vividly recalls the investigation of the murder of seven-year-old Kathy Hennessy. The child had been beaten, raped, and suffocated. "It was a tough case," he said, adding that "from the start we had several unusual suspects."[1] But while suspects were available, evidence was not. An intensive search for clues yielded nothing. The particularly brutal nature of the crime had infected the little community of Pemberton Township, New Jersey, with terror. Townspeople expected the authorities to make an arrest. Days passed without progress on the case. Then, looking for some way to find the murderer, one of Serafin's men, Detective Jim Bucs, suggested they try a psychic. Bucs showed him an article in *New Jersey's Finest,* a police magazine, about a Nutley, New Jersey, psychic.

Serafin later related that "his interest was piqued because the patrolman's magazine had written about a psychic detective."[2] He contacted the Nutley Police, and soon Dorothy Allison was on the case. Her first clue was that she saw "running water and brown uniforms."[3] In the first two weeks Allison worked with Serafin she provided him with information about the murder. Much of what she said concerned little details not released to the press, which he believed she could not have known.[4] She also had foretold that they would encounter a painter the first day she accompanied them on the investigation. As predicted, they ended the day in the courthouse where a worker was repairing the courtroom ceiling.

Thirty days into the investigation Serafin pressed Allison for more information about the murderer. She said that a suspect had "lots of little glass bottles in his basement. It's like a dark workshop . . . [and] he had problems with girls."[5] She added that "to get to Kathy's [house] he would have to drive a long distance. He doesn't live in New Jersey."[6] The descriptions fit a friend of the Hennessy family named Phil. Phil lived out of state, had lots of chemistry equipment in his basement, and was a bachelor. What's more, Phil was expected at the Hennessy home the day of the murder but never arrived. Serafin considered Phil a prime suspect but didn't move on him until Kathy's younger brother identified Phil as the assailant. (The brother's testimony was suspect due to his age, five, and because he gave conflicting stories.)

Based on Phil's less than perfect alibi, the little boy's statement, and Allison's matching description, Serafin decided to confront Phil.[7] Without sufficient evidence to make an arrest, the detective had to work cautiously. He asked Phil to meet him at the Hennessys' home. Phil agreed and arrived at the appointed time. Serafin and his partner got him to sit, and they explained his right to have an attorney present. The policemen then began asking questions. Phil was asked where he was the day of the murder. His reply was, "I stayed home; I couldn't get it together to drive here and back the same day."[8]

"Why didn't you let anyone know?"[9] Serafin's partner asked.

"I don't have to let anyone know," shot back Phil; "these people are my friends, I don't have to explain myself all the time."[10]

Serafin continued the interview, explaining that it was their job to check every possibility. Then, warming up the conversation, he challenged Phil. He told him that the Hennessys didn't think he could harm their child but that his own view was not clouded by friendship. "I think you could do it," he told the suspect.[11]

"Murder a kid? You BASTARDS ARE TOO MUCH,"[12] replied Phil.

The detectives asked more questions, turning the interview into an interrogation. Finally they dropped the bomb: They stated that Spanky, the younger brother, had fingered Phil as the assailant. Agitated, Phil managed to reply: "That little bastard doesn't know what he's talking about." Despite Phil's obvious anger and fear, he did not break down. He even agreed to a polygraph test.

Although the lie detector session proved nothing,[13] a few days later Phil was nevertheless off the hook: another man, David Geary, confessed to the murder of Kathy Hennessy! It should be mentioned that Geary resided in the general area, not out of state. Nor did he have a basement full of little glass bottles; he lived in a mobile home.

Individuals concerned that the use of "psychic detectives" in criminal cases is fraught with dangers might view the above case with considerable alarm. Dorothy Allison doesn't seem concerned, however. Much of the above narrative is based on Allison's autobiography.[14] The paradox of many psychic investigations is embodied in the Hennessy case: the same data as seen by different people lead them to separate conclusions.

Richard Serafin, now a captain with the Burlington County Prosecutors Office, is convinced that Allison has psychic abilities. "She was so accurate on so many details," Serafin explains; "I just can't see them as coincidence."[15]

Indeed, earlier in this case, according to her account, Allison had "seen" that the murderer would be forty or fifty and wear glasses and a wig. She further identified the murderer as living near a hangar for airships, being a highly decorated Navy man, and having a prior record of child molestation. She went on to say that his middle name was Harry, that he lived in a brown house, and that the house was only entered from a side door. She added that the house was on a dead end street and had a statue in the back yard. That same day a patrolman approached Serafin with a suspect in mind.

The patrolman's suspect had just been indicted for indecent conduct with minors, was in his late forties, and wore a toupee. The suspect's middle name was Harry, and he was a retired, decorated Navy man working at Lakehurst Naval Air Station. The Naval Air Station had a hangar for dirigibles. He lived in a brown house that was entered from a side door with a statue of Buddha in the back yard. He also had an airtight alibi for the day of the murder of the little girl.

So is the case of "Harry" a hit for Allison or a miss? She was specific and the suspect seemed a dead ringer for her description. Yet on the most important issue, the identity of the murderer, she had been dead wrong. And what if Harry had not had an alibi? Could he have been in jail while David Geary, the real killer, was free to murder another child? Yet if Allison is not sincere, why tell the story in so forthright a manner in her autobiography?[16]

Dorothy Allison, housewife, mother, and psychic detective, worked on her first case in December 1967. This first case involved finding the body of five-year-old Michael Kurscics. Since then, she says, she has worked on approximately four thousand cases. Her résumé lists the Patty Hearst, Robert F. Kennedy, and Atlanta child killings as "celebrated cases" she has worked on. She has been the subject of countless newspaper articles. A *partial* list of her national television appearances includes such shows as "Oprah Winfrey," "Donahue," "David Letterman," "Good Morning America," and "Unsolved Mysteries." Magazines such as *Newsweek, Time, People, Reader's Digest, Family Circle, True Detective, McCalls, Police Magazine,* and *Look* have all featured articles about her crime-solving activities. So great is her fame that in a recent book about psychic detectives the authors called her a "superstar psychic."[17]

Besides the impressive list of media recognition, Allison claims to have received "commendations from law enforcement agencies throughout the United States and Canada." All of these credentials pale in comparison to the ready testimony of police who have worked with her. Detective Bill Whildin of Fairfax County, Virginia, said that Allison "was very helpful, [and] truly concerned."[18] He said that he was sure she was sincere and cited the fact that she "came down from New Jersey for nothing. Other psychics," he said, "volunteered to help but they wanted some type of compensation."[19] He added that although Allison did not help find the body of Melissa Brannen or the murderer, Cable Hughes,[20] her predictions about the killer were astounding. Whildin remembered she had mentioned some twenty-one things related to the killer, eighteen of which were later confirmed. For example, she had said that the killer had pictures of horses in his house, that he was artistic, and that he walked with a limp.

I was impressed by the articulate and unquestionably honest testimony of Captain Serafin. Recounting the Hennessy case he assured me that Allison had made many accurate predictions. Yet his account differed slightly from the account in Allison's autobiography. Serafin remembered that Allison had said that the murderer's name would "sound like a car part." The killer's name, already mentioned, was David Geary. Serafin saw the "gear" in Geary as a hit. However, in her book Allison says that she identified the murderer's name as "David."

Because her strongest support comes from the recollections of police about her predictions, discrepancies like the one noted above pose a problem for the researcher. Human recollections, even over short periods, are often very subjective. A particularly pronounced example of blurred memory shows in the testimony of Detective Angelo Ferrara. On two separate accounts the Nutley detective was quoted as saying that Allison had led them to the location of a missing boy. He said Allison told them to dig up a drainage pipe, which they did. He then recounted that he had been present and that he had seen them find the Kurscics' boy, as Allison had predicted. True enough, Allison had identified a drainage pipe and a general location to dig, and the Nutley police did respond by digging up the pipe. (Allison had also predicted that they would find a bend in the culvert when all they could find was a break in the pipe.) Yet if Ferrara had been present on that day one would think he would have remembered that no body was found. Kurscics' body was not found until some time later, and not by Allison or the police. A man looking for a spot to bury a dead cat found the boy's body in a small pond along the river.[21]

How then can Allison and Jacobson write that "Finding Michael Kurscics changed Dorothy's life forever"? Allison's claim rests on the assertion that she had "seen" that the body would be found on February 7, that the boy was wearing a green snowsuit, and that his shoes were on the wrong feet. Allison reports a hit on these three issues, but by the account in her book her clues did not lead to the body. In other cases, too, Allison claims to have "found" a body or "solved" a case, but there are few facts to support these assertions. When I talked to Captain Serafin he told me that although he found her predictions accurate, "they were difficult to verify when initially given. The accuracy usually could not be verified until the investigation had come to a conclusion." Explaining, he told me that the clues she gave were only ascertainable after the fact.[22]

In several telephone interviews with Allison I asked for evidence that she had ever found a body or solved a case. Both Allison and her publicity manager, Tom Colamaria, told me that they had "hundreds" of letters from police departments confirming her successes. I asked for twenty of the most recent cases and was promised that they would be made available. At one point Colamaria even asked if twenty would be enough. When, after repeated requests, I finally received copies of the letters of commendation, there were not twenty but three.[23]

Only one of the three letters said that Allison's clues "contributed to solving" the crime. That was a letter from Chief of Police Harold N. Gingrich, Waynesboro, Pennsylvania, concerning the case of Debora Sue Kline. The Allison-Jacobson account of the case clearly shows that none of Allison's clues led to the arrest of the two assailants. (They were both in jail already but not for the Kline killing.) Nor did her clues lead to the body. Richard Dodson confessed to raping Kline, said his partner murdered her, and took police to the spot where they dumped the remains. The Allison-Jacobson account says that Allison picked Dodson's picture from several suspects, and that Dodson was apprised of the fact that a psychic had picked him as the murderer. The account implies that Dodson may have confessed out of fear of Allison's abilities.[24]

A second letter only thanks Allison for her efforts and time "attempting to uncover information which may be valuable." The third letter, from Detective Sergeant Ralph D. Courson, confirms the accuracy of her predictions. In his short letter Courson says, "all of the information Mrs. Allison provided me came true in one way or another." Local newspaper reports also seem to confirm the accuracy of her predictions. One newspaper even headlined, "Psychic Pinpoints Tot's Body." According to reporter Wanda Briggs, Allison told police to "look where they see doubles, like numbers or buildings." She also said "I see cars and parking lots," adding that the "numbers 7 and 8 were prominent." She also mentions "April."

On Wednesday, March 21, 1979, John Waibel found the body of Ryan Adams. Waibel said, "I read the story in *The Herald* and it was like Mrs. Allison was trying to tell me something. I was familiar with the area around Sacajawea [a park next to the Columbia River] and I remembered the double towers and bridges."[25] The paper went on to say the body was located "on the beach near Sacajawea Park almost directly in front of twin electrical transmission towers. Nearby in the Columbia River a navigation buoy was marked 44. Across the river is Two Rivers Park. . . . In plain sight just a short distance from where the body was found is Sacajawea's parking lot." Continuing on, reporter Briggs tells us the numbers 7 and 8 were found at the base of one of the nearby transmission towers.

The above account, although confirmed by both newspaper and police, is not as impressive as it seems. Examined carefully, the predictions are not as specific as they sound. In an earlier edition the newspaper reports that Allison "said the letter M was important" and that "a judge's house or a judge will live nearby." These were apparently misses, because they are not mentiomed again.[26] It was known from a confession that the mother of the children had thrown the two boys, Ryan and his brother Christopher, from a bridge over the Columbia River. So Allison's statement in the earlier edition, "I see water splashing over rocks," is not surprising. Nor is it surprising that the bodies would be found downriver from the bridge. Allison's clue about doubles was "like numbers or buildings," so Waibel's interpretation that the twin electrical transmission towers were the "doubles" does not fit. Realistically it appears that Waibel picked a downstream spot not in exact accord with the psychic's clues. The buoy marked 44 was identified only after the body was found.

Even Briggs tells us that the clues were not precise. She writes: "At first the prediction was interpreted to mean the body would be found on April 7-8. But painted in black and white on the concrete base of a nearby transmission tower was 78."[27] In the earlier edition Allison's prediction reported: "If he's not found before, he will be by April 7-8." What about Ryan's brother? Allison had said to look for both boys "near a bridge." However, the second boy was found on April 1, eleven days later, by twins fishing in the river—not near the bridge.

The big problem with this case is the action, or the lack of action, by the police. If Allison's predictions were specific, why did the police not act? She had worked just the month before with this sheriff's office, supposedly supplying similar predictions with similar accuracy on the previous case. Therefore, the lack of police response strongly suggests that the clues were not specific enough to enable them to locate the bodies.

I had originally requested from Allison letters from cases not more than six years old. Recent letters, I assumed, would be easier to verify. I also hoped to clarify any ambiguous statements by talking directly with the police who wrote them. The three letters supplied were from the period 1975–1981.

Fortunately I had three newspaper clippings from three cases that Allison had worked on in the past few years. One, the Melissa Brannen case, as already mentioned, was not an instance where Allison's clues helped solve the case or find the body. A second case, that of Lisa Anne O'Boyle, also proved no support for Allison's psychic powers. The assistant prosecutor for Morris County, New Jersey, Tom Critchley, said that the body was discovered by a hunter and the killer was apprehended "without help from any psychic." I read Allison's prediction from a newspaper article to Critchley, saying that O'Boyle's body would be found on Tuesday or Wednesday, October 6–7. He said the body was not found until Monday, October 12, 1987.

The third clipping involved the disappearance of Cassandia Hailey and Richard Keith Call in 1988. This case yielded no testimony to support the claim that Allison helped find the bodies or solve the case. Captain Ron Montgomery of the York County Sheriff's Department talked to me about the case.[28] He contacted Allison after seeing her on the television program "Unsolved Mysteries." Montgomery said he was "impressed with her as a person." He explained that they had talked on the phone a couple of times, but her information had not helped resolve the case. He told me that *all* her information was general. "Very general," he said, relating that she had said "the name of a street would have something to do with water." She did not specify how the street would have some connection with the case. Explaining, he said, "There are probably twenty-five to thirty streets that fit that description in York."[29]

No case identified in the many magazine articles, newspaper clippings or in her book provides independent, unambiguous verification that Allison's participation has resulted in her finding a body. Captain Montgomery told me that when he had talked with other police officers they also said that he would have to fit her data into the case after the facts were ascertained.

Not all of Allison's predictions are vague, however. On at least two occasions she has provided police with reasonably specific search locations.

In the first instance, already mentioned, the Nutley police wasted an entire afternoon digging up a drainage ditch in a park. In another case she identified the flooded basement in an abandoned building as the location of a missing boy.[30] The police had the fire department pump out the water but no body was found. Two weeks later the boy's remains were located across town.[31]

Allison claims that she is devoted to helping find lost kids and to apprehending their murderers. None of the people I contacted, including some critical of her activities, doubts her sincerity in wanting to help in the recovery of lost children. Nor do any think she is not generous in the devotion of her time. When the body of little Michael Kurscics was finally recovered and the family could not afford a funeral, Allison covered the expense. Good though her intentions might be, can such activity as already noted be considered prudent use of police resources?

I talked with Marilyn Green, a private investigator who specializes in finding lost and missing people. Green has been instrumental in finding over two hundred persons,[32] and she has made every effort to improve her techniques. She examined the claims that psychics, including Allison, can help find people. Green told me she found no evidence that "a psychic had helped find a missing person."[33]

Despite the lack of utility of her predictions, many see Allison's "hits" as significant. Again her record in this area does not stand up under close examination on those cases where data are abundant and from more than one source. In four thousand cases chance should have given her some astounding scores. This is especially so since Allison seems to provide an abundance of pronouncements. She apparently has made little attempt to document her predictions before a case is solved, relying instead on verification by participants after the search is concluded. She further maintains that her clues are independent of time. That is, if she "sees horses, horses along a trail," the clue is not time-specific. The horses could be in the future or the present or in the past. At the time Allison made the "horses" prediction quoted above, she was trying to help find Susan Jacobson. Later, after a thirteen-year-old boy found Jacobson's body, she was buried at St. Peter's Cemetery on Staten Island. Accordingly, Allison called her prediction correct because Susan's grave was "located not two hundred feet behind what had once been stables. . . . The tract of ground now used for burial had once been a bridle path."[34]

This is not Allison's only "out." According to Detective Lubertazzi, the psychic's longtime sidekick, her clues have to be studied. He explains: "Dorothy sees things, but she doesn't know geographical locations. Sometimes she'll say you have to go south to find a body. If we do, and we don't find anything, I'll tell the police department to go north. It's kind of hard to explain."[35]

Allison gets help along the way. Many if not most of the police she works with do not judge too quickly. Perhaps typical is the following quote from a police officer. Explaining that she contributed nothing to his investigation, he added: "She just seemed like a nice Italian lady, nicer than a lot of creeps I have to deal with. I can't say she helped, but maybe I didn't read her right."[36] One letter in the packet Allison's manager sent was from the newly appointed (1977) Chief of Police for Waynesboro, Pennsylvania. His letter, in response to a newspaper article, shows how far from being skeptical are some police. His entire letter, exactly as written, follows:

Dear Mrs. Allison:

When I was appointed to the position of Chief of Police in Waynesboro, the newspaper printed a story about your being in the area in reference to the Debbie Kline murder and a prediction that you made in reference to the new chief.

As I am a firm believer in the psychic world and am unfortunately not as familiar as I would like to be in this area, I did want to express my regard for you and your powers. Some day I would like to become more involved and possibly develop some ability.

As you predicted, I did teach, at the Philadelphia Police Academy, and at numerous community colleges, [sic] you mentioned that I maybe [sic] associated with the FBI. I was associated with them in that I received training at their school during that summer and the prior summer.

I read about your latest assistance to the police and would like to thank you as a police officer for your help in police work. enclosed [sic] is a copy of my natal horoscope [Allison uses astrology to complement her psychic powers], is it appropriate for a police officer?

Best wishes to you and if we have the opportunity to meet it will [be] my pleasure and honor.

Signed, Jude T. Walsh, Chief of Police.

Some of Allison's most spectacular "hits" have been numbers or dates, particularly the date a body would be found. We are told that she correctly predicted that Michael Kurscics would be found on February 7. We are not told how that date was given. In the Susan Jacobson case Allison "saw" the numbers 2562 and 405–408. Allison claims these as hits because Susan was born on 2-5-62 and that her time of birth was 4:05. In another case her numbers were the birth dates of the last two people to see a murder victim before that victim's death. In one case she saw the number 166. When the body was discovered it confirmed that the victim had fallen from a bridge. The body was not found near the bridge but next to the bridge where he had fallen was a tugboat with the number 166 painted on its side. Another number/date prediction of hers was that "if the plane was not found by July 15, it would be found on December 9th." In the Doreen Carlucci case Allison said "the number nine is important."[37] The Carlucci body was found near Route 9. For the Kline family, desperate to locate their daughter Debbie, Allison provided four dates: October 2 and 11, December 3, and April 4.[38] According to the Allison-Jacobson account, "The dates Dorothy had offered had surprised the family. Three of the dates were family wedding days, one of which Debbie had been planning to attend in October. The fourth date was important only to Debbie: in her journal it was the day highlighted for her first date with her boyfriend."[39] Detective Whildin said Allison gave him four numbers but they "did not fit."

In review, the numbers Allison "sees" can be interpreted in many ways. In the Jacobson case the numbers 405–408 were viewed to be a hit because the girl was born at 4:05. To make this a fit the other half of the number, 408, had to be jettisoned. When the April 7–8 prediction did not fit in the Ryan Adams case the 7–8 was separated from the month. Her numbers seem conveniently malleable. In other cases noted, the numbers were interpreted to be birthdays, wedding days, a date with a boyfriend (not related to the murder), a road number, and the number on a tugboat. The wide scope of how the numbers are interpreted looks suspiciously like painting the target on the tree after the arrow has been shot.

When I talked to Allison I asked her to name the most successful case she had worked on since her autobiography. I was surprised when she named the Atlanta child murders (1980).[40] I asked if she had not stumbled in Atlanta. She assured me she had been successful, telling me she had given the Atlanta police the killer's name. Others have not characterized her performance in the Georgia city in so positive a light. *Science* magazine, writing of her work in Atlanta, said, "City officials are reticent about Allison's visit, perhaps because they are awakening to a cold feeling that they were gulled."[41] According to the article, Allison's prophecy "that a major break in the case would occur on 12 November also proved wrong." *Science* concluded, "In Atlanta on her biggest consulting job so far, she proved a flop."[42]

A few weeks after I talked with her, Allison appeared on the "Ron Reagan Show" (Fox Broadcasting).[43] When the Atlanta case came up Allison said, "I gave the name Williams." (The 1990 Atlanta phone book lists 6,913 phone numbers to individuals or families with the last name of Williams.) Professor Ray Hyman, also a guest on the show, produced a letter from the Atlanta police saying that she had not helped them. Hyman explained that the Atlanta "Chief of Police said she did not name Williams but someone else." Allison shot back that she had a "tape" of her giving the name to the police. Hyman asked another guest on the show, author Arthur Lyons, if he could comment on the Atlanta case. Lyons, who had researched the case, confirmed the Chief's comment about Allison's not giving them the killer's name. He then added that "another [Atlanta police] investigator said she might have named Williams but she named everyone else in the phone book."[44]

Other newspaper and magazine reports, following her trip to Atlanta, confirm her pronouncements to have been many and varied. According to one newspaper story, "She gave two names."[45] Quoting Allison, the article continues: "I gave them specific descriptions. I told the police specific areas in which to track these people down. And I told them what areas to watch carefully because these people are getting ready to kill again." According to still another article, Atlanta Police Sergeant Gundlach said Allison "had given them some 42 possible names for the murderer(s) but not the correct one."[46] By Allison's own criteria for success, police endorsement, she failed on the Atlanta case.

Atlanta has not been the only failure for Allison. Chief of Police Curtis McClung, of Columbus, Georgia, was not impressed by the psychic. According to McClung, he spent two days with Allison but drew a blank. "She said a whole lot of things, a whole lot of opinions, partial information and descriptions. She said a lot. If you say enough, there's got to be something that fits."[47]

Woodbridge, New Jersey, Detective Tony Barcelona echoes McClung. "I believe in good police work. Good criminology will eventually pay off. The information she gave me didn't lead anywhere. It was very general."[48] Allison claimed credit for "pinpointing" the location of the bodies in the Woodbridge case. The bodies were found by a bicyclist. The bicyclist was not working from Allison's clues nor were the police. Said Barcelona, "I couldn't make any sense out of what she said."[49]

Another major goof by Allison was her series of pronouncements about missing Brian Timmerman. According to Lyons and Truzzi, Allison "told investigators that the boy [missing for over a month] had been murdered, that she had seen him suffocating. Her clues were a church, airplanes, construction equipment, a lot of digging, a yellow brick house, gold, and some kind of camp or park."[50] The police tried to follow up on these clues but were unsuccessful. A school guidance counselor eventually found Timmerman, "not dead, but in front of New York's Pan Am Building, peddling religious tracts. He had been living with the Moonies."[51]

According to an unpublished manuscript described by Lyons and Truzzi, "Allison explained away her error by saying she had been confused because the boy was spiritually dead. Her airplane clue she rated as a hit because the Pan Am Building then had a heliport on the roof."[52] On the Ron Reagan show Lyons singled this case out as a particularly "bad blunder." The host of the show tried to soften Lyons' criticism by saying "Well, people make mistakes." Lyons shot back, "To tell someone their child is dead is not a good mistake to make!"

Allison, quiet during the beginning of this exchange, now spoke up, saying, "I have never told a mother that in my life!"

Perhaps Allison did not tell the mother directly, but she must have realized the potential for such information to find its way back to the parents. In 1976 Allison worked on the case of a missing Palm Springs teenager. She informed Imperial County, California, officials that the missing boy was dead. Captain Bill Valkenberg of the Palm Springs Police told me the boy's parents knew of Allison's pronouncement. He did not know if Allison told the parents herself, but he believed that they did not learn of the vision from the police. Allison had also "seen" that the boy's body was "under water" in an area generally fitting the description of the Salton Sea. A deputy with the county sheriff's office, believing in Allison's abilities, began organizing a search. However, Captain Valkenberg did not think a search effort was merited and squelched the operation. Two months later the boy was arrested attempting to burglarize a house.

I found this episode difficult to reconcile with Allison's statement on the "Ron Reagan Show." Troubling, too, was the nature of her prediction. When a child is missing for more than a few days the chance he or she is dead is very high. Similarly a guess that the body would be found "under water" would seem a strong possibility. Most difficult to understand is Allison's claimed ability to identify very specific aspects of a crime, like the murderer's first or last name, although she is unable to accurately ascertain if the subject is alive or dead.[53]

In the March 1980 issue of *Family Circle* magazine Allison told the readers about one of her recent cases. Receiving a call about a missing boy, she wrote: "I immediately began getting a picture of him, but the images I got were of a dead child. I knew instantly that Delvis [Mattias] had been murdered and sexually molested. I told Sylvia Rodriguez that I would look for her son, but only through the police. I did not tell her Delvis was dead."

Continuing on, she tells of contacting the Paterson, New Jersey, police and working with them for several days. "I saw the little boy's body buried under slats of wood near what appeared to be a lumber yard. Within view of the body, there would be some sort of castle with a statue of a man and lions in front." She also said she told police the "murderer's name was something close to Robert or Charles (in Spanish they came up with Roberto, Gilberto, and Carlos), that he had a capital M in his name and that he was connected to Marshall Street." According to Allison's account the killer turned out to be "Gilberto Morales" who was living on Marshall Street. Her other clues were also to prove correct, she said.

The Mattias case sounds like other episodes described by Allison. She does not claim that she led police either to the body or to the killer. Her predictions, however, are semi-specific and confirmed. The Paterson police *do not verify her account.* According to Detective, now Lieutenant, George J. Brejack, "She was in for seven days, but she kept making wrong predictions. We went all over the place with her."[54]

"She said, 'I see railroad cars and steeples,' " the detective recounts, adding: "The whole city fit that description. Then we went up on a hill and she stood there and looking at the city she says the body will be found there. You could see the whole city from that spot." I asked Brejack if I could safely call the last example a "miss." He replied that "everything was a fucking miss."[55]

Following the discovery of the body Allison requested "an official letter documenting her contribution. Brejack alleged that Allison, denied the letter, then offered him and his partner money to say she located the body, which they refused."[56] Later, when Allison claimed credit for the case in a local newspaper story, Brejack went public with his story about the alleged bribe attempt.

Brejack's statements that Allison's clues were nebulous are almost identical with statements already detailed by Detective Barcelona, Chief McClung, and Captain Montgomery. Brejack's elaboration, that Allison justified her desire for a letter from him on the Mattias case to promote her book, also sounds true.[57] Allison complained to me, more than ten years later, that Scott Jacobson, her co-author, did not sufficiently promote the book. She seemed very disappointed over the sales of her autobiography.[58]

Her lack of supporting evidence and her evasiveness do not lend credibility to her case. For example, when the argument over the Atlanta case erupted on the "Ron Reagan Show" she claimed she had a "tape"; however, when Ray Hyman challenged this by saying that "the tape has not been seen," Allison's reply, more a put-down, was "Why should I show it to you? Who are you? [Raising her voice] WHO ARE YOU!"[59]

Allison has made very little money from her work, other than royalties from her book. "Money's not my God. My gift came from God, and I would never sell it," she says.[60] While she earns only expenses on some cases and nothing on most, it is possible that she enjoys the attention and prestige of being a famous psychic. It is also possible that her involvement as a psychic trying to help children fills an emotional need within her. Allison believed her mother was a clairvoyant. In the dedication of her book she writes: "To my mother . . . she understood and believed in me. She encouraged me to accept God's psychic gift." From an early age Allison was exposed to the "truth" of her mother's psychic abilities. Allison experienced an unusually traumatic adolescence capped by the early death of her father.[61] Like most people, she may not be able to objectively review her activities. I think it possible Allison believes that many of her clues are correct.

Other pronouncements by Allison seem contradictory. She maintains that she "hates publicity."[62] Her long list of television appearances and newspaper interviews does not support this contention. Her record resembles more that of a skillful entertainer complete with a publicity manager.

Allison told me, "I was tested at Duke University,"[63] a statement I could not verify. When Mary Jo Patterson interviewed her, Allison said, "I don't need anybody to test me, either, putting wires on my head or cards down in front of me." If she has already been tested, why not refer people to the study?

Speaking of her psychic abilities, Allison says: "I wouldn't use it for other purposes, either, so long as there are mothers crying. If some ass asked me about an election or what horse was coming in, I would take it as an insult."[64] Nevertheless, in her information package I found a letter from Hoda S. Elemary, detailing what appears to be tabloid-style predictions. In the letter Ms. Elemary says that Allison has "given me accurate information" about Saddam Hussein. Continuing, she writes: "On February 4, 1991, you stated that around the 14th or 15th of February, Saddam Hussein will give in and begin to seek peace. Having worked with you for so long, I was not surprised to hear on CNN that Saddam Hussein did in fact act in accordance with your prediction."

Although I was able to research most of the cases described above, they represent only a small portion of the total involvement by Allison with the police. All but a few cases mentioned in this chapter were singled out by Allison or her publicity manager as among her best cases.[65] It is possible that some of her other cases provide more support for her abilities. No doubt she could provide testimonials, especially from the parents of victims. Testimonials cannot erase the fact that her success rate in solving crimes or in finding bodies is very close to, if not actually, zero. In reviewing a case in Des Plaines, Illinois, Lyons and Truzzi emphasize her lack of utility. Allison and another psychic, Carol Broman, were brought onto the case by Detective, now Chief of Police, Joseph Kozenczak. The two authors write, "Virtually none of the leads given by either psychic was helpful in solving the case." They continue: "[C]onsiderable police manpower and equipment—including dogs, helicopters, boats, and trained divers—seem to have been wasted pursuing the psychics' pronouncements. Detailed searches were carried out of vacant lots, a boy's [sic] camp, a cemetery, and a solid waste incinerator, all for naught. Over the period of a week, Kozenczak drove Allison around for over one thousand miles, searching for the boy's body."[66] Eventually the body was found in the Des Plaines River.[67]

Marilyn Green, the private investigator mentioned earlier, told me that she "could be the top psychic in the country" just by using her accumulated experience and proven search techniques. Brejack also expressed the opinion that he could be a successful psychic based on his police experience. It seems inconsistent that if Allison has psychic powers, she cannot produce evidence of positive results.

NOTES

1. Captain Richard Serafin, telephone conversations, July 10, 1991 and December 4, 1991. Correspondence dated November 4 and December 7, 1991.
2. Dorothy Allison and Scott Jacobson, *Dorothy Allison: A Psychic Story* (New York: Jove Publications, 1980), p. 145.
3. Ibid., p. 146.
4. According to her autobiography, Allison "saw" that the girl had been raped anally. Serafin told me in a telephone conversation that her autobiography was accurate where it covered the Hennessy case.
5. Allison and Jacobson, *Dorothy Allison,* p. 169.
6. Ibid.
7. See note 1.
8. Allison and Jacobson, *Dorothy Allison,* p. 171.
9. Ibid.
10. Ibid.
11. Ibid., p. 172.
12. Ibid.
13. When he took the test, he was so agitated that the technician could draw no conclusions.

14. The autobiography was co-written by Scott Jacobson and clearly shows the hand of a competent professional writer.

15. See note 1.

16. It is possible that the factual manner of the autobiography is primarily due to Allison's co-author, Scott Jacobson. I was unable to contact Jacobson to talk with him about the book.

17. Arthur Lyons and Marcello Truzzi, *The Blue Sense* (New York: The Mysterious Press, 1991), p. 61.

18. Detective Bill Whildin, telephone interview May 21, 1991, and correspondence of November 10, 1991.

19. Ibid. In this conversation Detective Whildin told me that "hundreds of psychics had offered clues in the Melissa Brannen case." I asked if he might be exaggerating the number of psychics and he said no. He had kept notes, and filed them away. The total was in fact 272. He further stated that there was no consistency in the information from the psychics and they did not help in the case.

20. Cable Hughes is currently serving a fifty-year prison sentence for the murder of Melissa Brannen. Melissa's body has never been recovered.

21. Lyons and Truzzi, *The Blue Sense,* p. 142; Allison and Jacobson, *Dorothy Allison,* p. 73.

22. See note 1.

23. From Chief of Police Harold Gingrich, Waynesboro, Pa., April 13, 1977; from Asst. Director in Charge, J. Wallace LaPrade, FBI New York Office, April 10, 1975; from Det. Sgt. Ralph D. Courson, Franklin Co., Washington, Sheriff's Dept., May 14, 1981.

24. In two of Allison's cases, murderers were advised that a psychic was on the case. In both instances the individuals were prime suspects. It is possible that they were influenced into making a confession in part because they may have believed in Allison's psychic abilities. It is also possible that both would have confessed anyway. Dodson might have thought he could minimize his sentence by testifying against his partner Ronald Henninger. Regardless, the fact that someone would confess because he believed in a psychic is not a confirmation of psychic abilities.

25. Wanda Briggs, "Psychic Pinpoints Tot's Body," *Tri-City Herald,* Pasco, Washington, March 22, 1979.

26. While I was working on this chapter I decided to go to Pasco, Washington. I located Sacajawea Park on a map and drove there. I found that the park is in a desolate area bordered by desert, wetlands, a large industrial park, and the Columbia River. No residential sections are even remotely close to the park, making the clue about a "judge's house" a miss.

27. Briggs, "Psychic Pinpoints Tot's Body."

28. Because this case has never been solved, Captain Montgomery was limited in the type of information he could supply.

29. Captain Ron Montgomery, telephone interview, April 25, 1991, and correspondence, November 11, 1991.

30. The missing boy was Delvis Mattias. This case is covered in more detail in the chapter.

31. Mary Jo Patterson, "Dorothy Allison: 'Extrasensory Detective,' " *Police Magazine* (March 1981): 49.

32. Green has participated in some search efforts where the missing individual was still alive. Many other instances involved people who were dead when found. When I asked Green if she could supply information about some of her search efforts, she promptly supplied detailed and unambiguous documentation of several cases.

33. Marilyn Green, telephone interview, July 16, 1991, and correspondence, November 10, 1991. In a subsequent phone conversation Green said that her examination of psychic detectives was more cursory than comprehensive.

34. Allison and Jacobson, *Dorothy Allison,* p. 220.

35. Patterson, "Dorothy Allison: 'Extrasensory Detective,' " p. 48.

36. Ibid., p. 49.

37. Allison and Jacobson, *Dorothy Allison,* p. 93.

38. Ibid., p. 122.

39. Ibid., p. 123.

40. She also talked about a case in Canada. However, because the case was still unfolding, she could not give me the names of any of the people involved or the police department she was working with.

41. Eliot Marshall, "Police Science and Psychics," *Science* (November 28, 1980): 994.

42. Ibid.

43. The "Ron Reagan Sho.,' was a talk show hosted by the son of former President Reagan. The snow aired September 19, 1991.

44. Arthur Lyons and Marcello Truzzi are the authors of the book *The Blue Sense,* already noted. The book takes a mildly pro-paranormal view. In general it is an excellent review of the "evidence" for psychic detectives. Most of the psychics they examine in the book do not receive their endorsement. On the "Ron Reagan Show" Lyons said that psychic detectives had caused a "tremendous waste of manpower and money." He added that he was not a total skeptic.

45. Marian Christy, "Psychic Dorothy Allison Devotes Talents to Tracking Down Killers," *Buffalo Courier-Express* (January 7, 1981): 29.

46. James Randi, "Allison and the Atlanta Murders: A Follow-up," *Skeptical Inquirer* (Winter 1982–83): 7.

47. Patterson, "Dorothy Allison: 'Extrasensory Detective,' " p. 49.

48. "Skeptical Eye," *Discover* (December 1980): 8.

49. Ibid.

50. Lyons and Truzzi, *The Blue Sense,* p. 72.

51. Ibid., pp. 72–73.

52. Ibid., p. 73.

53. Captain Bill Valkenberg, telephone interview November 25, 1991.

54. Patterson, "Dorothy Allison: 'Extrasensory Detective,' " p. 49.

55. Lt. George J. Brejack, telephone interview July 15, 1991.

56. Patterson, "Dorothy Allison: 'Extrasensory Detective,' " 49.

57. According to newspaper accounts, Brejack has a reputation for solving tough cases. One account said he looks the part of a tough B-movie flatfoot, another called him "Paterson's version of Kojak." In my several telephone conversations with him I found him forthright. Information I requested from him was readily supplied. Because Brejack's testimony is so damaging to Allison's case I contacted writer Michael Kaplan. Kaplan is the author of a book titled *Buried Mistakes* (New York: Penguin, 1992). The book is about a homicide case that Brejack brought to a successful conclusion. In researching the book the author was in constant contact with Brejack for over a year. Kaplan told me without hesitation that he considered Brejack to be "competely honest."

58. Dorothy Allison, telephone interviews, July 8, 16, and 22, 1991.

59. I requested documentation from both Hyman and Allison regarding this exchange. Hyman promptly sent me a copy of the letter from the Atlanta police. I wrote both Allison and her publicity manager requesting a copy of the alleged "tape" of Allison giving the name Wayne Williams to the Atlanta police. In my letters (dated: January 9, 1991, December 14, 1991, and March 1, 1992), I offered them the opportunity to present the tape and other data they had as a reply to Hyman's comments. Allison and her publicity manager have not responded to my letters.

60. Patterson, "Dorothy Allison: 'Extrasensory Detective,' " p. 49.

61. According to her autobiography, she was one of thirteen children. At age fifteen she married and, although a devout Catholic, she divorced and remarried.

62. Patterson, "Dorothy Allison: 'Extrasensory Detective,' " p. 48.

63. See note 58.

64. Patterson, "Dorothy Allison: 'Extrasensory Detective,' " p. 48.

65. By singled out, I mean that the cases were mentioned directly by her, were prominent cases in her autobiography, or were featured in material provided by her publicity agent.

66. Lyons and Truzzi, *The Blue Sense*, p. 140.

67. Ibid.

5

The Media's Rising Star Psychic Sleuth: Noreen Renier

Gary P. Posner

Our next guest is helping to put a bite on crime in an unusual way. She has used her psychic skills in helping to solve 120 police cases. She is the only psychic to ever work with the FBI. She predicted the assassination attempt on President Reagan in vivid detail three months before it happened. Welcome psychic detective Noreen Renier.

—Host Gary Collins introducing Noreen Renier
on "Hour Magazine," November 7, 1988

Such plaudits from media celebrities have helped catapult Orlando, Florida's Noreen Renier to star status among the nation's psychics. Now earning her living as a "homicide detective," Renier, age fifty-seven, has in the past few years also been featured on other national TV programs such as "Geraldo," the "Joan Rivers Show," ABC's "Incredible Sunday," and CBS's "48 Hours," as well as in the December 5, 1988, *US News & World Report* article entitled, "The Twilight Zone in Washington: There Are Some Important People in Government Who Have Enlisted Psychics' Help."

Renier has also taught a non-credit course in "ESP and Awareness" at the Rollins College Center for Life-long Education, although she does not hold faculty status at Rollins College, which is located in Winter Park near Orlando.[1] Further occupying a great deal of her time for a half-dozen years, until its unexpectedly sudden settlement in March 1992, was her long-standing and bitter legal battle with skeptic John Merrell, whom Renier successfully sued for libel in 1986 following his allegations of "fraudulent" activity. (The case will be discussed further throughout this chapter.)

Supporters of Renier's alleged psychic abilities can be found in the law enforcement and academic communities. Her promotional packet, entitled "Book a Spellbinder: Psychic Noreen Renier—Meetings/Conventions/Workshops/Seminars," includes copies of letters, on impressive letterheads, containing passages such as the following:

> [Renier's] class was outstanding. She worked on two local cases and taught officers how to work with a psychic. All the students requested I find a way to bring her back.
>
> —In a memo to "All Florida Academy Directors" from
> David E. Walsh, Director
> Southwest Florida Criminal Justice Academy
> Lee County Area Vocational Technical School,
> Fort Myers, Florida

> It is a pleasure to extend to you an invitation to address . . . students attending the National Academy class entitled, "Applied Criminology." As you know, the National Academy students are police managers from throughout the United States and several foreign countries.
>
> —James W. Greenleaf, Assistant Director
> FBI Academy, Quantico, Virginia

> You definitely opened my eyes to the potential investigative tool of the psychic. Obviously, many a doubting Thomas had to revise his ideas concerning this somewhat esoteric area.
>
> —Daniel Grinnan, Jr., Training Coordinator
> Commonwealth of Virginia Bureau of Forensic Science, Richmond

> I have observed Ms. Renier in several situations where she has demonstrated her psychic talents and I was very impressed with these demonstrations. She has been willing to have her abilities scientifically evaluated in a laboratory setting which is rare for most psychics.
>
> —Robert L. Van de Castle, Ph.D., Professor
> Dept. of Behavioral Medicine & Psychiatry
> University of Virginia School of Medicine, Charlottesville

Your demonstrations and predictions were most accurate and although there still will be skeptics, you're able to have a lot of people leave with an open mind.

—Peter Slusar, Director
Peninsula/Tidewater Regional Academy of
Criminal Justice, Hampton, Virginia

Though her career as a "psychic" was barely a year old, University of Central Florida anthropologist David E. Jones selected Renier as one of four test subjects for his 1979 book, *Visions of Time: Experiments in Psychic Archeology.* The ability of Renier (and the others) to "psychically" describe the origins of various artifacts led Jones to declare, ". . . I feel a positive conclusion is unavoidable. There are individuals who have abilities which we now refer to as paranormal or psychic. They can help the archeologist, and all historical sciences and disciplines, to recapture in great detail human events heretofore lost and frozen in time."[2]

An April 1, 1981, article ("Psychic Predicts Shooting") in the Charlottesville, Virginia, *Daily Progress* (and perhaps carried elsewhere via AP, as indicated at the article's heading) begins: "It was there in the March 10 issue of the Canadian tabloid: A prediction from [then] Virginia psychic Noreen Renier that President Ronald Reagan would be shot—but not killed—in the left upper chest. . . . [S]he included it in her list of predictions for the [then] Montreal-based *National Examiner.*"

The *Daily Progress* article further states that WXAM (where Renier hosted a weekly radio call-in show) news director Elliot Wizer played for the reporter a tape from Ms. Renier's show of November 5, 1980, containing the following prediction: "Right now I feel very insecure about saying this, but I keep feeling problems in [Reagan's] chest. It's not a natural problem, perhaps it might come from outside. . . . I see an illness coming around him. Part of me is blocking it because I don't want to see the answer. . . . I feel like it would happen within a four-month period."

I spoke with Elliot Wizer, who is now the news director at WTVR-TV in Richmond:

I was the host of Noreen's radio show, in addition to being the station's news director. It was the most popular radio show in Charlottesville in the early '80s. I went into the show a skeptic of hers but I came away a believer. I think that she has ability. She did predict the thing with Reagan extremely accurately. She hit it right on the head—I was there when she did it. She even predicted things about me that came true. I don't believe in that stuff at all, for the most part, but I think she does have a gift. I've been in this business a long time, and out of everyone I've ever met claiming to have similar abilities, I think Noreen comes the closest. I found her to be the most accurate of the people that I've seen in the business.[3]

Renier was one of three "psychic detectives" featured on the May 30, 1991, edition of "Geraldo." An Albany, New York, couple had been shot to death in 1986 while the murdered mother was speaking on the telephone with her daughter, but the police had yet to make an arrest. After reading a *National Enquirer* article about Renier, the couple's son requested that Detective Ray Krolak call her in on the case. Explained Krolak from Geraldo's studio audience, "We'd just about run out of leads after two years of investigation. . . . I checked out her credibility through police agencies I knew, through articles I had read about her. I spoke to the officers involved with Noreen. . . . Noreen described the crime scene like she was standing at the crime scene. She described the victims. . . . She described the killer. I presented her with ten photographs and she picked out the killer's picture. She also told us where the killer went after the crime, and that fit exactly into where the alibi was." Krolak acknowledged that "She more or less reaffirmed what we knew previously," but said that her "leads" led him to take a closer look at the alibis of the suspects, and charges have now been filed against them.

In *Practical Homicide Investigation: Tactics, Procedures, and Forensic Techniques,* written by New York City Police Squad Commander Vernon J. Geberth and used as a textbook by the FBI and other police academies, Renier's insights are prominently featured in the "Psychics" portion of the section on "Identification of Suspects." Geberth identifies Renier as "a psychic and recognized authority on the phenomena of extrasensory perception [who] has worked with various police agencies including the FBI on homicide cases and other criminal investigations."[4]

As stated in the 1988 *US News & World Report* article, "The Federal Bureau of Investigation has hosted lectures to police officers by psychic Noreen Renier at its Quantico, Virginia, training center. She impressed her listeners by predicting in January 1981, that there would be an assassination attempt on President Reagan in the spring, which indeed took place [on March 30]."

Robert K. Ressler, a supervisory special agent assigned to the Behavioral Science unit of the Quantico center, attended that performance, and was questioned about it during his 1986 deposition in the *Renier v. Merrell* case. Ressler testified that "she said she felt that [Reagan] was having a heart attack in the future . . . some sort of chest pains . . . and then she clarified it by saying no, it's a sharper pain and it is a gunshot. . . . I believe she said in the left chest because she was patting her left side, and that he would not die. . . ."[5]

But, says Ressler, Renier's vision went further, as "she went on to say that . . . later in the fall, October, November, he would be killed in a machine gun assault on a parade stand by many in foreign uniforms. . . . " The following exchange then ensued:

> Question: Do you recall if she specifically said the second shooting would be President Reagan?
> Ressler: She thought it was President Reagan.
> Question: She was wrong on which President it was, then?
> Ressler: Yeah . . . circumstances were uncanny in their accuracy [but] it turned out that it was not Reagan, it was Sadat."[6]

Yes, Noreen Renier is also known for having successfully predicted the assassination of Egypt's President Anwar Sadat. However, in her version of the story, the U.S. Secret Service seems responsible for her apparent ambiguity. In a 1988 *New York Post* article included in her promotional packet, Renier says that following the Reagan shooting, and after hearing that she had predicted it, agents from the Secret Service paid her a visit. "They thought I might actually know John Hinckley. I didn't. Then they came back again and asked what I saw in the future for the president. I said I saw a parade, a reviewing stand, foreign uniforms, and gunfire. After Sadat was shot, I realized they never asked me *which* president" (emphasis in original).[7]

When I called the FBI Academy, I was informed that Robert Ressler has since retired from duty. In his stead, I spoke with Richard Ault, also a supervisory special agent in the Behavioral Science Unit and instructor at the FBI Academy, and long-time co-worker with Ressler. Ault, who holds a Ph.D. in counseling psychology, informed me that indeed "Bob [Ressler] did have Renier down here to the Academy to speak. It was against my recommendations [but] he did it anyway." Ault says that he attended a couple of Renier's lectures, and recalls that, "At no time during any of her lectures, or any of the time that I was associated with her, did she make any 'uncanny' predictions, nor was I impressed with anything that she did say. . . . I've seen that same technique used by a lot of people."[8]

Ault added that although he did not attend Renier's January 1981 presentation, "I've questioned Bob about it on several occasions, and it sounded like the same stuff I've heard before. . . . The way he described her prediction sounded to me rather bland. It didn't really sound 'uncannily accurate.' . . . What he said to me was she made this prediction, and to him it sounded neat. When I asked him exactly what all did she say, he wasn't real clear to me on it. He came up with some things that sounded pretty general." Ault added that, in retrospect, Ressler "has often expressed [to me] regrets at having brought Renier here to lecture. She's just caused him a lot of [paperwork] problems over the years [regarding] the kinds of claims that she's made."[9]

Yet Ressler continues to endorse publicly (and perhaps even embellish, if the following account is accurate) Renier's abilities. According to a recent newspaper story: "Ressler . . . said he wasn't a believer until [Renier] predicted the attempted assassination of President Ronald Reagan three months—*down to the date*—before it occurred during a lecture at the academy. He didn't report it to the Secret Service, who fumed when they later learned of the advance warning" (emphasis added).[10]

Readers may recall the audacious Reagan assassination prediction hoax by Tamara Rand, a Los Angeles psychic to the stars, who predicted in a TV interview allegedly taped on January 6, 1981, that the president would be shot in late March or early April by a sandy-haired man with the initials "J. H." Within days of the shooting, the tape was being shown on the network news, as evidence of Rand's startling abilities. However, skeptical AP reporter Paul Simon discovered that the tape had actually been produced the day *after* Reagan was shot, with the complicity of Rand's friend, Las Vegas columnist and TV personality Dick Maurice.[11]

With regard to Renier's predictions of the shooting, I know of no evidence of any such hoax. I asked Elliot Wizer if the 1980 radio tape was still available, but he informed me that he does not have it, and that the station has long since changed format and management. Judging by the *Daily Progress'* description of that prediction, it seems to have been somewhat more vague than Wizer recalls. In fact, if Robert Ressler's version of events at the FBI Academy in 1981 is correct, Renier's scenario had not yet involved a *shooting,* but rather a *heart attack,* until it underwent a mid-course correction during that lecture. And the precision of even that revised prediction has been questioned by Richard Ault. But Renier's *National Examiner* prediction sounds quite precise, assuming that it was hers. Renier was asked to address this point during the 1986 libel trial:

Q: Do you recall the predictions that you made in the same article that appeared in the *National Examiner* where you predicted President Reagan was going to be shot?
A: Some of those predictions were not mine. The newspaper put in three or four jazzy ones without my—I didn't do two or three of those predictions.

Q: So the list of predictions that are under your name with your picture, they just threw in some without your knowledge; is that correct?
A: Yes, they did, yes.
Q: So the wrong ones weren't yours and the right ones were?
A: No, some of mine were wrong, but where they went wrong was they had put some sort of what I call jazzy predictions in.[12]

Renier had apparently also made some rather "jazzy" predictions in 1979 about President Reagan's predecessor. According to *The Blue Sense*, a book generally favorable to the notion of psychic detectives, Renier had forecast that President Jimmy Carter would be reelected in 1980, and subsequently assassinated on the White House lawn. She had added for good measure that Vice President Mondale would commit suicide.[13]

Richard Ault had remarked during my interview with him that, "If you throw out enough predictions, you know how it is. All you have to do is pull any given tabloid off of the newsstand and read the latest predictions, and you'll find that finally something's going to have to happen— the odds are in that favor—especially if you say a prominent figure is going to be shot at or harmed. In this day and age it stands as a fairly safe prediction." Given that such predictions seem as popular as the one about UFOs finally landing on the White House lawn, wouldn't it be more remarkable if the president were to die, or suffer some other health-related crisis, and *no* psychic were to come forward to reap his or her just reward for having made such a prediction? Considering his age, I suspect that *scores* of the nation's "psychics" had predicted that President Reagan would not survive two terms in office (I had doubts myself).

If Renier's Reagan/Sadat predictions are indicative of a remarkably keen "psychic" ability to foresee such earth-shaking events, one might hope that she would make it a practice to offer her sage counsel to the world's leaders. If, on the other hand, after having struck out with Carter/Mondale, Renier simply lucked out with Reagan/Sadat, one might perhaps anticipate a retreat from the presidential death watch, so as not to risk further lowering her batting average with another series of misses.

Since I admit to a lack of ESP, I cannot read Renier's mind to divine why she has chosen to move on. But on the May 22, 1990, "Joan Rivers Show" she said, "I don't do presidents any more because I had so many people on me when I did the Reagan one that I just decided that I wasn't going to do presidents any more. I get too much attention." Renier is now strictly a "homicide detective." Her fee: about $400 per case.[14]

When asked by Rivers about how she first discovered her psychic power, Renier explained that she "used to be a skeptic. . . . And then one day a psychic did some stuff on me, body scars and things like that. And I didn't really believe even then. And then I started practicing what I didn't believe in, trying to disprove that this stuff existed, and . . ." She soon realized that, with practice, she had become as "psychic" as those who make their livings at it.

Renier told Rivers that, "The police have to invite me in on a case." Law enforcement agencies hear of her, she said, by "word of mouth" from other police agencies who "are proud of what I do, and they tell another agency. . . . I don't advertise and I don't solicit."

Yet, her promotional packet, as noted earlier, contains letters of recommendation ideal for use in solicitation. Renier mailed one such packet in October 1989 to "Director Richard N. Harris, Department of Criminal Justice Services," in Richmond, Virginia. The packet appears to have then been forwarded to a skeptical organization, along with Renier's accompanying cover letter which begins:

> Some say ESP and Psychic Phenomena does [sic] not exist. Some say the police who have used psychics had negative results. They say all psychics are frauds.
>
> Others say they have used psychics with excellent results. They say psychics can help bring an unsolved crime to a successful conclusion. They say they would use a psychic again.
>
> As a professional psychic with extensive experience in police work, backed up by recommendations from the FBI, I offer your training center a bold new understanding about psychics and their work with law enforcment officers.[15]

Although one might infer an eagerness to travel the country to lecture to police agencies, Renier told Joan Rivers that she has grown "tired of going all around the country to police stations and scenes of crime," preferring instead to conduct her homicide investigations in the comfort of her own home. The police, Renier says, "just send me objects off the body," such as a bullet or a piece of clothing, for her to "tune in" on. By so doing, she is able to relive the crime (e.g., while holding a bloody shirt, she in effect *becomes* the murder victim, experiencing agony as the bullets impact), and is able to visualize the murderer as if through the victim's eyes. Recounts Renier, "I have had my throat slit, I have been stabbed, I've been a man and shotgunned down here [pointing to her lower abdomen]. I can actually feel it for a few moments."

Then, says Renier, "I have a police artist who works with me, and he draws the face, and we send the face to whatever department we are working with. And then they're real happy, usually."

A potential source of *un*happiness for the police is adroitly handled by this sensitive seer. As she told Rivers, "I try not to tune in to X-rated stuff. The police are always worried that I'm going to see things about their sexual life or about who they went out with last night, or who they're cheating on. So I tell them, 'No X-rated stuff—I don't do that.' "

Nevertheless, PG-rated demonstrations of her "psychic" skills have dazzled national television audiences. For example, for her November 7, 1988, performance on "Hour Magazine," Renier brought along a collection of what she described as police evidence from "current cases," including a belt and bloody shirt allegedly from a shooting victim. Renier closed her eyes, held the belt in her hand, and began to describe the circumstances of the murder as if she herself were the victim. She claimed to feel the impact of the bullets in her neck and elsewhere, and after a few moments asked Collins if she could stop, since "I get a little upset."

Renier also displayed "a piece of a bone they sent me . . . for me to describe who it belonged to . . . and where the rest of the body was." She recounted how "when I first picked it up and tuned in to see what this person looked like, I saw this enormous animal in front of me. . . . It turned out to be a rat. . . . I thought they gave me an animal bone. So I waited until the police called and I said, 'Did you send me [a rat] bone?' They said, 'No, Noreen. . . . The rat probably chewed the hand off the body, and that's what you were picking up. Could you just go past the rat and see the person?' So I did, and it's a girl, college age. . . . They're going to find her. . . . It's in Virginia."

Another guest on that day's program was Dr. Eugenie Scott, executive director of the Berkeley, California, based National Center for Science Education, with whom I discussed the show when I met her at a conference in May 1991. During a commercial break, Scott had mentioned to host Gary Collins that Renier's parading of such items across the country would be a gross violation of police procedure since, once allowed out of their custody, such "evidence" would no longer be admissible in court. When Collins again chatted with Renier during the show's final segment, he asked her if law enforcement agencies really "let that evidence go around the country, police evidence, the kind of stuff that you brought today." An apparently flustered Renier stammered in response, "Uh, no, I don't think so, really. I, I, I, I, they don't know I have it here. And I haven't worked on it either." Responded Collins, looking directly into the camera, ". . . and that's why there are skeptics."

As alluded to in Collins' remarks that introduce this chapter, Renier's promotional "bio" said that her law enforcement cases have included "several for the Federal Bureau of Investigation." It added that "Mrs. Renier will not accept a case unless an officially authorized representative of the agency having jurisdiction contacts her directly. At that time an agreement outlining fees, expenses, and confidentiality requirements will be sent."[16]

However, Robert Ressler testified in his deposition that Renier's claim to having worked as a psychic for the FBI "is not true from the standpoint of being a paid employee and is not true from the standpoint of her being on a retainer or being used in any regular capacity. She does not work on FBI cases."[17] Added Ressler: "Merrell wanted to know whether the FBI used psychics in our investigative process. And I told him that was absolutely something I wouldn't discuss, but, in reality, we don't."[18] Additionally, Renier was compelled to modify her promotional literature as a result of a reproach by Ressler, who testified that she had claimed "that she was an instructor for the FBI, something along that line, and I told her she could not say that."[19]

During a July 16, 1990, return engagement on the "Joan Rivers Show," which emanates from New York, Renier participated in a panel discussion of that city's fearsome "Zodiac" killer (along with *New York Post* reporter Anne Murray, and criminology professor Candice Skrapec). At one point, Renier was handed photocopies of two letters that "Zodiac" had sent to authorities, with the hope that she would be able to perform a "psychometry" reading and assist in the identification and capture of this dangerous criminal.

After first apologizing for what she feared might be inaccurate information because she was not working with evidence "off the body," within seconds Renier began speaking in the first person, as if she had become "Zodiac," saying such things as "My beard is now shaved," "I feel like maybe Spanish is very prominent in me," and "I don't know if they called me 'stupido' or what when I was younger." She then adopted a hostile expression and tone of voice, and said, "I'm killing because these men are worthless anyway, so it doesn't matter if they're dead. I don't care if they're dead, no one else cares if they're dead. I'm just killing people that no one cares [about] anyways. I have two more before I'm caught." She then emerged from the first person and added, "I don't know if he'll kill them both, but I feel two more attempts—maybe one will be killed."

When asked by an enthralled Rivers, "Where does he live?" Renier began gesticulating in all directions, eyes closed, describing how "I felt a river there, and I felt a very dark brick building . . . not real tall, maybe four, six stories high. Then I lived across the street, and the road here. The bridge is up here. There's a bridge and it looks metal—big. And over here is a traffic light . . . the closest traffic light is to my left. . . . The apartments are over here—the seventh, eighth story I live on. We walk up the stairway, and it's open on two sides but it's closed on two sides."

When asked by Rivers if he lives with anyone, Renier bounced in her seat and blurted, "Yes, yes, yes, yes. I saw a younger man, I saw a younger man, younger man, younger man."

Unfortunately for the terrorized citizenry of New York City, Renier was apparently unable to specify the stretch of river, the bridge, the apartment building, the traffic light/intersection, or the identity of the "younger man." Even more regrettable was her apparent inability, when she "became" the killer, to discern *her own name!*

Following this performance, Rivers asked, "Would you give this information to the police, or would the police come and ask you for it?" Renier responded by saying, "I'm sure if I asked them and told them about me, they would, I'm sure. And there's a possibility we'll do some contacting with them after the show." Rivers then reluctantly read a disclaimer on behalf of the show (which she said she found "embarrassing" to have to do) to the effect that Renier's information "is only theory," and that if "police investigation in the capture of this criminal" should confirm its accuracy, "we'll have you back." (She has been back anyway.)

On the following day's show, Rivers proudly announced that as a result of that appearance, Renier was now working with the New York Police Department on the "Zodiac" case. However, when I called NYPD in an effort to confirm this claim, I was informed by Officer St. Just of the NYPD Public Information Office that Renier was "not working with the Police Department" on the case. Although, he said, as a matter of policy he could/would not exclude the possibility that Renier might have called or visited NYPD to offer information as might any other citizen, "We didn't reach out [for her]."[20]

But faced with a 1½-year-old unsolved murder case of their own and an ice cold trail, south Florida detectives Ralph Pauldine and Henry Mackey definitely did reach out for Renier, as the nation learned during the May 13, 1992, telecast of CBS-TV's weekly newsmagazine "48 Hours" in a segment entitled "Hard Evidence." With CBS camera crews taping simultaneously at the detectives' office and at Renier's home (the two locales were also connected by speakerphones), reporter Doug Tunnell explains how "just for starters, [Renier] transports herself back to the crime scene and enters the victim's body." She then accurately describes the murder scene (a portly, middle-aged shirtless man, mortally wounded in the neck). The police, Tunnell reports, are convinced that Renier had no advance knowledge of the case. But given the elaborate choreography required to put this TV spectacle together, a skeptic might suspect that a person with police contacts (such as a professional "psychic detective"), or perhaps even a national television news department, could have made prior inquiries about the nature of the case to be televised.

Renier then opens a package of evidence (a bloody towel and a beer can believed to have been handled by the murderer). Says Tunnell, "Noreen now enters the body of the killer . . . [and] describes the killer's appearance," as she offers enough of a description (". . . I do have some flare in my nostril . . . ") to allow a police artist to make a sketch that may or may not bear any resemblance to the real killer. As in the Zodiac case, she didn't seem even to know her own name, though this time she was able to name an alleged accomplice, "Wanda," a prostitute with a butterfly tattoo on her shoulder. Within one week, says Tunnell, police had already picked up for questioning five women fitting that description.

To further bolster the credibility of Renier and of his uncritical journalistic effort, Tunnell also interviewed Ray Krolak about the upstate New York murder case discussed earlier in this chapter. Says Tunnell, "One of the people Noreen led police to was a new suspect, a member of the victims' family . . . the grandson." The viewer must assume that this was told to Tunnell by Krolak. Geraldo Rivera had made the same claim on his show a year earlier (perhaps the result of a pre-show interview with Krolak?). But the murdered couple's daughter, sitting next to Krolak in Geraldo's studio audience, had responded unequivocally, "[Renier] did not do that. She did not finger my son. She did finger the other two." (They were already suspects.) Krolak did not comment.

Renier's claims of "psychic" communication extend into the realm of "ghosts" and "poltergeists" as well. For example, she has described assisting a Durham, N.C., group called the Psychical Research Foundation (PRF) in an investigation of "a haunting" at a spa where "every Wednesday at exactly [the] same time the whirlpool would overflow" for no apparent reason (mechanical difficulties were excluded). "Telephones would ring and people would pick them up and there would be no one on the line. There'd be footsteps. . . . Then I came in and I did go into a trance, contacted whatever was there, and I found out it was a woman who had died in the whirlpool on a Wednesday at 10:00. She gave me the name of her husband and . . . her attorney. . . . [She] was haunting the spa . . . she said, because her attorney hadn't finished the . . . lawsuit. . . . Her husband [then] got in touch with the attorney, he fixed everything up, and the haunting stopped. It was all under scientific research. It wasn't foolishness."[21]

Renier also tells of how, "A police officer called me one day and he said, 'Noreen, we're having some strange things happening in a house in Leesburg [Florida]. . . . [T]here's phones ringing and when people pick them up there's a voice on the other end that tells them what they have just done, what they're planning to do, what they're wearing.' Every time this one little girl . . . went into the bathroom, all the water would start overflowing in the toilets. Things would fly around the room. . . . Police people, the press, everyone had seen this. . . . So I called the PRF up and I said, 'Is this a haunting?' They said, 'No, it sounds like a poltergeist' [where usually] a small child is involved . . . going through a change of life . . . maybe mentally and emotionally out of kilter, and she wouldn't know it, but her energy, by being out of kilter, is creating all of this. . . . A scientific paper was written on it by the PRF. It's called the Leesburg poltergeist case. . . ."[22]

Renier has also functioned more formally as a "medium." The following appears in a previous version of her promotional packet: "An optional trance is held in the evening with workshop members encouraged to make contact with deceased relatives, friends, or famous people, and questions may be posed to 'Sing' and 'Robert,' Noreen's two main spiritual entities, who have something to say about everything!"[23] Renier says, "I have really no conclusions on who Robert and Sing are—if they're my alter-ego or if they're entities coming from without—as long as the information I receive is accurate. . . . My voice changes [when they speak through me]."[24]

My initial contact with Renier occurred on October 28, 1986, when she and I were guests on Bev Smith's former radio program on WKIS in Orlando. Shortly before air time, as we introduced ourselves, Renier informed me of her recent victory in her libel action against John Merrell, a co-founder of the Northwest Skeptics. Renier seemed to believe that her claims of "psychic power" had been vindicated by the jury, and that her legal battle with Merrell was now behind her. Never in her worst nightmares could she have imagined that, for the next five and one-half years, her life would remain largely consumed by their continued litigation. And never in my wildest dreams could I have imagined what fortuitous discovery, yet to come, would help elevate this already notable dispute to a truly bizarre level.

Merrell informs me that he first heard of Noreen Renier in mid–1985, at a time when she was making the rounds in his home state of Oregon. After conducting some research (which included a telephone conversation with Renier), Merrell composed a lengthy "Letter to the Editor" of the Ashland *Daily Tidings* in which he alleged "evidence of fraudulent claims [by Renier] involving police agencies, questionable background credentials, and current ongoing investigations by representatives of the National Council Against Health Fraud. . . ."[25] Although never published, a copy of Merrell's letter eventually made its way to Renier through an acquaintance at the paper, and ultimately formed the basis of Renier's libel action against him. Following a three-day trial in Oregon, the jury awarded Renier $25,000 in general damages (9 percent of the $275,000 requested by her). Merrell's subsequent appeal was unsuccessful.

In a further effort to nullify the award to Renier, Merrell, after first guaranteeing payment to all of his other creditors, elected to declare bankruptcy. The law specifies that a debt may not be discharged through bankruptcy if it resulted from an act of "malice," i.e., an injurious charge that not only is false, but is *knowingly* (rather than inadvertently) so. Renier contended that ten allegations within Merrell's letter were indeed malicious. Following three days of testimony, the federal bankruptcy court judge agreed that four of the ten fulfilled the criteria for "malice" (one would have sufficed), and the $25,000 debt was reaffirmed. As one cited example, regarding Merrell's claim of "current ongoing investigations by representatives of the National Council Against Health Fraud," the judge ruled that Merrell, though himself an NCAHF member, "knew there was no such investigation [by NCAHF as an organization] at the time he made this statement."[26]

The seeds of this legal entanglement had been planted in May 1985, when an article favorable to Renier appeared in the *Daily Tidings*.[27] Leroy Coppedge, a Northwest Skeptics colleague of Merrell, responded with a "Letter to the Editor" which stated in part, "Not everyone who claims to have psychic abilities is a fraud or a charlatan; some are sincere lunatics, and some are simply sincerely misguided. . . . I don't know which, if any, of the above people Noreen Renier is. . . . A simple demonstration, under controlled conditions, would prove [her abilities] to James Randi [a noted challenger of psychic claims], and to most rational people."[28] Shortly thereafter, Coppedge received and forwarded to Merrell a handwritten letter from "Nancy Uzdavinis" of Ashland, who was requesting information about Noreen Renier. Within days, Merrell received a similar letter of his own from Uzdavinis which read in part: ". . . Coppedge . . . suggested I write to you because you are investigating that psychic Noreen Renier and had lots of information. And hopefully could enlighten me. I'm confused about her abilities and need to know if she's real or not. She's planning a workshop in July and I need to make a decision."[29]

Merrell, who had already conducted a brief inquiry about Renier after receiving the *Daily Tidings* article from Coppedge, intensified his investigation as a result of Uzdavinis' request, and claims to have kept Uzdavinis closely informed of his progress. Shortly before writing his letter to the *Daily Tidings,* he wrote one to Uzdavinis which began: "Following your phone call Monday I am enclosing some additional information on Noreen Renier which I've gathered while attending a conference with other members of the National Council Against Health Fraud. . . . This conference was timely in that many representatives of the NCAHF were able to examine together the brochures and clippings about Ms. Renier [that] you sent [to me] in August. After reading the material and listening to portions of my tape recorded telephone conversation with Noreen Renier, Dr. Ben Wilson concluded her claimed ability to heal using her 'psychic vibrations' borders on . . . medical quackery. Dr. William Jarvis, the President of the NCAHF, and NCAHF chapter President James Lowell agreed that the investigation of Ms. Renier should continue since her claims appear to involve quackery and fraud."[30]

Four years later, during a several-week-long hiatus in the federal bankruptcy proceedings, Coppedge happened to recognize that within the text of the two handwritten "Uzdavinis" letters, Noreen Renier's name appeared in script identical to Renier's actual signature. This led to the suspicion that Merrell had actually been corresponding with Renier herself, rather than with the seemingly skeptical "Nancy Uzdavinis," about the concerns of himself and other NCAHF members.

Accordingly, after the trial's resumption, Merrell's attorney asked Renier: "Has anyone identifying themself with that organization [NCAHF] ever contacted you or requested information from you?" "Has anyone identifying themself with that organization ever advised you that they had concerns about . . . medical quackery and fraud in regard to you?" Renier's answers to these questions were "No" and "No, sir."[31] When later asked, "Do you have any knowledge of Mr. Merrell's attempts to investigate your claims?" Renier replied, ". . . I heard what happened in the Court, in the [1986 Oregon] trial, but I don't know anything other than that." When reminded that Merrell had called her on the phone, she added, "We had one conversation, sir." When asked again, "You don't have any other knowledge of any other investigation that he made?" Renier answered "No."[32]

Though he had been unable to do so prior to the judge's verdict, Merrell later obtained the services of a forensic handwriting expert, Dorothy Lehman of Portland. After examining the "Uzdavinis" letters, as well as other relevant documents, Lehman "arrived at a firm conclusion. It is my opinion that the two questioned letters purportedly written by Nancy Uzdavinis . . . were actually executed by Noreen Renier."[33] Merrell had by then also discovered that there really is a "Nancy Uzdavinis"—Renier's sister-in-law, who lives in Ashland.

Armed with these startling new allegations, Merrell's attorney filed another motion for dismissal of the $25,000 debt, arguing that the original Oregon judgment "was based in part on fraud, misrepresentation, and other misconduct of Noreen Renier. . . . Renier used a false name and tricked the Defendant into investigating her claims of psychic ability. . . . Assuming that the handwriting expert is correct, Ms. Renier has perjured herself."[34] In response, Renier filed a sworn affidavit with the court attesting that, "Because I had . . . become aware that . . . Merrell and certain of his associates were making . . . inquiries and representations concerning me . . . to impair and undermine my pursuit of my profession . . . I requested my sister-in-law, Nancy Uzdavinis, to make an inquiry to determine the nature and content of the representations. . . . [She] told me that since I knew precisely what I wished to find out, I could make the inquiry myself in her name. . . . I have never denied or concealed this inquiry. . . . I did not 'trick' or 'entrap' the Defendant. . . ."[35]

Regarding Merrell's letter to Uzdavinis, Renier's affidavit states: "I have never seen or received the purported . . . letter. . . . Nor has my sister-in-law ever seen or received the letter. . . . Nor has the purported letter even been produced in the extensive discovery and document production activity engaged in during the course of this litigation. . . ."[36] During a later deposition, Renier went further: "John Merrell wrote a bogus letter and backdated it, pretending he was writing to Nancy Uzdavinis. It was filled with fraudulent statements and quotes."[37] The real Uzdavinis also filed an affidavit in which she attests that although Merrell's letter was correctly addressed, "I have never received that letter or any other letter from Mr. Merrell. In the letter I have been shown . . . I purportedly made a phone call to Mr. Merrell on the Monday preceding the date of the letter. I never made any such telephone call and have no knowledge whatsoever regarding any such phone call. . . . [M]y sister-in-law, Noreen Renier, at about that time had sent to Mr. Merrell a letter under my name. She did so with my knowledge and consent. . . . I have no knowledge of [her] ever having made any phone calls to Mr. Merrell using my name."[38]

Merrell's motion for dismissal of the $25,000 libel judgment was denied, but in a curiously ambiguous manner. Although the motion had requested relief due to alleged misconduct tainting the *original Oregon trial,* the federal bankruptcy judge's ruling, without elaboration, states, "Upon consideration of the defendant's Motion and accompanying exhibits . . . the court concludes that *its* Judgment [i.e., the *bankruptcy* judgment] was not based in any part on perjury, fraud, misrepresentation or any other misconduct" by Renier (emphasis added).[39] The integrity of the original *libel trial* was thus not commented upon.

FATE magazine, in its June 1991 issue, published a comprehensive article about *Renier* v. *Merrell,* which even in nine pages didn't come close to doing the case justice.[40] (For that matter, neither have I, with my emphasis on the NCAHF and Uzdavinis material to the exclusion of the matters of Renier's police associations and credentials, which I do however touch upon elsewhere throughout this chapter.) I highly recommend that the *FATE* article be read, to see how the writer (a consulting editor to the pro-paranormal magazine), who even cites my previous writings on the subject, has nevertheless presented an unswervingly pro-Renier, anti-Merrell scenario.

Merrell attempted to turn the tables against Renier by filing suit in Orlando, Florida, in June 1990, alleging malicious misconduct by her. During the pre-trial discovery process, he confronted Renier with what may be the most penetrating questioning that she has ever faced in her professional career. Among much information demanded of her were the names of the police agencies that had provided the various pieces of alleged "evidence" that she had used during her televised "psychometry" performances.

But Renier countersued with similar charges of her own. And as the "wheels of justice" ground and creaked, with the judge granting Renier several extensions on her obligation to supply the information demanded by Merrell, her multiple liens on Merrell's home threatened his ability to accept a job promotion and transfer. Under growing financial and professional pressures, Merrell decided to make his legal "peace" with Renier in March 1992, the terms of which are being kept under wraps by both parties as per a stipulation (which Merrell tells me he did not favor) of the final settlement.

During the original Oregon libel trial, Merrell had disputed the accuracy of many of Renier's claimed psychic successes. The case I find the most fascinating, and for which the most documentary evidence is available, deals with her role in locating an airplane that had crashed in Massachusetts. To this day, Merrell remains convinced that the verdict in Renier's favor resulted, in large part, from her having moved several female jurors to tears with her "psychic" rendition of the tragic death scene of a young man and his female companion. For these reasons I have selected this case to present in detail, to illustrate the importance of employing intensely critical scrutiny when evaluating even the most impressively corroborated paranormal claims.

The Blue Sense correctly states, in its single-sentence reference to this remarkable case, that "special agent Mark Babyak [of the FBI] testified that Ms. Renier had successfully helped him locate a crashed plane."[41] And Renier continues to promote this case as one of her most amazing success stories, as she did in the April 1, 1992, *Woman's Day* article, "Can Psychics Solve Crimes?" The following is her dramatic and emotional description of events as recounted on the May 22, 1990, "Joan Rivers Show":

A lady [Jessica Herbert] called me on the phone and told me she was an FBI agent's wife [Note: actually Babyak's ex-wife], and her brother was missing up north in the Massachusetts area. . . . I was in Virginia and she was from Washington [D.C.] . . . and would I help find a plane. . . . I'm a homicide detective and I usually just work with the police, but for some reason I decided to take the case. . . . She brought me a metal cup . . . and a wallet [both belonging to her brother] . . . and she came to my house. . . . And I prove—I always prove—I described what her brother looked like. . . . And then I could see the plane. It was right in the middle of these trees. . . . So I went up high [like an airplane or a bird], and I could see this little gas station down below . . . and I could see a woman with no teeth, I could hear dogs barking, I could see a dirt road. And about halfway up the mountain—that's where the plane was—numbers started coming into my head—they turned out to be longitude and latitude. . . . Then she said, "Tell me, is my brother alive? What do you see?" And I saw the two people up front [in the plane], their necks were broken. And then I saw her brother, and he was carrying something, and he placed it under a tree, and he started walking away. . . . When they found the plane, the two people in the front, their necks were broken. *Her brother had carried a headless woman, and sat this headless woman against a tree, and had walked several yards away.* And the longitude and latitude were right, [and] the gas station with the barking dogs. The woman with no teeth had owned that gas station for years and had died the year before.

Jessica Herbert had testified that within days of her visit to Renier, the plane was found in "an area exactly the way [Renier] had described it . . . very thickly forested, very primitive . . . very rocky. . . . [S]he mentioned also that there was a down draft that had sucked the plane down, she could feel the—well, in fact, this down draft caused by that hill being there, the way the air current flowed off the runway and . . . they were flying too low . . . and it had caught in a down draft. That's exactly what happened. And she also described the injuries. . . . *[My brother] had survived the crash and he'd tried to help the girl . . .*" (emphasis added).[42]

The following is from the testimony of FBI special agent Babyak:

[T]hey had been unable to find any evidence of a plane and were going to call off the search, so Jessica was quite frantic. . . . I had heard from a friend of mine at work here of someone whom I could contact . . . Noreen Renier . . . Jessica went to see her. . . . [S]he did come away with a description of an area and events that transpired leading up to the crash which was substantial enough that I obtained the assistance of a friend of mine who is a pilot with the bureau, and we rented a small plane and flew up to the area. . . . [T]his was off-duty, totally unrelated to bureau activities. . . . [F]ollowing the directions that Noreen had provided us from the standpoint of landmarks, speed, turns, things of this nature . . . [we began circling an area]. . . . [It had become late and was getting dark]. . . . [W]e got a firm conviction from the man who was running the search that they would put a foot party in [the area we were circling] . . . [and] then our presence basically became unnecessary and both Mr. Crause [the pilot] and myself did have to be back [home] the next day. . . . [T]he following day a resident of that area and his daughter, due to our circling over that area constantly [the day before] went out in that area themselves and they found it prior to a search party finding it. . . . But it was in basically the area that we had been circling over and that's what, again, drew them to look in that area.[43]

According to newspaper accounts, the January 28, 1984, crash and explosion were heard by local pilot Ronald Richards and a companion, moments after they noted a low-flying plane pass over the Gardner, Massachusetts, airport.[44] An exhaustive but fruitless ground and air search was commenced on January 31, and called off on February 7.[45] But efforts were resumed on February 9 at the request of Jessica Herbert, who arrived on the scene that day in a chartered plane from Washington.[46]

Finally, on February 10, the wreckage of the plane was located. The following is from John Monahan's front-page story in the Worcester, Massachusetts, Telegram:

Four bodies were recovered from the twisted wreck. . . . The bodies of two of the victims were found dismembered amid snow-covered debris strewn in a wide area. Two others were found inside the crumpled body of the craft. . . . Inspector Murphy said last night from the appearance of the wreckage all four probably died on impact. The search . . . ended when a Templeton man, Carl F. Wilber, 40, and his 18-year-old daughter, Cheryl L. Wilber, found the wreckage shortly before noon in woods about a mile from their South Main Street home. They were among a number of area residents who continued searching on their own in the hilly and swampy woods southwest of the [Gardner] airport. They continued the search, they said, based on reports from two area pilots who insisted they witnessed a plane crash while at the airport the night of January 28. The Wilbers set out on foot and, using a compass, followed the last known direction of the aircraft as reported by the two witnesses. Once in the area yesterday, the Wilbers said, Cheryl suggested they follow a set of deer tracks, thinking the curious animals may have already gone to the crash site. The deer tracks, they said, led them to the wreckage one hour into their search (all emphases added).[47]

Newspaper accounts on February 13[48] and 14[49] reported upon the results of the post-mortem examinations performed by the medical examiner. Arthur Herbert, 28, brother of Jessica Herbert, was positively identified as one of the four victims, all of whom, according to Dr. Paul Hart's findings, *"died immediately" upon impact* (emphasis added).

Two years later, the National Transportation Safety Board (NTSB) issued its official determination of the causes of the crash. Inadequate pre-flight preparations, including lack of adequate winterization of the engine, had created unsafe conditions aboard the craft. The NTSB report said the crash occurred *"during a forced landing after a fire ignited in the aircraft"* (emphasis added).[50]

Special Agent Babyak had more than just Renier's "psychic" impressions to guide him in his search for the missing plane. The following exchange had occurred during the deposing of Babyak by Merrell's attorney: "Q: Your ex-wife indicated in her deposition that there had been a report of a crash right off that airport, and that crash was supposed to have happened on the night that her brother's plane was missing. Were you aware of that report? A: I was aware of that through her, yes."[51]

Jessica Herbert had further testified during her deposition that her visit to Renier had taken place one day after their initial telephone conversation about the case.[52] At the time, Herbert had obviously been keeping herself well-informed as to the progress of the investigation into the plane's disappearance, though she, like everyone else, was unaware of two facts that would only later be discovered: the condition of her brother (dead on impact), and the cause of the crash (fire). Even if Renier had used the one day available to her to research the published accounts of the then week-long search for the missing plane, witnessed to have crashed in a hilly, wooded region near the Gardner, Massachusetts, airport, these two facts would have remained unknown to her—unless, of course, she was "psychic."

In her *Practical Homicide Investigation* commentary, Renier emphasizes that, "As I describe the victim and the scene . . . I insist on feedback. A simple 'Yes' or 'I understand' is sufficient."[53] Coincidentally, this is precisely the sort of feedback that magicians and psychology instructors rely upon in their very convincing "cold reading" demonstrations in which, *pretending* to have "psychic" power, they are able to convince strangers that they know all about them. On the following page, the textbook's author cautions that, although Renier is presumably beyond reproach in this regard, "It is important to note that charlatans and frauds exist in all professions . . . [and] flourish in the area of extrasensory perception. . . . [M]any frauds merely 'feed back' information . . . which is already a matter of public record, having read a newspaper account. . . . Or a fraud may have access to information on the case through family members . . . which give[s] the impression that he or she has some psychic knowledge of events."[54]

If Renier really does possess "psychic" abilities, such should be a simple enough matter to confirm unambiguously, by means of a carefully controlled test, under conditions that eliminate the possibility of cheating or self-delusion. During my 1986 radio appearance with her, Renier initially expressed resistance to being tested by a group of skeptics. But under pressure from Mark Plummer, then Executive Director of the Committee for the Scientific Investigation of Claims of the Paranormal (who participated by phone from CSICOP's Buffalo headquarters), Renier commented to the effect that, "You know where I am if you want to test me." Immediately after the show, both Bev Smith and her producer expressed to me their interest in doing a follow-up program, and in possibly assisting in the arrangements for a controlled test of Renier, who was billed as the "Bev Smith Show" 's "resident psychic." I attempted to pursue this matter in two subsequent letters to Smith's producer, but never received a reply.

During a February 1990 telephone conversation with Terry Smiljanich, chairman of the Tampa Bay Skeptics (TBS), Renier agreed to receive from TBS a proposal for just such a test, though she did remain noncommittal.[55] (I founded TBS in 1988, and since 1989 we have been offering $1,000 for *any* successful demonstration of *any* paranormal phenomenon.) In Smiljanich's follow-up letter to Renier, he referred to her May 14, 1989, appearance on ABC-TV's "Incredible Sunday," "in which you performed 'psychometry' on police officers' keys and rings, which were sealed in envelopes. . . . If you are indeed able to read the vibrations from such objects [and then to give a 'cold reading' of the person's life], you ought to be able to determine if a hidden ring or key is one of *your own,* or that of a stranger. I propose that we employ keys and/or rings. . . . After touching or holding the [envelopes or] boxes, you would choose which contained your own object. . . ."[56] A test of this nature, in contrast to her typical "cold reading," allows the odds of "success" and "failure" to be mathematically predetermined, and the results to be immediately and objectively self-evident.

Renier never replied directly to Smiljanich, but in a later telephone call to me she expressed her disinterest in being tested "by a doctor and an attorney" (referring to myself and Smiljanich), since she was "working on too many police cases and with too many scientists to have the time. . . . I'll let the scientists do it."[57] The names of these scientists and the dates and results of any such tests were among the information that Merrell had hoped to obtain from Renier during the course of his now-settled lawsuit against her.[58] Renier's attorney has since informed Smiljanich that he has advised his client not to speak with us further, citing TBS's "predisposition" in our newsletter's coverage of Renier's activities.[59]

But TBS remains willing and able to carry out a test—perhaps the one suggested by Smiljanich, or even an appropriate one designed by Renier herself—should she ever reconsider. A prior version of Renier's promotional packet contained a newspaper article alleging another easily testable ability: "She intimidates some people, such as opponents in billiards, where she uses her powers to block shots."[60] And given Renier's claim on the May 22, 1990, "Joan Rivers Show" that she has the ability to see right through one's clothing, any number of far more entertaining test possibilities come to mind.

NOTES

1. Letter from Dr. Joan Straumanis, Dean of the Faculty, Rollins College, to Terry Smiljanich, February 16, 1990.

2. David E. Jones, *Visions of Time: Experiments in Psychic Archeology* (Wheaton, Ill.: Theosophical Publishing House, 1979), p. 16. This book was the subject of an article by anthropologist Kenneth L. Feder entitled, "Psychic Archaeology: The Anatomy of Irrationalist Prehistoric Studies," *Skeptical Inquirer* (Summer 1980): 32–43. Among Feder's observations were these: "[P]sychic archaeology has gained an unfortunate professional tolerance, if not acceptance, in some quarters. . . . [F]ar and away the most disturbing work is that of David E. Jones. . . . It makes no sense, in an objective test of a hypothesis, to propose a phenomenon, design an experiment . . . and then seek to explain all experimental results within the context of the assumption that the hypothesis is, in fact, valid and true. This constitutes post-hoc rationalization . . . *not* science. . . . All of the results of [Jones'] experiment, including those that quite clearly contradict the hypothesis, are interpreted, squeezed, fudged, and rationalized away as actually supporting the hypothesis. . . . The abandonment of statistical analysis by a person with an advanced degree in anthropology is appalling. . . . Jones [has] abandoned science, reasoning, and rationality."

3. Minutes of telephone conversation with Elliot Wizer, June 27, 1991.

4. Vernon J. Geberth, *Practical Homicide Investigation: Tactics, Procedures, and Forensic Techniques* (New York: Elsevier, 1983), p. 420. Geberth acknowledges in his introductory remarks (p. 420) that the use of psychics is "somewhat sensational and often controversial," but offers that "anything which has proven to be successful in one investigation should certainly be considered in other cases. . . . [Psychics] may not always be accurate and in some instances may have no value to the

investigation. However, this should not discourage authorities from using a psychic, especially in homicide cases where there is limited information."

And from his concluding "Summary" (p. 425): "[I]nvestigatively speaking, there has been sufficient documentation of successes to merit the consideration of this technique on a case-by-case basis. . . . [T]here is a definite need for an evaluation of the successes and failures of psychic phenomena as they relate to law enforcement before they can be recognized as a 'legitimate' investigative tool. Perhaps in time, the psychic and the homicide investigator may form the perfect partnership against crime. In any event, I neither encourage or [sic] discourage the use of psychics in homicide investigations."

5. Deposition of Robert Ressler in the Circuit Court of the State of Oregon for the County of Jackson, September 5, 1986, p. 12.

6. Ibid., p. 13.

7. "Psychic Sees Death Try, FBI Listens," *New York Post,* June 4, 1988.

8. Richard Ault, telephone conversation (recorded with permission), May 20, 1991.

9. Ibid.

10. Chris Doyle, "Psychic Asked to Solve Keys Murder Case," *The Key West Citizen,* April 2, 1993.

11. Kendrick Frazier and James Randi, "Prediction after the Fact: Lessons of the Tamara Rand Hoax," *Skeptical Inquirer* 6, no. 1 (Fall 1981): 4–7.

12. Transcript of Proceedings in the Circuit Court of the State of Oregon for the County of Jackson, *Noreen Renier* v. *John Merrell* (Case No. 85-3781-J-2), September 10, 1986, p. 84. (Note: In the transcripts of the *depositions* referred to, the case number is recorded as ending in "J-1" rather than "J-2.") I should also mention that I have been unable to secure a copy of the *National Examiner* item in question. John Merrell informs me that his copy disappeared sometime during the Oregon trial. The *National Examiner,* now headquartered in Florida, informs me that it does not keep issues from so many years back. During our telecon, Elliot Wizer had offered to send me a copy from his personal file, provided that I submit the request in writing, attesting that the article would not be used for "legal purposes." I wrote such a letter to Wizer on July 2, 1991, as well as a reminder letter on August 29, but never received a response.

13. Arthur Lyons and Marcello Truzzi, *The Blue Sense* (New York: The Mysterious Press, 1991), p. 84. (Note: This point is footnoted in *The Blue Sense* and credited to an article in the Charlottesville, Virginia, *Daily Progress* by Anne Richardson entitled "Ruckersville Psychic on Trial of Rapist," December 11, 1979. [It appears that the word "Trial" may be a misprint of "Trail."])

14. Rex Springston, " 'Impressions' Give Clues in Cases," *Richmond Times-Dispatch,* June 21, 1992, C1. The fee is said to include "two sessions of 60 to 90 minutes each and a sketch of the crime suspect done by a member of her staff."

15. Noreen Renier, letter to Richard N. Harris, October 6, 1989.

16. "The Psychic Connection: Using Psychic Assistance in Law Enforcement" (p. 6 of a previous version of Renier's promotional packet).

17. Robert Ressler, deposition, p. 14.

18. Ibid., p. 11.

19. Ibid., p. 16.

20. Officer St. Just, NYPD Public Information Office, telephone conversation, September 12, 1990.

21. Transcript of Proceedings in the Circuit Court of the State of Oregon for the County of Jackson, *Noreen Renier* v. *John Merrell,* September 12, 1986, pp. 287–88.

22. Ibid., pp. 289–90.

23. "Workshops—ESP: An Awareness," (p. 5 of a previous version of Renier's promotional packet).

24. Transcript of Proceedings, *Renier* v. *Merrell,* September 11, 1986, pp. 253–54.

25. John Merrell, letter to *Ashland Daily Tidings,* October 10, 1985 (unpublished).

26. Richard Stair, Jr., United States Bankruptcy Judge, Eastern District of Tennessee, "Memorandum" of October 19, 1989, p. 10. (Note: Merrell had since moved to Tennessee from Oregon.) The ruling centers around the distinction between being a "member" vs. a "representative" of NCAHF. Stair ruled that "the debtor [Merrell], a member of the NCAHF, was not an authorized spokesperson for that institution . . . [and] was never asked by the NCAHF to conduct an investigation of the plaintiff [Renier] . . .," although Merrell had held "conversations [about Renier] with NCAHF co-members [Dr. Benjamin] Wilson, [Robert] Steiner and [Dr. Robert A.] Mendelsohn [sic] at a Portland, Oregon [NCAHF] conference" and had made an "inquiry to the president of the NCAHF . . . to see if it had any background material on [Renier]" (which it did not) (p. 11). The Dr. Mendelson (proper spelling) referred to is not to be confused with the late Dr. Robert S. Mendelsohn, a frequent guest on national TV talk shows in the 1980s as a "medical heretic" claiming that doctors do more harm than good.

27. Tony Hazarian, "Using the Power of the Mind," *Ashland Daily Tidings,* May 4, 1985.

28. Leroy Coppedge, letter to *Daily Tidings,* published June 4, 1985.

29. "Nancy Uzdavinis," letter to John Merrell, June 26, 1985.

30. John Merrell, letter to "Nancy Uzdavinis," September 14, 1985.

31. Transcript of Proceedings, *Noreen Renier* v. *John Douglas Merrell* (Case No. 3-88-00616), United States Bankruptcy Court for the Eastern District of Tennessee, Northern Division, April 17, 1989, p. 19.

32. Ibid., p. 50.

33. Dorothy V. Lehman, affidavit, State of Oregon, County of Clackamas, sworn November 21, 1989.

34. "Motion of Defendant John Merrell for Relief of Final Judgment," January 9, 1990.

35. Noreen Renier, affidavit sworn January 31, 1990.

36. Ibid. When I questioned Merrell as to why the letter had not surfaced

earlier, he told me that he had stored his "Nancy Uzdavinis" material in his general correspondence file along with the many other letters from people inquiring about the Northwest Skeptics, rather than in his "Renier" file.

37. Noreen Renier, deposition, Circuit Court of the Ninth Judicial Circuit in and for Orange County, Florida, May 21, 1991, p. 73.

38. Nancy Uzdavinis, affidavit, State of Oregon, County of Jackson, sworn January 17, 1990.

39. Richard Stair, Jr., United States Bankruptcy Judge, "Order" of February 14, 1990.

40. Loyd Auerbach, "Taking a Skeptic to Court," FATE (June 1991): 60–68.

41. Lyons and Truzzi, The Blue Sense, p. 7.

42. Jessica Herbert, deposition, in the Circuit Court of the State of Oregon for the County of Jackson, August 28, 1986, p. 16.

43. Mark Babyak, deposition, in the Circuit Court of the State of Oregon for the County of Jackson, September 4, 1986, pp. 5–11.

44. John J. Monahan, "Missing Plane Reportedly Seen in Gardner," The Telegram, Worcester, Mass., February 7, 1984.

45. Monahan, "Air Force Calls Off Hunt for Missing Plane," Telegram, February 8, 1984.

46. Monahan, "Search for Plane On Again," Evening Gazette, Worcester, Mass., February 10, 1984. (Note: The Telegram and Evening Gazette have since merged into a single daily paper.)

47. Monahan, "Plane Found in Templeton; 4 Dead," Telegram, February 11, 1984.

48. "Examiner Says Plane Victims Died Instantly," Telegram, February 13, 1984.

49. "Two Plane Crash Victims Are Identified," Telegram, February 14, 1984.

50. Mark E. Ellis, "Several Causes Listed for 1984 Plane Crash," Evening Gazette, February 27, 1986.

51. Mark Babyak, deposition, p. 12.

52. Jessica Herbert, deposition, p. 23.

53. Geberth, Practical Homicide Investigation, p. 422.

54. Ibid., pp. 423–24.

55. Minutes (prepared by Terry Smiljanich) of telephone conversation with Noreen Renier, February 5, 1990.

56. Terry Smiljanich, letter to Noreen Renier, February 27, 1990.

57. Noreen Renier, telephone conversation, March 15, 1990.

58. Since one might perhaps infer from Dr. Robert Van de Castle's letter of recommendation (see early in chapter) that he has had personal involvement in scientifically evaluating, in a laboratory setting, Renier's alleged "psychic" powers, I wrote to him on October 24, 1991, for clarification. In his reply (undated but postmarked on November 5), he expressed his favorable impression of Renier's "psychometry" demonstrations on patients of his ("I felt she described many aspects of their past history or current personality features . . ."), and noted that "an

anthropologist/archeologist in Florida who compared her 'psychometry' impressions with archeological information he had available for this Georgia site . . . described her abilities in 'psychic archeology' very favorably in his book" (see my note 2). As to the point of scientific/laboratory testing, Dr. Van de Castle stated, "I accompanied Ms. Renier to the laboratory facilities of the Psychical Research Foundation in Durham, N.C. She was being evaluated to see whether there would be EEG and other physiological changes produced when she went into a trance state and attempted to contact some spiritual guides. Changes were found but there were also considerable artifacts which made precise evaluation difficult. There were no card tests, etc., attempted. Renier was very willing to return for further evaluation."

59. Carey N. Bos and Terry Smiljanich, personal communication (as reported to me by Smiljanich).

60. "Psychic's Career Began with $5 Readings," *Lakeland Ledger* (Florida), July 29, 1986.

6

Veteran Psychic Detective: Bill Ward

Jim Lippard

In September 1965, 23-year-old army medic Bill Ward and his fellow soldiers found themselves under heavy fire in Vietnam. Enemy bullets struck a nearby officer, who collapsed and fell into a water-filled ditch. Ward moved to the officer's side, administering mouth-to-mouth resuscitation and applying first aid. As fighting continued, Ward supervised the helicopter evacuation of the wounded officer. The officer's life was saved, and Bill Ward was decorated with a Bronze Star Medal with valor for his efforts.[1] In the course of his ten-month military service, Ward also earned two Purple Hearts.[2]

After returning home from Vietnam in 1967, Ward resumed his work at the Will County Printing Company in Lockport, Illinois, from which he has only recently retired. But for Ward, as for many other Vietnam veterans, his life was not quite the same. Before he had been back home for a year, he found that his exposure to many violent deaths had affected his perceptions of the world in a radical way: he had developed psychic abilities.[3]

Since 1971, Ward has assisted in over 400 homicide cases, for which he has claimed a 75-to-80 percent success rate.[4] He is supported in his claims of psychic powers by private and police investigators around the country who say he has provided them with assistance in solving crimes. In the course of his more than two decades of psychic sleuthing, Ward has shunned most publicity (initially he even required anonymity as a condition of assistance) regarding his police work and, until recently, has worked entirely on a volunteer basis.[5] His motivation, therefore, has been neither fame nor money. Investigators he has worked with are quite convinced of his sincerity.

What is it, exactly, that Bill Ward claims to be able to do, and what evidence is there to support his claims? Is the evidence strong enough to establish the validity of paranormal abilities, or the usefulness of Bill Ward as an investigative tool? The following is an attempt to critically analyze Bill Ward's claims and answer these questions, despite objections from Ward's publicist, Gayle Crnkovic, that it is an attempt to do the impossible.[6]

The objection is frequently made that the scientific examination of paranormal abilities is futile, because somehow these abilities evade attempts to study them.[7] But how could this be the case? Even if Ward has little or no control over his abilities, even if he doesn't know when he's on the mark, any genuine ability should show up as an above-chance effect in a controlled experiment.[8] Those who have worked with Ward seem to think that he *can* tell when he is accurate or not; he frequently supplies not only his impressions, but how strongly he feels about a particular statement. If he really can do this, then testing his abilities is even easier. Unfortunately, Ward refuses to undergo testing, which he refers to as "play[ing] games."[9] As a result, this examination of his claims relies mostly on testimonial evidence, with all of its limitations.[10]

WHAT DOES BILL WARD DO?

"I get pictures as soon as [investigators] say something—faces, scenes, areas, just like you turn on TV,"[11] says Ward, who indicates that violence is the easiest thing for him to pick up on. In addition to using his innate (or, as he would probably prefer, God-given) ability to receive images from spatially and temporally distant locations, Ward makes use of some other tools in his practice of psychic detection—including psychometry (handling objects in order to obtain information about people who have been in contact with them), seeing auras, biorhythms, and both Chinese and Western astrology.[12] A flyer advertising "Bill Ward: Psychic Investigator of Crimes" lists "HYPNOSIS & ADVISOR" and "PSYCHOMETRY & CHIROMANCY" among his skills.[13] One published article about Ward states that he "reportedly can read minds and bend objects, such as keys, by concentrating on them," but also notes that he refers to such feats as "junk" and "circus tricks."[14]

The ABCs of Ward's paranormal toolkit (astrology and auras, biorhythms, and chiromancy) involve widely made claims which are not only subject to scientific examination but have also been carefully examined. Proponents of astrology, biorhythms, and chiromancy, at least, have even frequently claimed scientific validity for their practices. They claim that anyone, using them properly, can achieve repeatable success. But these claims are not supported by the experimental results. None of them has any demonstrated ability to predict human behavior or personality characteristics, contrary to their practitioners.[15] No reliable correlations have been observed between astrological horoscopes and personality characteristics, between biorhythm cycles and human performance, or between palm creases and future actions. Astrological readings from incorrectly drawn horoscopes, biorhythms based on incorrect dates, and palm readings opposite what the lines are supposed to indicate are perceived by their recipients to be just as accurate as those based on the correct information.[16]

The detection of human auras has also failed the test. Since auras are claimed to extend beyond the boundaries of the skin, they should be detectable in some cases when the body they surround is not. For example, a person standing to just one side of an open doorway, behind a wall, should be visible to an aura reader when the aura extends into the doorway. But the ability of aura readers to detect persons in such conditions at a rate better than expected by chance has yet to be demonstrated.[17]

Rosalyn Bruyere, the founder and director of the Healing Light Center Church in Glendale, California, has published a description of how anyone can learn to see human auras.[18] Her method requires the would-be aura reader to "Focus on a person, setting your focal length on their forehead. As you look, your peripheral vision will give you a kind of shadow image. . . . The way to improve is by relaxing and letting your peripheral vision come into play."[19] This technique will produce "a kind of shadow image" for any kind of object in your field of vision, not just people or other biological organisms. If you focus at one point and look at another, the separate images from your two eyes will not be consistent with each other. The image from one eye will be shifted with respect to the other, which can appear as a transparent "fuzz" on the edge of the object— an "aura."[20]

This evidence strongly suggests that any success Bill Ward has achieved is not due to his use of these ABC tools, but due to some other skill he possesses. The above-mentioned candidates remaining are his ability to see images of spatially and temporally distant occurrences (perhaps a form of telepathy or clairvoyance) and psychometry. These are abilities which have been widely claimed, and which have also been subjected to scientific experiments. The results here, however, are not so clear cut as with the ABCs. The Parapsychological Association (PA), whose members are devoted to the scientific examination of such abilities, is affiliated with the prestigious American Association for the Advancement of Science (AAAS). There are several active journals in the field which regularly publish both successful and failed experimental results. Unfortunately, there is no consensus about what, exactly, has been established in the field. While most parapsychologists are confident that anomalies have been clearly demonstrated, there is significant disagreement about the proper explanation for these anomalies. Outside the field of parapsychology, critics claim that the existence of anomalies themselves is not well established.[21]

Perhaps most relevant to Ward's claimed abilities to see distant events as though watching a movie are experiments testing what is known as "remote viewing." Some experiments in remote viewing have produced above-chance results, but even ignoring the criticisms that have been made of these experiments, they do not provide support for claims of psychic powers as dramatic as those claimed by most psychics.[22] While Ward has claimed to be more than 80 percent accurate in his work in over four hundred homicide cases,[23] psychologist Louise Ludwig, who has worked with many psychic detectives and advocates their use by police, suggests that a more reasonable figure is 20–25 percent accurate, with higher accuracy on rare occasions.[24] Even this lower figure, however, is a rough estimate rather than the result of careful calculation. Accuracy figures are also subject to varied interpretations. Does "accuracy" refer to number of accurate statements made, number of verified statements, number of cases in which the police believed the psychic to be right, number of cases in which a conviction was obtained, or number of cases in which some useful information was provided?

Ward has given one answer to this question in his claim that arrests have been made due to information he provided in 75 percent of his homicide cases.[25] Of the eight homicide cases this author has specifically discussed with investigators who have worked with Ward, arrests have been made in two. In neither of those cases is the arrest attributable to evidence provided by Ward. (In one case, the suspect turned himself in; in the other, the suspect was arrested in another state on other charges. Both cases are described below.) An examination of all the published articles on Ward cited in this investigation reveals a total of eleven homicide cases, six of which are included in the above figures. Of the five additional cases, arrests were apparently made in all of them, all possibly on the basis of information provided by Ward. This makes a total of thirteen cases, with arrests in eight, five possibly due to Ward, giving a "success" rate (by Ward's definition) of 42 percent. The published information about all five of these cases comes, directly or indirectly, from Bill Ward's publicist, Gayle Crnkovic.[26]

BILL WARD'S CASE FILE

Despite the fact that none of the cases examined as part of this investigation resulted in arrests due to information provided by Ward, all but one of the investigators contacted were convinced that Ward was helpful. Most have used him in more than one case and said that they would gladly use him again as the need arose. What follows are descriptions of several of Ward's cases, focusing on his contribution to each.[27]

THE JEANIE BENNETT CASE

In February 1978, 37-year-old Floy Jean "Jeanie" Bennett, a court re-porter in Beaverton, Oregon, disappeared. She had left home, reportedly to go shopping. She has not been seen since. Her checks and credit cards have remained unused, but most of a $90,000 inheritance vanished with her.[28]

Jeanie Bennett's husband, Robert Eugene "Bob" Bennett, reported her disappearance to the police. According to Bennett, he and his wife had fought and she had left him for another man. Bennett became the prime suspect in his wife's disappearance, but police were unable to collect enough evidence to charge him with any crime. The case remained open but inactive.

In 1988, Portland private investigator Ray Montee, working on the Bennett case, decided to contact Ward after reading about him in the *National Examiner*. Montee sent Ward copies of materials regarding the Bennett case and spoke to him on the telephone. Bill Ward told Montee that either Jeanie Bennett's body or something belonging to her was buried in the back yard of the home of Bob Bennett's deceased brother-in-law. The outdoor barbecue was specifically mentioned as the most important place to dig.

Bob and Jeanie Bennett had themselves once lived in this house, which was noteworthy for various do-it-yourself improvements that had been made. The driveway had been repaved, a former greenhouse in the back yard had been converted into a storage shed, and a concrete patio and outdoor brick barbecue had been built in the back yard.

Montee obtained permission from the present owner of the house to do some digging, and began to remove bricks from the barbecue "with a soup spoon and a screwdriver."[29] The Beaverton Police Department learned of Montee's activities, and had him removed from the site so they could dig it up themselves. According to Detective Dan Kelly, this was done "to preserve evidence and the integrity of the site."[30] Two holes, three feet by five feet in area, were dug in the backyard by police and public works employees, but no body was found. The case of the disappearance of Jeanie Bennett remains unsolved.

What does this case demonstrate about the psychic abilities of Bill Ward? Not much, unfortunately. Ray Montee still has a positive view of Ward, and still thinks that the body of Jeanie Bennett may be buried in the backyard of Bob Bennett's brother-in-law. The Beaverton Police Department's search was less than exhaustive: two holes in the back yard, neither of which involved digging under the concrete patio or the barbecue (though one of them was next to the barbecue).

There are more ambiguities in the case. In a newspaper report, Montee was quoted as saying, "I had never even thought about the barbecue and never mentioned it to Ward" and that Ward said the body would be found on one side or another of the barbecue.[31] In a 1991 interview, however, Montee said that he had had a hunch that the barbecue was important even before he had spoken to Ward, and that he had mentioned it to him.[32] Montee also reported Ward saying that "either she or something of hers is under that fireplace," rather than on one side or the other. According to Montee, kids had dug up bones on the site before his abortive attempt to dig. When asked about this, Detective Kelly stated that no human bones were found.

Around 1989, according to Montee, Bob Bennett was captured in Las Vegas attempting to use the identification and credit cards of a coworker who had been murdered in Utah. Bennett was convicted and imprisoned for this murder. (Detective Kelly confirmed that Bennett is in prison.) The Jeanie Bennett case remains open but inactive.

The evidence does not clearly show Ward to be either right or wrong. However, neither does it give any support to his claim to have psychic abilities. Even if Jeanie Bennett's body were discovered under (or in the vicinity of) the outdoor barbecue, it is not clear that the source of this prediction was Ward rather than Montee's hunch.

THE JOLIET GRAIN ELEVATOR EXPLOSION

On April 23, 1988, an explosion in a grain elevator at Archer Daniels Midland in Joliet, Illinois, left five men dead and buried under tons of corn and debris. A nearby bridge tender reported seeing a man blown off a barge into the Des Plaines river by the explosion. During the first day of the thirty-hour search for bodies, Bill Ward arrived at the scene to offer assistance. Ward apparently confirmed the bridge tender's report, stating that a body would be found in water. His impressions of the incident also included one person having trouble breathing and another's legs entwined in something.[33] He also offered suggestions on how the search should proceed. In the UPI account of the explosion and search, Ward was quoted as saying, "I just more or less gave them an idea of where to start digging . . . I just sense it. I feel it."[34]

As it turned out, the bridge tender's report was in error: no one had been thrown into the river by the explosion. Gayle Crnkovic, Ward's publicist, wrote in correspondence to the author that this "is probably the only public error [Ward] has ever made.[35] She continues, "It turned out that the man believed to have been thrown into the river was found submerged in water in the lower level" and investigators on the site were willing to give Ward the benefit of the doubt. But Ward himself, she writes, "simply stated he was wrong."

According to Lieutenant Joe Drick of the Joliet Fire Department, however, Ward was "totally incorrect in his predictions" and was "more trouble than he was worth," contributing to a circus-like atmosphere.[36] Drick, who was the battalion chief's driver the day of the explosion, said that no bodies were found in water. Ward's suggested search procedure, says Drick, was to begin at the perimeter of the explosion area and work to the center, but this was simply stating the obvious. It was the only possible way to search due to the way the 70,000 bushels of grain and other debris were situated. Drick also emphasized that Ward was not called in by the Joliet Fire Department.

But according to Detective Louie Silich of the Joliet Police Department, who worked closely with Bill Ward that day and who continues to use Ward as an investigative aid, a water main in the basement of the grain elevator had burst, and one of the bodies was found there. Another body was found with its legs entwined in twisted metal rebar, and the autopsy on another revealed corn grain in the throat.[37]

Here, as in the Jeanie Bennett case, the evidence is not very persuasive. The report of the bridge tender likely inspired Ward's statement that a body would be found "in water," but even though the bridge tender's report was false, another interpretation of the statement turned out to be correct. The statement that someone involved had difficulty in breathing is a fair guess in a case where people were known to be buried under tons of grain. Likewise, the prediction that a body's legs were entwined in something was vague and unsurprising.

THE CANDACE AND GREGORY AUGUSTUS MURDERS

In October 1987, Candace Augustus, age thirty, and her son Gregory, age eleven, were found beaten to death in their trailer home in Dixmoor, Illinois.[38] Robert L. Fair, who lived in the same trailer park, disappeared, as did the murdered woman's car. Fair immediately became the prime suspect in the murders.

Dixmoor police contacted Bill Ward for assistance in the case. Of the probable suspects, Ward concurred with the police that Fair was the most likely.[39] Ward informed the police that Fair had taken the murdered woman's car and driven it part of the way to his mother's house, taking a bus or hitchhiking the remainder of the way. Fair ended up turning himself in to the Cohoma County Sheriff's Department in Clarksdale, Mississippi, near his mother's and brother's home in Friar's Point. Cohoma County Sheriff Andrew Thompson said he thought the car was found in Friar's Point, but Dixmoor Police Deputy Chief Michael Morgan said it was found in Champaign, Illinois, where Fair had stayed in a motel and then traveled on by bus. According to Morgan, "Bill didn't know where the car was."[40] Two independent newspaper reports said the car was found in Mississippi.[41]

According to Deputy Chief Morgan, who took Fair into custody, Fair confessed in Mississippi at about 6 P.M. About an hour earlier, Ward was in the trailer park in Dixmoor with Chief Anton Graff, describing the details of the murders as they examined the scene of the crime. Morgan reports that when he told Graff the details of the confession, they matched what Ward had described. The most impressive point of correspondence, according to Morgan, was Ward's explanation of a bloodstain found in a hallway as the spot where Fair had set down the murder weapon (a baseball bat) after killing Gregory Augustus and before killing the boy's mother. Ward "made a believer out of me," Morgan said.

Other information supplied by Ward included a psychological profile of Fair, apparently based on biorhythms, designed to help with the interrogation process. Ward told Morgan that he should not "be in a room alone with him. You are going to be the focal point of his anger," but Morgan says that Fair was "pretty passive."[42] Ward also advised Morgan not to "say things about the woman—focus on the child." According to Morgan, he didn't follow this advice, and whenever he mentioned Candace Augustus' name, Fair would "clam up." As a result of his assistance on the case, the Dixmoor Police Department presented Ward a certificate for supplying "invaluable information" which "gave the investigators a greater insight of the crime and of the offender" for his "psychic rendition of the crime and psychological profile of the offender."[43]

The evidence for Ward's abilities in this case is again rather weak. At least one piece of information about the murderer (that he would focus his anger on Morgan, his interrogator) proved false, and the rest may well have been just common sense (e.g., provoke a confession by talking about the murder of the child). The suspect had already been identified before Ward was contacted, and checking with relatives is certainly a good investigative strategy independent of psychic advice. Ward may have been correct about Fair's driving the murdered woman's car only part way to his mother's house, but given the conflicting information about where the car was found, one can't be sure.

THE ANNA SANDERS MURDER

On April 10, 1989, Anna L. Sanders was stabbed to death in her apartment on Lois Place in Joliet, Illinois. Bill Ward was called to the scene after it had been partially gone over by technicians, and pointed out a fingerprint on a dining room window that they had missed, although that did not prove useful.[44] There were three or four possible means of egress from the apartment complex, of which Ward indicated one as the route the murderer took when leaving. Investigators found people in the area who were in the process of moving at the approximate time of the murder, but none of them saw anything. The case remains unsolved.

According to Joliet Police Sergeant Robert Kelly, Ward is "quite accurate" and is used by his department "quite a bit."[45] The first case Sergeant Kelly used Ward in, over a decade ago, involved a missing eight-year-old boy from the northeast side of town. Ward reported that he saw the boy on the street talking to neighbor kids, and that he would be found in a two-story red building next to a one-story white building. The boy was found, dead, in just such a building (though the body's discovery was not made on the basis of Ward's description). Tracing the boy's steps backward, witnesses were found who had seen him standing in the street talking to people. The suspect in this case was arrested and convicted of murders in Texas, but has not been charged for this murder.

Sergeant Kelly says that occasionally Ward will be given six or seven fingerprint cards of possible suspects, and "he's picked the right one several times."[46] Without more detailed information, it is impossible to conclude anything about Ward's abilities on the basis of the fingerprint card test. Nor is the other evidence in these cases very strong. Finding a fingerprint at a crime scene is not particularly remarkable. The description of the building where the boy would be found is fairly vague and unsurprising, as is the description of him talking to "neighbor kids."

MISCELLANEOUS CASE ANECDOTES

Some of Ward's most impressive cases have been with the Kendall County State Attorney's Office. One case which several investigators mentioned that they had heard about was a 1981 case involving a 24-year-old female found stabbed to death in a bathtub. According to former Kendall County Investigator Ricky M. Holman, when he called for Ward's assistance, Ward was able to describe the scene without any prompting, despite the fact that police processing of the scene had only just begun and the press knew nothing about it. When told that investigators had no clues, Ward asked, "Did you get the fingerprint?" Ward said he saw bookshelves on the ground, things strewn about, and a picture tilted on the wall which had been touched by the killer. Investigators followed his description into the living room, where a tilted picture was found to have a smudged partial fingerprint on the bottom right side. On the telephone with investigator Randy Clawson, Ward instructed him to "send Rick outside over to the parking lot." There, Ward said, he would find two men drinking beer under a street light who might be able to answer some questions. According to Holman, there were men there, just as Ward described, who were talking about a salesman who had been in the apartment complex the night before. (The salesman and the fingerprint both turned out to be dead ends, and the crime remains unsolved.)[47]

Another case involved a nurse who disappeared the night before she was supposed to testify against her rapist in Naperville, Illinois, in the mid-1980s. Ward was called in by the Naperville Police Department, for whom he drew a map of the area where her body would be found, which he believed to be northeast of Naperville. Despite the investigators' best efforts, no body was located. About a year and a half later, a farmer in Aurora, Illinois (west of Naperville), noticed a depressed area of ground in one of his fields. The farmer guessed that one of the clay tiles buried under the surface of the ground to drain water properly had broken and began to dig. When he uncovered a white shoe—still being worn—he called the police. When Holman compared Ward's map to the field in which the body was found, he discovered that it matched very well. The map showed a highway running east and west at the north end, another road running north and south on the east side, a water tower in the northwest corner, railroad tracks and a creek running north and south on the west side, and trees in the northeast corner.[48]

Detective Michael Krause of the Naperville Police Department, one of two investigators working on this case, does not remember any involvement of Bill Ward. He reports that the suspect was found dead after he had stabbed himself in the femoral artery while killing a boy. Among evidence recovered was a wine bottle in the trunk of his car which matched a lid found with the nurse's body.[49]

Holman, the only source for this article who has indicated that Ward sees auras, related the phenomenon to another he says he has seen. While looking over photographs of death scenes, he and a fellow investigator noticed a bright blue pinpoint of light, sometimes with red and white wavy lines radiating out from it, on them. These blue dots were found only on death scenes. When he sent film to Kodak asking for an explanation, he was informed that it was "photographer error." Holman, however, found this explanation unconvincing, and told this author that taking photographs of a fresh grave at a cemetery at different film speeds with no light source would produce the same effect.[50]

A query of photo labs and police departments found that no one else was familiar with blue points of light associated with death scenes, including Victor Franz, one of Holman's former fellow investigators.[51] According to an employee of the Photographic Works Lab in Tucson, Arizona, there are a number of factors which can produce all sorts of unusual images on film. Chemical splashes during processing, water spots causing pieces of the film to stick to each other, light flare in the camera lens, or a defect in the camera lens could all produce such an effect.[52]

IS BILL WARD PSYCHIC?

There are serious problems involved in reliance upon testimonial evidence in answering a question such as this. The more independent confirming testimony there is, the better the case, but in the cases described above there is usually only the testimony of one or two investigators, who are not independent of each other.

The ideal way to answer the above question would be to subject Bill Ward to a controlled test of his abilities, something he refuses to permit. While such tests have been conducted with other psychic detectives[53] with the result that "the usefulness of psychics as an aid in criminal investigation has not been validated,"[54] they are open to the criticism that genuine psychics are rare (and weren't involved in the testing) or that psychics achieve success only under certain conditions which weren't properly duplicated by the experimenters. In order to evaluate a psychic who was not a participant in these experiments, it is necessary to look at his or her own track record, as has been done here.

Given the nature of the evidence, it is probably not possible to definitively answer the question "Is Bill Ward psychic?" Both apparent successes and apparent failures have been described, supported by the testimony of investigators. Those who have worked with Ward are generally enthusiastic about his abilities and usefulness as well as his sincerity. But this is not sufficient to establish the validity of his psychic abilities, given the social and psychological factors that are capable of convincing people of the accuracy of information provided even by phony psychics, palm readers, or astrologers—independently of any truly specific and accurate information provided by those sources.[55]

Still, some of the stories of Bill Ward's successes are fairly impressive. It cannot be said with certainty that belief and perceptual biases, "cold reading," and the like can constitute a complete explanation of what he does. In fact, if (and it's a big if) the accounts of his successes are correct in all their details, it seems unlikely that these factors alone could be such an explanation.

In order to justify a "yes" answer to the question "Is Bill Ward psychic?" some critics of the paranormal seem to require that he be able to solve cases all by himself—to take the police directly to the culprit, if not provide his name, address, and telephone number. Psychic detectives in general and Bill Ward in particular have not demonstrated such an ability. Instead, as former Kendall County investigator Ricky Holman puts it, "What Mr. Ward does is provide information that one could ordinarily not find without his insight. . . . He provides additional pieces to the puzzle."[56] If psychic detectives, in order to prove useful, were required to do more than this, then other tools of the police trade such as fingerprint technology would also fail the test.

Perhaps a better question to ask is whether or not Bill Ward has proved useful as an investigative tool. If the testimonial accounts of those who have worked with him are correct, then the answer is clearly yes. By these accounts, Ward has demonstrated his usefulness by pointing out details overlooked by on-site investigators, sometimes without even being present at the scene of the crime.

Unfortunately, however, those who have made use of Bill Ward generally have no official guidelines for the use of psychics,[57] and so it is difficult to gauge how much information Ward has provided independently and how much information he is given by the investigators to work with. It is possible that much of what he does is commonsense reasoning combined with a dash of speculative induction. As such, the case for Bill Ward's psychic abilities remains at best unproved, and certainly does not support his own claims of success and accuracy.

ACKNOWLEDGMENTS

This article could not have been written without the helpful cooperation of a number of law enforcement and private investigators and others who have encountered Bill Ward. I am especially grateful to Marcello Truzzi, who got the ball rolling by providing numerous references and news clippings.

NOTES

1. "Local GI Decorated As Hero," *Joliet* (Ill.) *Herald-News,* undated clipping (between January 26 and March 10, 1966).
2. Gayle Crnkovic, "Will County Psychic Aids Investigations: Work in Murder Case Earns Honors," *Joliet* (Ill.) *Herald-News,* November 15, 1987; Crnkovic, "Mind over Murder! Psychic Aid in Investigations," *Police Times* 21, no. 2 (March–April 1987): 6.
3. Arthur Lyons and Marcello Truzzi, *The Blue Sense: Psychic Detectives and Crime* (New York: The Mysterious Press, 1991), p. 60; Crnkovic, "Mind over Murder!" p. 6.
4. John Jeter, "Psychic Tie Aids Arrest of Suspect in 2 Killings," *Chicago Sun-Times,* October 25, 1987, reports an "80-plus percent accuracy rate" for "400 homicide cases," while Molly Woulfe, "Television Viewers Can See Lockport Psychic: Ward Stars as Himself in ABC's 'Crime Busters,' " *Joliet* (Ill.) *Herald-News,* May 25, 1989, reports Ward's estimate as 479 cases since 1971, with arrests due to information he provided in 75 percent of those cases.
5. Crnkovic (personal communication, January 8, 1992), Ward's publicist, has confirmed that since his retirement from the printing business in June 1991, he has required payment for most of his work. He is, however, willing to forgo payment in certain cases, e.g., finding a lost child. Ward and Crnkovic refused to answer written questions from this author or submit to any kind of extended interview on the basis of time constraints and the fact that they are collaborating on a book about Ward's life. Ward, however, suggested that something might possibly be arranged provided that he be paid for his time (personal communication, December 10, 1991).
6. Personal communication with Gayle Crnkovic, January 8, 1992. She expressed similar doubts in correspondence dated March 26, 1991.
7. Robert Sheaffer, in his book *The UFO Verdict: Examining the Evidence* (Buffalo, N.Y.: Prometheus Books, 1980), p. 159, refers to phenomena that exhibit this kind of shyness as "jealous phenomena."

8. Such an experiment could be set up within the context of the very work Ward does in his present investigations. For example, items known to be unrelated to a crime could be given to him along with items associated with the crime to see if he could tell the difference or if his impressions for unrelated items matched the results of mundane investigations as well as his impressions for the associated items. Ideally, such an experiment would be double-blind. That is, the person conducting the experiment with Ward would not know which items were related and which were not. For examples of similar experiments which found no confirmation of psychic crime-solving ability, see Martin Reiser, Louise Ludwig, Susan Saxe, and Clare Wagner, "An Evaluation of the Use of Psychics in the Investigation of Major Crimes," *Journal of Police Science and Administration* 7, no. 1 (1979): 19, and Nels Klyverand and Martin Reiser, "A Comparison of Psychics, Detectives, and Students in the Investigation of Major Crimes," in Martin Reiser, *Police Psychology: Collected Papers* (Los Angeles: Lehi Publishing Co., 1982), pp. 260–67. For some criticisms of these experiments, see Lyons and Truzzi, *The Blue Sense,* pp. 52–53.

9. Crnkovic, "Mind over Murder!" p. 6.

10. Some of these limitations are described in the Introduction.

11. Crnkovic, "Mind over Murder: Psychic Aids in Investigation," *Law and Order,* September 1986, p. 44. Ward makes similar remarks in Molly Woulfe, "Television Viewers Can See Lockport Psychic": "He can visualize a crime as soon as an officer calls, Ward said. . . . 'It's just like watching a movie,' he explained."

12. For biorhythms and astrology: Lyons and Truzzi, *The Blue Sense,* p. 60 and John Jeter, "Psychic Tie Aids Arrest of Suspect in 2 Killings," *Chicago Sun-Times,* October 25, 1987. For psychometry: "Bill Ward: Psychic Investigator of Crimes," undated flyer. For seeing auras: personal communication with Ricky M. Holman, Deputy Public Defender, Juvenile Division, DuPage County, Illinois, November 30, 1991.

13. This flyer is the same one mentioned in the previous note. Ward apparently uses hypnosis and chiromancy (palm reading) in his role as a psychic advisor but not in his sleuthing. Of other occult/paranormal activities, Ward has been involved in hunting for and photographing ghosts, allegedly with success (personal communication with Gayle Crnkovic, January 8, 1992).

14. Woulfe, "Television Viewers Can See Lockport Psychic." None of the people interviewed for this investigation reported any such claims, and several expressed skepticism that Ward would ever claim to be able to do such things.

15. For biorhythms, see William Sims Bainbridge, "Biorhythms: Evaluating a Pseudoscience," *Skeptical Inquirer* 2, no. 2 (Spring/Summer 1978): 40–56, and Terence Hines, "Biorhythm Theory: A Critical Review," *Skeptical Inquirer* 3, no. 4 (Summer 1979): 26–36. For astrology, see Geoffrey Dean, "Does Astrology Need to Be True? Part 1: A Look at the Real Thing," *Skeptical Inquirer* 11, no. 2 (Winter 1986–87): 166–84, and Dean, "Does Astrology Need to Be True? Part 2: The Answer Is No," *Skeptical Inquirer* 11, no. 3 (Spring 1987): 257–73; John H. McGrew and Richard M. McFall, "A Scientific Inquiry into the

Validity of Astrology," *Journal of Scientific Exploration* 4, no. 1 (1990): 75–83; Ivan W. Kelly, Roger Culver, and Peter J. Loptson, "Astrology and Science: An Examination of the Evidence," in S. K. Biswas, D. C. V. Mallik, and C. V. Vishveshwara, eds., *Cosmic Perspectives* (Cambridge: Cambridge University Press, 1989), pp. 207–231; and I. W. Kelly, G. A. Dean, and D. H. Saklofske, "Astrology: A Critical Review," in Patrick Grim, ed., *Philosophy of Science and the Occult,* 2d. ed. (Albany, N.Y.: SUNY Press, 1990), pp. 51–81. For chiromancy, see Michael Alan Park, "Palmistry: Science or Hand-Jive?" *Skeptical Inquirer* 7, no. 2 (Winter 1982–83): 21–32.

It is important to note regarding astrology that the work of "cosmobiologist" Michel Gauquelin (discussed briefly by Kelly, Culver, and Loptson and more extensively by Kelly, Dean, and Saklofske and, more recently, by Suitbert Ertel in "Update on the 'Mars Effect,' " *Skeptical Inquirer* 16, no. 2 [Winter 1992]: 150–60) has thus far managed to withstand criticism. Gauquelin apparently found correlations between positions of the planets and certain personality traits, but these do not correspond to traditional astrology, of which Gauquelin was himself quite critical.

16. A firsthand (pardon the pun) account of the last of these may be found in Ray Hyman, " 'Cold Reading': How to Convince Strangers That You Know All about Them," *The Zetetic* (now *Skeptical Inquirer*) 1, no. 2 (1977): 29 (reprinted in Ray Hyman, *The Elusive Quarry: A Scientific Appraisal of Psychical Research* [Buffalo, N.Y.: Prometheus Books, 1989], pp. 402–419). For the other two, see the references given in the previous note.

17. Two tests of aura readers' abilities to identify persons standing behind screens are reported in Robert Steiner, "News and Comment: Live TV Special Explores, Tests Psychic Powers," *Skeptical Inquirer* 14, no. 1 (Fall 1989): 3, and *James Randi: Psychic Investigator* (London: Boxtree Limited, 1991), pp. 26–27.

18. Rosalyn Bruyere, "How to See the Human Aura," in Jerry Dunn, ed., *Tricks of the Trade: Over 79 Experts Reveal the Secrets behind What They Do Best* (Boston: Houghton Mifflin, 1991), pp. 23–28.

19. Ibid., p. 26.

20. This is not the only way one can see "auras." Some "auras" are afterimages, some are produced by various kinds of contrast, and so on. See Geoffrey Dean, "Physiological Explanation of Human 'Auras,' " *Skeptical Inquirer* 15 (Summer 1991): 402–403, and Andrew Neher, *The Psychology of Transcendence* (New York: Dover, 1990), pp. 186–92.

21. This is perhaps another way of saying that there are anomalies, but they are explainable in terms of methodological problems, statistical artifacts, and so forth. For an overview of the parapsychological evidence and a wide variety of opinions on the matter, see K. Ramakrishna Rao and John Palmer, "The Anomaly Called Psi: Recent Research and Criticism," and James E. Alcock, "Parapsychology: Science of the Anomalous or Search for the Soul," and their subsequent commentaries in *Behavioral and Brain Sciences* 10, no. 4 (December 1987): 539–643. Alcock's contribution is reprinted in his book, *Science and Supernature: A Critical Appraisal of Parapsychology* (Buffalo, N.Y.: Prometheus Books, 1990).

22. For work skeptical of remote viewing, see David Marks and Richard Kammann, *The Psychology of the Psychic* (Buffalo, N.Y.: Prometheus Books, 1980), pp. 12–41 and their article, "Information Transmission in Remote Viewing Experiments," *Nature* 214 (August 17, 1978): 680–81; David Marks and Christopher Scott, "Remote Viewing Exposed," *Nature* 319 (February 6, 1986): 444; Ray Hyman and James McClenon, "A Remote Viewing Experiment Conducted by a Skeptic and a Believer," *Zetetic Scholar* no. 12/13 (1987): 21–33 (reprinted in Hyman, *The Elusive Quarry,* pp. 347–61); and Alcock, *Science and Supernature,* pp. 111–25. Work supportive of remote viewing has been conducted by researchers at the Princeton Engineering Anomalies Research Laboratory. For references, see Roger D. Nelson and Dean I. Radin, "When Immovable Objections Meet Irresistable Evidence: A Case of Selective Reporting," *Behavioral and Brain Sciences* 10, no. 4 (December 1987): 600–601, as well as Hyman and McClenon, and Alcock.

23. Jeter, see note 4.

24. Lyons and Truzzi, *The Blue Sense,* pp. 186–87.

25. Woulfe, see note 4.

26. The five cases apparently due to Ward are two cases with arrests by Jack Watters (formerly of the Will County [Ill.] Sheriff's Department), one by Andrew Barto of the Romeoville (Ill.) Police Department, one by Grundy County (Ill.) Sheriff James Olsen, and one by Orland Park (Ill.) Police Chief Melbourne Gorris. All are described in Crnkovic's "Mind over Murder!" articles. One of Watters' arrests, for the murder of "James Blue," is also described in the "Psychic Vietnam Veteran" segment of the ABC-TV show "Psychic Crime Busters," which aired December 21, 1989 (for which Crnkovic is credited as "researcher") and in Woulfe, "Television Viewers Can See Lockport Psychic," which is a report about the television program.

27. Since writing this report, I have come across another case involving Bill Ward. Laura Henderson was last seen on March 28, 1986, in Kodiak, Alaska. Police suspected Jack Ibach, her ex-husband, hired Donald McDonald and James Kerwin to murder her, as she was last seen in McDonald's van. Officer Michael Andre of the Kodiak Police Department called Bill Ward in October, who suggested that something of Laura's was still in the van—"something smaller than a comb"— even though it had already been searched on March 29. A new search warrant was issued on the basis of a "citizen's informant tip," and an earring was found in the van. The defense attorneys challenged this evidence and the use of a psychic, leading Judge Edmond Burke to state, "A psychic is not probable cause for a search warrant in my court. In my opinion it is nonsense, resorted to by desperate people." After two trials, Ibach and McDonald were convicted of first degree murder and kidnapping while Kerwin was acquitted. The key piece of evidence was a gun of Ibach's which demonstrated a link between Ibach and McDonald. (The story is told in Tony Durr, "Psychic Tip Leads to Laura's Earring Months after Van Held," *The Kodiak Daily Mirror,* November 14, 1986, and Karen Durr, "Ibach, McDonald Found Guilty: Jury Reaches Decision after Barely 5 Hours," *The Kodiak Daily Mirror,* April 28, 1987.)

28. John Painter, Jr., "Backyard Dig Finds No Clues to Missing Woman," *Portland Oregonian,* March 3, 1988. Much of the following is based on this newspaper account and on information provided by Ray Montee (note 32, below).

29. Ibid.

30. Personal communication with Detective Dan Kelly, Beaverton (Oregon) Police Department, June 11 and November 1, 1991.

31. Painter, "Backyard Dig Finds No Clues to Missing Woman."

32. Personal communication with Ray Montee, Private Investigator, Portland, Oregon, June 13, 1991.

33. Personal communication with Detective Louie Silich, Joliet (Ill.) Police Department, January 8, 1992.

34. "Investigators Search for Clues at Joliet Blast," UPI story of April 24, 1988, via Lexis. (Also untitled UPI story of April 23.)

35. Personal communication with Gayle Crnkovic, March 26, 1991.

36. Personal communication with Lieutenant Joe Drick, Joliet (Ill.) Fire Department, July 22, 1991. Also contacted was Fire Chief (now retired) George Plese, Joliet Fire Department, on July 23, 1991. Plese chose not to comment, stating that whatever Drick said should be allowed to stand.

37. Personal communication with Louie Silich.

38. Jeter, "Psychic Tie Aids Arrest of Suspect in 2 Killings"; Crnkovic, "Will County Psychic Aids Investigations."

39. According to Crnkovic. Dixmoor Police Deputy Chief Michael Morgan, however, states that Ward did not assist in identifying the suspect.

40. Personal communication with Andrew Thompson, Sheriff, Cohoma County, Clarksdale, Mississippi, October 17, 1991; personal communication with Deputy Chief Michael Morgan, Dixmoor Police Department, October 17, 1991.

41. Jeter, "Psychic Tie Aids Arrest of Suspect in 2 Killings"; Crnkovic, "Will County Psychic Aids Investigations."

42. Personal communication with Michael Morgan.

43. Crnkovic, "Will County Psychic Aids Investigations."

44. Personal communication with Sergeant Robert Kelly, Joliet Police Department, September 26, 1991, and January 8, 1992; Woulfe, "Television Viewers Can See Lockport Psychic."

45. Personal communication with Robert Kelly, September 26, 1991.

46. Ibid.

47. Personal communication with Ricky M. Holman (formerly Investigator, Kendall County Sheriff's Office and Kendall County State Attorney's Office); Crnkovic, "Mind over Murder!"

48. Personal communication with Ricky M. Holman; Crnkovic, "Mind Over Murder! Psychic Aid in Investigation," p. 6.

49. Personal communication with Detective Michael Krause, Naperville Police Department, January 10, 1992; Crnkovic, "Mind over Murder! Psychic Aid in Investigation," p. 6.

50. Personal communication with Ricky M. Holman.

51. Personal communication with Victor Franz, Investigator, (Illinois) State's Attorney's Appellate Prosecutors, January 9, 1992 (formerly Sheriff, Kendall County, 1966–70 and 1978–82; also formerly Investigator, Kendall County Sheriff's Office and Kendall County State Attorney's Office).

52. Personal communication, January 8, 1992.

53. See note 8.

54. Reiser et al., "An Evaluation of the Use of Psychics," p. 24. See also Kendrick Frazier, "Psychics and Crime," *Skeptical Inquirer* 3, no. 4 (Summer 1979): 7.

55. Hyman, " 'Cold Reading' "; David Marks and Richard Kammann, *The Psychology of the Psychic* (Buffalo, N.Y.: Prometheus Books, 1980); Dean, "Does Astrology Need To Be True? Part 2: The Answer Is No." Also see the Introduction.

56. Personal communication with Ricky M. Holman.

57. Lyons and Truzzi, *The Blue Sense*, pp. 230–31, give a set of guidelines adopted by the Pomona (California) Police Department in 1981 which, if followed, would greatly improve the quality of evidence for or against the abilities of psychic detectives.

7

A Reticent Psychic Sleuth: Rosemarie Kerr

Lee Roger Taylor, Jr., and Michael R. Dennett

One of the several flaws in man is that he is constrained by the limits of his ordinary senses (sight, sound, touch, smell, and taste), which are poorly developed relative to the superiority of other animals in an environment that he often finds complex and hostile. One probable end product of this limitation is that man for several centuries has created gods and heroes with superior powers, that is, with all that ordinary man lacks but desires: flight, precognition, invulnerability, lightning bolts, omnipotent sight, and so forth. These mythical creatures which man persists in creating and idolizing regard the common man as puny and insignificant but, for that very reason and out of a strange sense of kinship, feel obligated to watch over and protect him—as long, that is, as the proper respect is paid.

Within man's mythology, however, whenever he has given himself an extrasensory power, it has been badly flawed. One of the first great psychics of the ancient world was Cassandra. In return for one evening of love, Apollo gave her the ability to foretell the future. Cassandra accepted the gift but reneged on her part of the bargain. Apollo, thus, in anger left her with his gift but added the stipulation that no one would ever believe her. So, in Aeschylus' *Agamemnon,* Cassandra accurately predicts Agamemnon's death at the hands of Clytemnestra and Aegisthus, but no one, unfortunately, comes to their aid.

Again, Oedipus of Sophocles' *Oedipus Tyrannus,* is tormented by the seer Teiresias, who accurately describes all the circumstances that have led Oedipus on his self-destructive quest for truth. Unfortunately, Teiresias fails badly in the one key psychic responsibility: he fails to recognize that Oedipus is in fact the one responsible for the misery of Thebes. If indeed Teiresias had had the psychic abilities he seems to display early in the play, then he should have seen Oedipus as the real villain who had murdered the former king. The easy answer is, of course, that this is a built-in flaw; there would have been no play if he had. The Greeks, after all, it might be argued, believed as strongly in psychic ability as they believed in and laughed at their gods. Just as this Greek tragedy is built on Oedipus' efforts to thwart the fate foretold by the Oracle of Delphi, so are those very efforts thwarted by his failure to accurately interpret the oracle until *after* the events foretold.

In 2,500 years, man has not advanced much further. The truth lay not so much in the prediction as in the interpretation. The truth of the psychic, the Oracle of Delphi, was cast like the dim shadows on the wall of Plato's cave. The truth was finally perceived after the foretold event—or the event was reinterpreted to fit the prediction, in which case the reality of actual events must be recast into the mold created by one or more persons to fit the power given by a false or cryptic prediction.

Today the paranormal, with its seers and psychics, has become a subculture unto itself. Communities of people alleging psychic abilities blossom and fade away with the same voracious energy as the claims which seem to support them. Proof of success is apocryphal while examination is elusive, and so it appeared in a television broadcast of one apparent psychic.

The authors had worked together on a previous project of paranormal investigation[1] and have jointly or singly examined other fringe science areas. Because of the claims and disclaimers made, we were attracted to the broadcast of a network television program hosted by actor Anthony Zerbe in December 1989. The program featured four so-called "psychic detectives," who had successfully assisted police in their investigations and resolutions of certain identified crimes. The lead segment in the television program was what it called "The Daigle Murder."

In a dramatized documentary format, the program re-enacted the events of the case. André Daigle was a member of a large extended family in the New Orleans suburb of Metaire. On the evening of June 9, 1987, he met Thelma Horne in a bar. André Daigle left with Horne and disappeared. The family, which had expected him home that night, immediately notified the police. Receiving no immediate satisfaction, the family began distributing fliers with André's picture. Meanwhile, on June 13, four days after the disappearance, a sister, Elise McGinley, living in California, consulted psychic Rosemarie Kerr. Kerr stated that André had been injured about the head and that she saw water around him, a bridge, and a railroad track and the number 7. Then with an apparent sense of urgency, Kerr urged McGinley to contact the family and have them "go toward Slidell." McGinley did as she was told. A number of family members got into their cars and drove from New Orleans along Highway 10 to Slidell. At some point never clearly identified, one group spotted André's truck, but André was not the driver. They followed the truck for several miles before finally persuading a patrolman in Pearl River, several miles beyond Slidell, to stop the truck. The occupants of the truck, Charles Gervais and Michael Phillips, were arrested. The following day, Charles Gervais, a self-proclaimed Satanist, confessed to the murder of André. Then, according to the program, Gervais led police to the body. Without providing specifics, the program visually showed an Exit 7 in following the route to the body and stated that the body was found in water with a railroad bridge nearby. The program segment concluded with a statement from James Gallagher, a sergeant with the Kenner Police Department, testifying that he believed Rosemarie Kerr was invaluable in providing a solution to the case.

The "Daigle Murder" offered everything that television could hope for. An ineffective or unresponsive police department is superseded by an extended yet unified family which takes action on its own: the family that prays together stays together. For us, however, there were a number of aspects of the presentation that caught our attention which seemed to set this psychic incident above others. One, for example, was the immediacy of Kerr's injunction to "go toward Slidell" and the "psychic circumstance" of encountering the murderers driving André's truck. Another was the apparent, "meanwhile-back-at-the-ranch" scenario. In other words, while the family hunted for André in New Orleans, way out in California— 2,000 miles away—another family member consults a psychic who then is impelled to contact the family. Most psychic "revelations" lack such immediate spontaneity. Cinematically, it was almost too good to be true; it could almost be described as "The Waltons Take Charge in Louisiana." Still another was an interesting coincidence of names. The friend who saw André leave the bar with Thelma Horne was Nick Shelley. The Associate Producer of the segment was Angela Shelley. And, finally, we were curious as to just how accurate Rosemarie Kerr's "psychic insights" were.

Our first step was to try to locate Rosemarie Kerr to get her input concerning the Daigle case. Tracking her down proved to be an arduous task. The producers of the television program (Clearlight Productions) were uncooperative and tightlipped. In a telephone conversation, Les Sinclair, credited in the program as one of the writers, stated that he "didn't have time to talk about the show" and that other members of the production team "were not available to talk about a show that was two years old." He did, however, provide an address for Rosemarie Kerr. The address was old, and letters were returned. After three months of inquiry, Rosemarie Kerr was located in what she described as a "spiritualist community" in Escondido, California.[2]

In the television program, Rosemarie had re-enacted for the camera her psychic session with Elise. On camera, she appeared as a diminutive, unassuming woman not unlike the character played by Zelda Rubenstein in the *Poltergeist* film series. When we first contacted her, she seemed willing to discuss herself and events, but she also seemed somewhat unaccustomed to talking to skeptics. She revealed vague details about her work but virtually nothing about the Daigle murder. Among her revelations she stated that when she was working on a case (such as a missing person) she liked to have an object from the person but that it was not necessary.

She made vague references to a number of "cases" she was working or had worked on. The first involved a plane crash in Missouri that was being looked into "by a family." Another was in connection with a "little girl in Kentucky." Her somewhat sensational references included her investigation of a "snuff murder" about which she could not give details because the FBI had "asked her to keep her involvement quiet." In still another potentially sensational case, she said she had helped find a "lawyer from Washington, D.C."

In all instances, Rosemarie refused to reveal any details and very often only referred to these cases in the vaguest of terms.[3] She said that she would contact the parties concerned with each case in order to obtain permission to discuss their details with us, but in further telephone conversations the cases were never mentioned again. The only reference to the Daigle case came in connection with the plane crash in which she said the parties involved had been referred to her by the Daigle family.

Following the second telephone conversation, Rosemarie Kerr promptly began to add to the stone wall she had already begun to erect with further vague, unspecific references. Finally, repeated calls to her residence were unreturned, and letters unanswered. We had, during our last conversation with her, revealed that our work was to be published by Prometheus Books.

We contacted Christian Daigle, brother to the deceased, André, and the only member of the Daigle family who did not appear in the program. We explained that we wanted to objectively analyze the case and would like his and the family's cooperation in providing details. He replied that he would talk to the family about it. He returned our call a few days later and said that the family would only work with us on two conditions: (1) that we assure them *in advance* that everything we said/wrote would be positive about Rosemarie Kerr and (2) that Rosemarie request the family to cooperate with us. This request effectively brought this avenue to a dead halt inasmuch as we could not guarantee the outcome prior to the investigation.

This ultimately left us with little to go on but the details provided by the television program. Despite the usually justified assumption that television elaborates and changes details to suit its own purposes, we felt fairly comfortable that we had accurate facts concerning Rosemarie's "psychic insights." We were also comfortable in discarding anything resembling interpretation of her "insight."

The pre-Rosemarie Kerr circumstances are in themselves somewhat unusual. André Daigle was lured out of the bar by Thelma Horne, who was in there to find a victim for Charles Gervais and Michael Phillips, on Tuesday night, June 9, 1987. The last of his friends to see André alive was Nick Shelley. André at the time was housesitting for his brother, Christian. It wasn't Christian, however, who first noticed André's absence. Another brother, unidentified, noticed that "Christian's home was not being taken care of and the cats not fed." Assuming that André had been home at some time during Tuesday to pick up around the house or possibly give the cats some food, the absence is not likely to have been noticed until sometime Wednesday, June 10.

Thus, this is the earliest that the police could have been notified. We do not suspect that any of the police departments in the New Orleans area are so diligent that an immediate all-points bulletin was broadcast on this one missing person report. Missing persons reports typically do not get acted on until several days after the event unless there is sufficient evidence to suspect foul play. The television program, as one might suspect, however, stresses the failure of the police to find André *before* Rosemarie was consulted on Saturday, June 13. Despite the "repeated failures of the police," as noted in the television program, the family took matters into its own hands. First, they launched a massive poster campaign, papering the city with posters of André's picture—with no results. Second, they divided the city up into sections and searched each section—also with no results. Once again, all this was accomplished, after the failure of the police, probably within a two-day period. Not only was the family impatient for immediate results but they were also impatient with their own efforts. The family, while extended and living in different communities, could not apparently tolerate a loss of contact with one of its own members. One might even suspect that Elise McGinley had an enormous phone bill from the required constant contact with the family. For our part, we suspect that the family might have suspected that foul play was in the works before the police were actually notified. This, of course, is merely supposition based on the unusually short time span and the demand for immediate (and, perhaps, unreasonable) results.

What we had, on the other hand, concerning Rosemarie's insights was straightforward. With a Louisiana road map and a picture of André Daigle in her hands, Rosemarie said (which was verified by a tape she made of the session)[4]:

- André had "water around him."

- Nearby was a "bridge—not the Golden Gate."

- Also nearby was a "railroad track and the number 7."

- She sensed generalized head pain.

We were able to dismiss a number of these "descriptions" as opportunistic guesses. We define an "opportunistic guess" as a statement so obvious that it requires an enormous stretch of the imagination to accept it as anything other than the overstated obvious. For example, we made the basic assumption that when Elise McGinley first contacted Rosemarie, the assumption was made that André, a responsible and beloved family member, was dead; otherwise he would have contacted his family. Thus, Rosemarie's statement that there was "water around him" falls into the opportunistic guess category. Since most of Louisiana and especially the New Orleans area is barely above sea level or in fact under water, a discarded body or even a body entrapped in a car wreck away from visible or prying eyes is very likely to be in water. If one takes for granted that André met with foul play, the villains in this set piece are likely to have few choices in the disposal of the body. To say then that he has water around him comes as no big surprise and offers no depth of insight. The presence of a bridge likewise comes as no surprise, since in an area like New Orleans, which is covered by water and swamp land (no matter how recovered), bridges are likely to be everywhere. Once again, if the assumption is taken that he had met with foul play, bridges are often in the annals of crimes opportunistic dumping points. To consider these "predictions" as "hits," as paranormal investigators are wont to say, is to say that Tinker Bell is real because she is in a movie.

One of Rosemarie's most tangible "insights" pinpointed a "railroad track and the number 7," which she apparently linked together. As the television show had done, we tended to link this "insight" with Rosemarie's description of where André's body was located. We were never able to determine precisely where the body was dumped. The television show had said a bridge was nearby without actually pinpointing a location. As a consequence, we dismissed that assertion. In one of the few newspaper accounts of the crime, *The Times-Picayune* stated that "his body was dumped in a swamp near Lake Maurepas in St. John the Baptist Parish."[5] This limits the spot to an eight-mile stretch of Highway 55 between Ruddock and Manchac. Highway 55 parallels a railroad track which is readily visible on even the poorest road map. The problem here is establishing a connection between the two. The television program's suspect interpretation has the police exiting near Ruddock at Exit 7. Through the information available to us, we were not able to confirm the accuracy of this. The railroad, however, is on the *opposite side* of Highway 55 from Lake Maurepas. Had the body been found near the railroad tracks, the report most likely would have been phrased as "dumped in a swamp near Lake Pontchartrain" which is noticeably closer to the railroad. This assumption, however, has its flaws inasmuch as we were not able to determine whether or not any railroad spurs branched off in the direction of Lake Maurepas; the most detailed maps we could obtain of the area did not show any. The most likely conclusion then is that a railroad track was not in the immediate vicinity of the body.

This would likely rule out the number 7. A nice, mystical number, 7 was given prominent attention by the producers as an obvious hit in Rosemarie's favor. As noted above, they clearly showed a highway interstate sign reading "Exit 7." This appears incontrovertible except for one minor flaw. In an interview with the policeman who found the body, Sergeant James Gallagher of the Kenner Police Department, Gallagher noted that "one of the murderer's addresses was #7,"[6] thus confirming in his mind a hit by Rosemarie. Therefore, there is a difference of opinion on the interpretation of the number 7, neither of which is attached in any way to a railroad. We might add that we were slightly skeptical of Sergeant Gallagher's interpretation, since few addresses have a single number in them, as in 7. More likely, although Sergeant Gallagher did not elaborate, he may have "extracted" the significant number 7 from several others that may have been in the address in question. If that is indeed the case, then the sergeant is probably reaching about as far as the television program. Once again, we have to underscore the fact that we were not able to obtain confirming evidence that might make one believe one interpretation over another—or an altogether different view.

The most solid, hard-core description of André provided by Rosemarie was her statement about "generalized head pain" without any specifics. Our first interpretation was that this sounded like a case for the infamous "blunt instrument," and, we thought, a probable hit by Rosemarie—that is, until we read the news reports of the crime, which stated quite clearly that "Daigle was strangled."[7] It may be, one might argue, that he was hit over the head first before he was strangled. Still, if Rosemarie were describing his death or in psychic contact with his death pain, one might suspect that the more traumatic wound or death process might be the more "psychically evident." For us, this was a clear miss by Rosemarie.

Finally, on the Daigle case, one cannot escape the amazing immediacy of Kerr's urging the family to drive "toward Slidell." This is, perhaps, one of the most stunning, dramatic events of supposed psychic phenomena, and appears as though it is a clear, dramatic hit for Rosemarie. Neither of us will deny the credit to Rosemarie for this stunning coincidence, but we are both sure that that is exactly what it is. Our reasons lie in Rosemarie's implied "revelation," that this would lead the family to André. Neither of us is convinced that it led to André via the capture and confession and ultimately to the body. If the family was expecting to find André, Rosemarie sent them physically in the wrong direction (see maps). The body, as pointed out above, was dumped near Lake Maurepas, west of the family's residence. Slidell is in the opposite direction, to the east. Considering the directions open to Rosemarie, east and west were it. Also, considering Rosemarie's misses in this case, we are reluctant to attach credence to the fact that this was anything more than mere coincidence.

Our conclusion that Rosemarie's apparent success was a coincidence is also shared by at least one of the law enforcement officials involved in the case. When we spoke to Chief of Police, Benny Raynor, of the Pearl River Police Department, he said: "I don't believe a psychic solved this case. I think it was the effort of the family. It was just a coincidence that they traveled in that direction."[8] Chief Raynor further explained that he met Rosemarie at the trial. Confronting the psychic in the courtroom he said, "If you want me to believe in psychics, I have about thirty unsolved burglaries you could help me on." According to the Chief, Rosemarie declined to help him with the unsolved cases.

One facet of this case which drew our attention originally was the extended media hype, or rather the supposed media hype. It was stressed by the television program and some of the individuals involved that this case had received national attention. A computerized search of national publications produced only articles from *The Times-Picayune* and *The Orange County Register*. Reference was made to a Miami-based television station filming witnesses and even Thelma Horne for a television program which "often airs shows" about sensational murder cases. The producer of that "documentary" was Angela Shelley, sister of Nick Shelley. She apparently asserted that she was producing a documentary and "owns Real Life Productions in North Hollywood, California." Both of us were troubled by the rhyming names of Clear Light Productions, Los Angeles (producer of the television program) and Real Life Productions. Had there been significant media interest following the national broadcast we presume that they would have met with the same reluctance by the principles to answer questions about the circumstances of the crime. If the Daigle murder represents a true instance of psychic ability, why are the people most involved, the psychic, the Daigle family, and the television show's producers, unwilling to talk about the case?

NOTES

1. "The Saguaro Incident: A Study in CUFOS Methodology," *Skeptical Inquirer* (Fall 1985).

2. Rosemarie Kerr, telephone conversations, September 2, 1991, October 2, 1991, and October 14, 1991.

3. When we first talked to Rosemarie Kerr, she agreed to work with us. We asked her to identify several of her best cases in order that we might contact the police/individuals involved. We specifically asked for cases in which at least two other people could provide testimony about the case. We agreed to protect the identity of any witnesses should they wish anonymity. In all, Rosemarie provided only a single witness to a single case. She told us that one of her successful cases had been a "reading" for Jennet Griff of Long Beach, California. Ms. Griff agreed to an interview and on October 23, 1991, we spoke with her. Although Ms. Griff was very much impressed by Rosemarie both as a psychic and as a person, she did not provide corroborative evidence of Rosemarie's alleged psychic powers. Ms. Griff's son had left home and she had asked Rosemarie's help in finding her boy. Significantly, she told us, "But we didn't find him because of that [Rosemarie's help]."

4. We were unable to obtain a copy of the tape. We assume with reservation that the producers of the show made at least cursory efforts to verify the authenticity of the tape used on the program.

5. Richard Boyd, "Judge, Jurors Join Party to Celebrate Slay Verdict," *The Times-Picayune* (January 29, 1989): BB, B1.

6. Telephone interview with Sergeant James Gallagher, August 27, 1991.

7. Boyd, "Judge, Jurors Join Party to Celebrate Slay Verdict," p. B1.

8. Telephone interview with Chief Raynor, May 8, 1992.

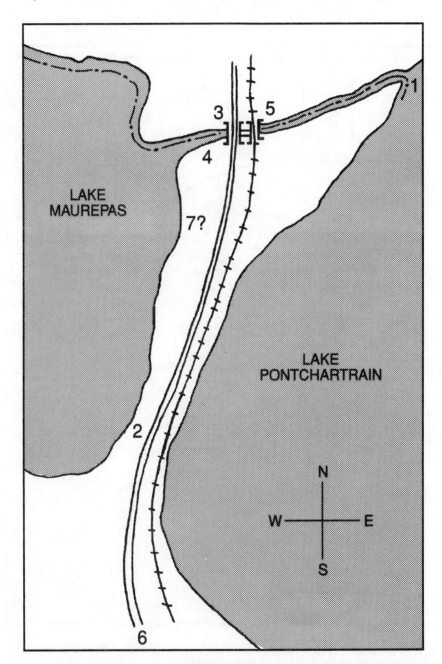

MAP 1. Area along Louisiana's Lake Pontchartrain relating to the "Daigle Murder" case. (1. Boundary line for St. John the Baptist Parish; 2. Ruddock; 3. Manchac; 4. Highway bridge; 5. Railroad bridge; 6. Highway 55; 7. Approximate location of body.)

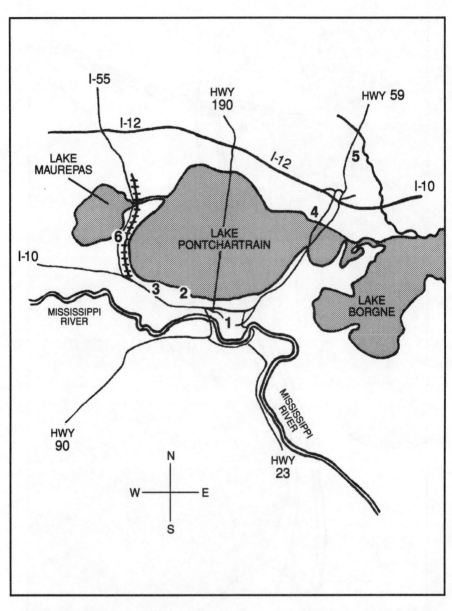

MAP 2. Extended area relating to the Daigle case. (1. New Orleans; 2. Metairie; 3. Kenner; 4. Slidell; 5. Pearl river; 6. Ruddock.)

8

The Mythologized Psychic Detective: Phil Jordan

Kenneth L. Feder and Michael Alan Park

INTRODUCTION

As confirmed skeptics, we believe it is fair to say that neither of us takes too much stock in signs or messages from "the beyond"—or, for that matter, from anywhere else. Still, things happen that do make you think.

While one of us (Feder) was sitting in front of his Macintosh computer, reading self-proclaimed psychic Phil Jordan's own description of one of his most celebrated cases, the "Talking Moose" popped up on the computer screen. For you non-Mac users, the Talking Moose is a completely silly, useless, and utterly indispensable piece of software that includes an endearing, animated, and yes, talking moose who every so often appears in the upper left hand corner of the computer screen to share with you some piece of arcane wisdom, or merely to ask if you can go get him a doughnut. Well, there I was, reading Jordan's own version of the events that led to his discovery of little Tommy Kennedy when up pops my moose to say, "There's less to this than meets the eye." "Out of the mouths of moose," as they say (well, sort of). It's almost enough to make one believe in a higher power—at least of the micro-chip kind.

In any event, it seems as though my moose was exactly right. After examining the claims, one sees there is quite a bit *less* to the story of psychic detective Phil Jordan than meets the eye.

115

Jordan lives in upstate New York; he was residing in Tioga County (where he later became a deputy with the county sheriff's department) when his better known cases occurred. His principal claims to fame include serving as a consultant for the lawyers on two major felony murder cases.[1] In 1977 Jordan was a consultant to Attorney Robert Miller, public defender in the New York murder trial of Lawrence Albro, Jr., who had been charged with hiring someone to kill his stepmother. In a better known case, Jordan was hired by Attorney Joel M. Aurnou, who represented Jean Harris in her trial for the murder of her boss and lover, Herbert Tarnower, the famous diet doctor. In both cases, Jordan was hired to help screen jurors—to counsel the counselors concerning which jurors might prudently be eliminated from consideration, and which might vote for acquittal. The fact that both Mr. Albro and Ms. Harris were convicted and sentenced appears not to provide great solace to those who might hope to rely on a psychic in such matters. Attorney Miller has maintained that Jordan was indeed quite helpful, although not so much as a direct result of any psychic skills. Miller believed that some prospective jurors were more honest and forthcoming when interviewed concerning their possible prejudgment of the case, since they may have believed that a psychic (whose presence, apparently, was known to them) could tell whether they were lying or not.[2]

But certainly Jordan's most spectacular "success story" concerns his assistance in the search for five-year-old Tommy Kennedy of Owego, New York, who disappeared near Empire Lake in Spencer, New York, on August 3, 1975. It is on this claimed impressive "psychic hit" that we will focus our attention.

THE MYTH OF THE PSYCHIC DETECTIVE

The Tommy Kennedy case is a useful example of the psychic detective genre of modern mythology. The term *myth* is popularly used as a synonym for a false or fictional story. Certainly, aspects of many myths turn out not to be supported by fact; creation myths are a good example. But the important thing about myths is not their verity or falsehood, but their meaning for and function within a particular cultural setting.

A myth is essentially a story that attempts to make sense out of some aspect of the world as a group of people sees it at a given time. It satisfies what seems to be a characteristic human need to place events in chronological order and in a sequence of causality. It asks and answers the same basic questions about the world that science does—how, what, why, when, who—

Gerard Croiset, the Dutch "clairvoyant" who gained fame as a psychic detective. (Photo: De Telegraaf, Amsterdam.)

Dorothy Allison, right front, walks the bank of the Raritan River with friends and relatives of two men presumed drowned (spring 1993). She was unable to provide any specific help but made numerous predictions. (Photo by Ed Pallarin, with permission of the *Courier-News*, Bridgewater, N.J.)

Noreen Renier, "the media's rising star psychic sleuth." (Photo by Carlos Santos, courtesy Richmond Newspapers, Inc., Richmond, Va.)

Bill Ward, army medic turned psychic sleuth, has reportedly assisted in over 400 homicide cases since 1971. (Photograph courtesy the *Herald-News,* Joliet, Ill.)

Publicity photo of Greta Alexander, billing her as a "parapsychologist." (Courtesy the *State Journal Register,* Springfield, Ill.)

Greta Alexander on the "Geraldo" show, holding the hand of a woman as she tells her that her missing son is dead. (Reproduced by permission of the "Geraldo" show.)

British "psychic" Nella Jones failing to pick up the "vibes" from an actual murder weapon, as magician James Randi looks on. (From "James Randi: Psychic Investigator," Granada Television, London.)

SKEPTICAL INQUIRER

Vol. 17, No. 2

Winter 1993 / $6.25

POLICE & PSYCHICS
QUESTIONING THE CLAIMS

The Big Sur 'UFO' Identified
Pseudoscience in Nursing
Hands-On Science Education
Martin Gardner:
The Great Samoan Hoax

Published by the Committee
for the Scientific Investigation
of Claims of the Paranormal

The *Skeptical Inquirer,* official journal of the Committee for the Scientific Investigation of Claims of the Paranormal, has frequently questioned the claims
of psychics in general and psychic sleuths in particular. (Reproduced by permission.)

but without the skepticism, testing, and reexamination that are science's hallmarks. A myth is taken for granted, held to be "true" in the sense that it satisfactorily answers these questions for the people asking them. Myths can become powerful determinants of a society's future ideas and actions, but this does not mean myths are static. Because myths relate to the world as perceived at a specific time, they obviously have to change as that world and a group's perception of it, changes in light of ongoing environmental and historical events. In other words, people create the myths as they go, adding and subtracting details as new real-life data emerge, so as to maintain an orderly and logical chronology.

Myths, as we deal with them in anthropology, are stories shared by entire societies, stories that hold meaning, and so are held to be true by a whole cultural system. But myths can arise on a smaller scale. They can be created out of the perceptions of a small group of individuals about a specific event for all the same reasons that societies create myths—to account for that event via a satisfyingly logical causal sequence. So powerful is this need, it seems, that the story created can hold sway over a more scientific, questioning, and skeptical examination of the facts.

It can be shown that this is precisely what happened in the Tommy Kennedy disappearance case. There is, of course, the actual series of events beginning with the recognition by his mother of the boy's disappearance on August 3, 1975, and ending with his safe recovery on August 4. In testing the accuracy of the stories now told concerning the disappearance, it is crucial to compare those tales to the verifiable facts of the occurrence; but it is important to remember that the actual chain of events is unrecoverable, untestable, and ultimately unknowable. There is no stenographic transcript of what self-proclaimed psychic Phil Jordan said and no way of proving what he did *not* say. The case did not proceed under conditions even vaguely approximating scientific controls or experimental protocols. There is no way of knowing exactly what part Jordan played in the recovery of Tommy Kennedy and to what extent his claimed psychic powers were involved. The story, or rather stor*ies,* that have emerged are plainly anecdotal, and based upon the individual, imperfect, idiosyncratic, and often contradictory recollections of people involved, none of whom can be considered an objective or dispassionate observer. Their stories are evocative and emotional *post hoc* interpretations, many of which have been rationalized, phrased, slanted, and filtered so as to amaze, impress, and move the listener. The stories are, in short, myths. This is not an indictment of Phil Jordan or of any of the people involved, especially not Tommy Kennedy's family. It is simply a statement of fact.

Now however, although we cannot assess the "real" story—the irrecov-

erable actual sequence of events surrounding Tommy Kennedy's disappearance and ultimate discovery—we can assess the anecdotal stories as they
have been told. In other words, we can analyze the *myth* of Tommy
Kennedy's disappearance and discovery, just as anthropology analyzes the
cultural myths of entire societies.

The most accessible version of the story comes from that oracle of
modern mythology, the television. Phil Jordan's role in the discovery of
the missing five-year-old was highlighted in a television program dedicated
to examining psychic detectives, in which Jordan is interviewed and plays
himself in the dramatic re-creation.[3]

The narrator prefaces the program by stating that "psychics are rarely
used in police investigation," and when they are, it is admitted, they are
"only sometimes helpful." Despite this prefatory disclaimer, it would be
fair to characterize the show as a less than skeptical treatment of the subject.
The narrator maintains that the program details cases where, indeed,
"psychics have proven useful," and remember that this show, produced
in 1989, is a compendium of "best cases" covering a long period of time.
One might expect that the individual instances selected for inclusion would
be pretty impressive. Let's see. We can briefly summarize the Tommy
Kennedy story as told in the television broadcast:

> Five-year-old Tommy Kennedy and his family, which included his mother,
> Mary, his siblings, and his stepfather, were visiting "Lake Empire" in
> upstate New York on August 3, 1975. Mary Kennedy remained at the
> picnic area while her husband and kids hiked around the lake. When
> they returned about forty-five minutes later, they noticed that Tommy
> was gone; Mary Kennedy had assumed that he had trailed along with
> his stepfather, while his stepfather had assumed that Tommy had remained
> behind with his mother. After a frantic search around the lake proved
> fruitless, Mary Kennedy alerted the authorities and an intensive search,
> that eventually included more than two hundred people, began. The
> weather turned quite bad and late that night the search was called off,
> to be resumed at dawn.
>
> Phil Jordan, a psychic who had helped police previously in tracking
> down missing persons, through a fortuitous coincidence lived next door
> to the home of one of the volunteer firemen leading one of the search
> parties. He was asked by the fireman's wife, who was familiar with his
> psychic abilities, to aid in the search. Applying his supernatural talents,
> Jordan immediately sensed that the boy was alive, well, and asleep under
> a tree. Though he had never visited the lake, he drew an accurate and
> detailed map of the surrounding terrain. In the meantime, Tommy's
> biological father sped to the lake after hearing of his son's disappearance

and hunted all night for his son. Jordan himself joined the search at the lake the next morning at 5:30 A.M. The search party followed Jordan and his map precisely. Several of the landmarks Jordan had drawn on the map remarkably were located that morning. Less than an hour later, Phil Jordan led the exhausted search team right to the ravine where he had seen the boy asleep in his psychic vision the night before. And, indeed, there they found little Tommy Kennedy, somewhat dirty, tired, scratched-up, and frightened, but unhurt, just as Jordan had said. Thus, a child's life was saved through the clearly remarkable and almost certainly supernatural skills of a psychic detective.

Thus, the story is here told by a television documentary writer as he extracted it some fourteen years after the facts had been allowed to ferment in the minds of the story-tellers: Phil Jordan, others involved in the search effort, and Tommy's mother. We can, at least in part, assess their stories, comparing those told by different people as well as those told by the same individual at different times. As we do so, a clear pattern emerges.

THE TOMMY KENNEDY CASE: WHAT REALLY HAPPENED

Tommy Kennedy was indeed reported missing on August 3, 1975, from the area around *Empire Lake* (it is labeled that on the topographic map of the New York State Department of Transportation, *not* "Lake Empire" as it was called in the broadcast; Figure 1). The *Binghamton Evening Press* carried articles about the disappearance on August 4[4] and August 5.[5] Two of the articles discussed the role Phil Jordan ostensibly played in the recovery of the missing boy.[6]

Having established that Tommy Kennedy had disappeared, almost immediately we ran into unsupported assertions and fundamental inconsistencies in the story, especially as it was later retold. For example, a central theme of the 1989 television broadcast was that through some psychic channel Phil Jordan *knew* that Tommy Kennedy was alive and that this, in and of itself, demonstrated Jordan's remarkable psychic ability.

Indeed, they make it sound quite impressive in the televised version of the myth. One of the searchers is quoted in the show: "The most common scenario in these types of searches is not too happy an ending." Much is made of the bad weather, in the form of a fierce thunderstorm with its attendant torrential downpour, that had rolled in on the evening of the third. Implicit throughout much of the telling of the story and explicit

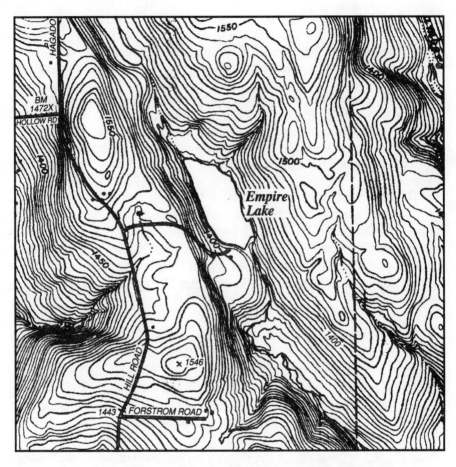

FIGURE 1. Topographic map of the area around Empire Lake.

in the narrator's summary at the end is the notion that by all rights Tommy Kennedy should have died that night. As the narrator intones, ". . . A small child lost in the woods with no food, wearing only swim trunks on a stormy night, doesn't have a great chance of survival." And yet, through it all, Phil Jordan knew that Tommy Kennedy was alive. He must be psychic! As represented in the program, Jordan's very first impression when asked by his neighbor to apply his psychic talents to the investigation was that Tommy Kennedy was okay and would be found: "I immediately began to see things," Jordan himself recounts in a voice-over, during the dramatic recreation of the events. "I saw that he was *asleep* under a tree. I felt that his head was on his right arm as if using it for a pillow. I *felt that he was all right. I didn't feel that he was hurt in any way*" (emphasis added).

If Phil Jordan really did know and state that Tommy Kennedy was alive and if the odds against a small boy's survival alone in the woods that night were enormous, then the truth behind this version of the myth would be buttressed. But is any of this true or reasonable?

Let us begin with the notion that the odds were against Tommy Kennedy's survival. Neither of us wishes to minimize the danger the Kennedy boy experienced. One of us has a child Tommy Kennedy's age at the time of his disappearance and can well imagine the terror experienced by his parents and by the boy. But the simple fact is that, as harrowing an experience as it must have been, the odds, though they cannot be mathematically calculated, were decidedly in his favor. Tommy Kennedy was five when he disappeared, and five-year-olds can be quite self-reliant when they need to be. Tommy had no food with him (at least none we are aware of), but he was missing for probably no more than twelve hours. Certainly he got hungry, but equally certainly he was in no danger of starving to death that night. He likely slept through most of the ordeal.

Further, much is made of the fact that the boy was wearing only his swimming trunks. Indeed, exposure can be deadly for those not properly dressed if they are outdoors during harsh weather. But here we are talking about August in New York State. The National Weather Service reports high daytime temperatures for the area of greater than 90 degrees on August 3, 1975. That evening when Tommy Kennedy was lost in the woods, temperatures certainly dropped, but remained in the upper 60s and low 70s. No healthy five-year-old is likely to be in danger of exposure at such temperatures. The thunderstorm that hit that evening may have been intense and frighteningly noisy for a lost child, but not terribly dangerous. The rain did not begin in the nearby Binghamton area until 8:15 P.M., and was characterized in the *Binghamton Evening Press* as being accompanied by only "occasional" thunder. Finally, this was, after all, upstate New York, rural to be sure, but certainly no wilderness with man- (or child-) eating beasts. Empire Lake is relatively small as shown by the fact that, according to Mary Kennedy's own testimony, her husband and other children walked around the entire lake in about forty-five minutes. In fact, the lake is not quite a mile in circumference, and Tommy, according to the televised version, was ultimately found only about a mile and a half from the picnic ground where he began. As long as the wet and frightened child knew enough to stay away from the water, he was not in very much immediate physical danger. There was no reason to suppose that anything terrible had happened to him. Accurately predicting that he would be found alive is not compelling evidence of psychic ability on Phil Jordan's part.

This brings up the general topic of missing children and the likelihood of their safe recovery. There is no intention here of belittling the fear felt by Mary Kennedy and her family; nevertheless, it must be said that, in fact, the common conception that children are constantly being kidnapped and then never seen again is quite fallacious. According to FBI estimates, only about 150 children are abducted in the United States by strangers each year, though estimates by the National Center for Missing and Exploited Children are considerably higher (between 4,000 and 20,000; the FBI considers the great majority of these to be runaways or the result of parental custody disputes).[7] Most children reported missing turn up quite soon, having run away, gotten lost, been taken by a parent in a custody dispute, or simply not having adequately communicated their whereabouts to their parents.

It would appear at this point that we have shown that Phil Jordan's knowledge that the Kennedy boy was all right did not take any psychic power. It was simply a good guess that would be right more often than not in the first twenty-four hours after any child's disappearance. But, in fact, even on this point, there is a surprising revelation to make. Though Phil Jordan has stated, as cited previously, that he knew the Kennedy boy was alive, there is a fundamental and seemingly inexplicable contradiction between this claim as made in the 1989 televised account of the story and two previously published versions.

In the August 5 article appearing in the *Binghamton Evening Press,* it is related that as of a little after 2:00 A.M. on the fourth, Jordan's "only insight," as he revealed it to the boy's biological father, was that "Tommy is in the woods, not the water."[8] There is no mention here of *any* knowledge of the boy's condition. This would seem to be a rather peculiar omission if, in fact, Jordan "knew" that the child was okay.

Beyond this, two years later, Jordan wrote his own description of the event, published in *FATE.*[9] Even more revealing than the newspaper account just cited, according to this version, when Jordan was initially asked to use his power to find the Kennedy boy on the night of August 3,

> I sat silently and suddenly the first of a series of visions came to me. I could see the boy lying on his stomach under a tree with his head on his arm *as if* asleep. *I could not tell if he were dead or alive* (emphasis added).[10]

This absolutely contradicts Jordan's claim from his own description in the broadcast version of the story where he said that virtually immediately he knew that the Kennedy boy was "asleep under a tree," that "he was all right," and that Jordan did not feel "he was hurt in any way." The *FATE* article makes it clear that, even up to the point immediately before the boy was found, Jordan clearly did not know if Tommy was alive or dead. Jordan confides to *FATE* readers that toward the end of the search on the morning of August 4, "I feared we would come upon the lifeless body of a small boy."[11]

So it turns out that the probability was great in the late hours of August 3 and the early morning of the next day that Tommy Kennedy would be found alive. It would have taken no supernatural powers, only the more prosaic power of deduction, to have accurately suggested that the boy would be found unhurt. Yet even here, it seems that Phil Jordan, with all of his alleged psychic ability, by his own admission did not know even this.

Two characteristics of myths are clearly demonstrated so far. Myths have influence and power in part because they are dramatic. Again, think of the creation myths of many cultures, for example, the Judeo-Christian story from Genesis—dramatic stuff indeed. The Tommy Kennedy story would hardly be dramatic if the boy were not perceived as being in grave danger, and the degree of that danger, as the story evolved, seems to have increased. Myths must also, as noted, link events in a causal sequence. Thus, the involvement of Phil Jordan is required to have some functional connection to the rest of the plot. Since Jordan claimed to have some insight into the boy's location, the story has come to accept that as given, and, in fact, Jordan's insight itself has become more profound. In earlier versions he knew only where the boy was and clearly not the boy's state; in later versions he knew Tommy was alive.

The next question of importance concerns the significance of the role played by Jordan in helping find the Kennedy boy. Specifically, we would like to know how accurate the map drawn by Jordan actually was. Is it the truth, as claimed, that Jordan had never visited the lake, and did the map or Jordan's own feelings or perceptions when out at the lake actually contribute (and how much) to the finding of Tommy Kennedy?

The map itself is at least a concrete piece of evidence, but it has not been published. The only image of the map we saw was a few fleeting glimpses of a recreated map on the televised broadcast. That map looked extremely general and vague. Even Jordan characterizes it as "crude"[12] and in the August 4 article in the *Binghamton Evening Press* it was described as "a general route."[13] It also should be pointed out that though the claim was made that Jordan had never visited the lake, no claim was made that Jordan was completely unfamiliar with the area which was, after all, not that far from his home. Had he ever seen a map of the lake and its environs, or an aerial photograph of the area? We do not know and we have no way of answering this question definitively.

Beyond this, there were a few c ncrete landmarks Jordan placed on the map, and these were specifically mentioned in the broadcast and published versions of the story. According to those involved, Jordan drew in the following features:

1) three overturned boats

2) a building with a peaked roof

3) a large rock

4) a stream

5) a waterfall

6) a clearing

7) a ravine, where Tommy Kennedy would be found.

According to both the televised and printed versions of the story, three overturned boats were found almost immediately when Jordan joined the search on the fourth. Interestingly, neither the house nor the large rock placed by Jordan on the map existed. Both, however, were rationalized into existence. In Jordan's version of events, he did not find or even recognize these landmarks, but others in the search party did: "And across the lake is the tent which you thought was a small building," one searcher informs Jordan, and someone else tells the party, "Here's a large pile of stones," to which Jordan responds, "I knew instantly I had mistaken [in the map] the pile for one large stone."[14] The other landmarks whose existence was verified are not terribly convincing either; clearings, ravines, streams, and cascading water (though Jordan drew a waterfall, he describes what actually was found as a "small cascade of water")[15] are all quite common, in fact, ubiquitous, in the vicinity of lakes. Overturned boats near lakes are quite common as well. Here, too, Jordan was not the one to recognize the boats he supposedly had drawn. In Jordan's own account, when he finally "recognizes" the boats, one of the searchers exasperatedly says, "I've been trying to tell you that for 10 minutes. . . ."[16]

What is perhaps more interesting is the fact that while Jordan's vague map supposedly was used to find the Kennedy boy, Jordan himself, by his own description in *FATE,* was not much use in the search itself. As he describes it,

I walked through the woods as if a magnet were pulling me. Much of the time I was scarcely aware of the others. When the vibrations weakened I'd rub Tommy's sneaker which I had stuffed in my belt. We would

walk 200 yards and *I would feel to turn left or to turn right, to go
here to go there. But Dick insisted on following the map.* "That's what
we are here for, so let's follow it," he persisted (emphasis added).[17]

In other words, in the published 1977 account, the psychic detective
was receiving vibrations to turn, "to go here, to go there," but the other
searchers paid him no mind, "following" the map instead. And, as we
will soon see, it was the others in the party who actually found the boy.

Interestingly, by the time the story becomes a television re-creation
in 1989, it changes again. Now, according to one of the searchers, "We
followed the map exactly as it was drawn, and *we went exactly as Phil
basically instructed us from landmark to landmark"* (emphasis added).
No longer is Jordan getting vibrations to turn off the trail, no longer
are the others in the search party redirecting the hunt by using his map,
and no longer are others finding the supposed landmarks from the map.

Finally, as just mentioned, it was the others who actually located the
boy. The *Binghamton Evening Press* reported on August 4 that it was
the "party which Jordan accompanied that found little Thomas Kennedy."[18] As Jordan puts it, "The others reached him first but God had showed
me the path."[19] We can reasonably assume that it was not God who kept
inducing Jordan to lead the search party to the left or right—away, it
turns out, from where Tommy Kennedy actually would be found.

Here we see another characteristic of good myths: their flexibility as
they are altered to account for the ever-changing world they are charged
with explaining. Note how the need to include Phil Jordan in a functional,
causal role was so important that the specific details of his role were
essentially created "on the run," as the events were actually taking place.
In fact, those details—specifically, the accuracy of his map—were added
not by Jordan but by some of the other searchers. As reflected in the
televised version, as time has passed, the myth has evolved to elevate Jordan's
actual role; Jordan is now leading the search party directly to the boy,
no longer being "pulled" in other directions, and no longer are others
finding the supposed landmarks on the map he had drawn the night before.

When we look at other important details of the story, we find additional
contradictions. There is more of that pattern, typical of the process of
myth-making, of exaggerating aspects of the story with the result, if not
the conscious intent, of making it more dramatic—in this case, making
Jordan's accomplishments seem all the more amazing. For example, in
the televised version of the story, Mary Kennedy states that Tommy was
found one and a half miles from where he disappeared. The *Binghamton
Evening Press* on August 4 reported that it was three miles.[20]

Oddly, there is no mention in *FATE* or in the televised account of the time when Tommy's disappearance was first recognized by his mother, the time when it was reported, or the time the search actually began. Jordan recalls in *FATE* that he heard the sirens summoning the volunteer fire department on the evening of the third around dinner time. (The *psychic* initially thought there must have been a big fire in town. He determined that the sirens were, instead, summoning volunteers to search for a missing boy only through the more prosaic source of his next-door neighbor.) In the television re-creation of the events, it is dark when Tommy's mother summons help. This would seem to indicate that Tommy was noticed missing sometime in the evening of the third. In the *Binghamton Evening Press* on August 4,[21] it is reported that the police were informed of Tommy's disappearance at 6:00 P.M. It is unlikely, therefore, that the search could have begun in earnest any earlier than about seven o'clock. Because of the bad weather and the dark night, the search was called off sometime between 12:30 and 1:00 A.M. on the fourth and resumed again at 5:30–6:00 A.M.[22] It then took the team only about an hour to find Tommy. At most, therefore, Tommy was missing for about twelve hours, and the large search party was out for a maximum of about seven hours (7:00 P.M. on the third to 1:00 A.M. on the fourth and 6:00 to 7:00 A.M. on the fourth). Yet in a recently published version of the events in *The Blue Sense,* Lyons and Truzzi report that police had been searching for the boy for *seventeen hours* before Jordan located him.[23] This is five hours or so *more* than the boy was even missing and a good ten hours more than the actual duration of the search!

There is also the question of the number of searchers involved. Again according to the *Binghamton Evening Press* in their account of the day of Tommy's recovery, the search party is put at one hundred or a little more.[24] Fourteen years after the fact, in the televised version, this has burgeoned to "more than two hundred." It may seem a minor point, but it exemplifies the consistent pattern of exaggeration that characterizes myth-making. Jordan's alleged achievement, and the supposed supernatural quality of it, becomes all the more amazing as the number of hours the boy was searched for fruitlessly increases and as the number of searchers involved inflates.

The most recent version of the myth as set out by Lyons and Truzzi adds further embellishments. They state that Jordan used the boy's T-shirt to get psychic vibrations before drawing the map.[25] This must be factually wrong if we are to believe Jordan's own account. He mentions no T-shirt —and why would his next-door neighbor, who had induced him to draw the map in the first place, have the boy's shirt? Moreover, while the televised version of the story mentions no article of clothing, Jordan, in the *FATE* article, mentions a sneaker which he had only during the actual search on the fourth. But again, the myth need bear little relation to the truth. It must only be a good story, and the image of the psychic clutching the missing boy's T-shirt as he is drawing the map is evocative indeed.

There is also a curious coincidence, not mentioned in either the broadcast version or the Lyons and Truzzi version. Jordan informs *FATE* readers that he knew, if only slightly, Tommy Kennedy's biological father, Don. Don Kennedy, a free-lance writer, had previously interviewed Jordan for a newspaper article about his claimed psychic abilities. He later wrote another article about Jordan—specifically on Jordan's role in finding his son Tommy, published in the *Binghamton Evening Press* on August 5, 1975, the day after Tommy was found.[26] Certainly, this could have been entirely coincidental. On the other hand, such a connection might reasonably raise doubts in the minds of even the least skeptical concerning this psychic detective story. It is curious indeed that this case, with all of its contradictions and odd coincidences, is considered an example compelling enough to be singled out in a television documentary more than a decade after the fact.

CONCLUSIONS

Ultimately then, we are left with very little indeed. A small boy gets lost in the woods and is found the next day. Nevertheless, years after the fact, the tale, having been told and retold, has evolved into a remarkable yarn of psychic detective work. Indeed, even by loose scientific standards, it simply does not hold up under scrutiny; there *is* less to this than meets the eye.

Has Jordan ever had his alleged psychic abilities put to a test where scientific controls were in place? Sort of. In a case mentioned by Lyons and Truzzi, in 1977 Jordan was called in on a multiple child-killing case by the Michigan police. In what those police called "Operation ESP," under somewhat controlled conditions, according to those investigators, Jordan provided information that was "vague, contradictory, and basically useless."[27]

Ultimately, though they may weave a good yarn, the psychic detectives simply have not proven their case, any more than other so-called psychics have been able to verify their telepathic, clairvoyant, or psychokinetic skills.

Author Colin Wilson cites a self-styled "archaeologist," Stan Gooch, who claims that human psychic abilities are derived from our Neanderthal heritage.[28] According to Gooch, our Cro-Magnon ancestors spent tens of thousands of years developing our ablity to use the left side of our brain like a microscope—to focus on problems close and to stay focused on them for long periods. And "close-up" focus is the opposite of that broad, intuitive state of consciousness in which we receive psychic "flashes."[29]

Again according to Gooch via Colin Wilson, we modern humans have inherited our psychic abilities through our ancestors, who mated with Neanderthals. Today we can attain "Neanderthal consciousness," apparently, only when we are "pleasantly drunk." Of course.

It is valuable to point out in the midst of such gibberish, however, that the Neanderthals are extinct, having been replaced 32,000 years ago by anatomically modern human beings. It would seem that their supposed ESP provided them little in the way of adaptive advantage. Unfortunately for those with missing relatives, it should also be clear that they can no more rely on the abilities of a psychic than the Neanderthals, apparently, could depend on their psychic abilities in their evolutionary struggle with Cro-Magnon.

NOTES

1. M. A. Galante, *The National Law Journal* (January 27, 1986): 1, 32–33.

2. Arthur Lyons and Marcello Truzzi, *The Blue Sense: Psychic Detectives and Crime* (New York: The Mysterious Press, 1991).

3. "Psychic Detectives," ABC television broadcast, December 21, 1989.

4. "Searchers Use Map of Psychic," *Binghamton Evening Press* (August 4, 1975): 3-A; F. Kourt, "Owego Boy Found After 12-Hour Hunt by 100 Volunteers," *Binghamton Evening Press* (August 4, 1975): 3-A; F. Kourt, "12-Hour Hunt Finds Owego Boy," *Binghamton Evening Press* (August 4, 1975): 3-A.

5. D. K. Kennedy, "How Dark the Woods Where Son Is Lost," *Binghamton Evening Press* (August 5, 1975): 1-A, 5-A.

6. "Searchers Use Map of Psychic," p. 3-A; Kennedy, "How Dark the Woods," pp. 1-A, 5-A.

7. S. Pease, personal communication, 1991.

8. Kennedy, "How Dark the Woods," pp. 1-A, 5-A.

9. P. Jordan, *FATE* (1977): 60–65.

10. Ibid., p. 61.

11. Ibid., p. 64.

12. Ibid.

13. "Searchers Use Map of Psychic," p. 3-A.

14. Jordan, *FATE* article (above, n. 9), p. 64.
15. Ibid., p. 65.
16. Ibid., p. 64.
17. Ibid.
18. "Searchers Use Map of Psychic," p. 3-A.
19. Jordan, *FATE* article (above, n. 9), p. 65.
20. See note 4.
21. Kourt, "12-Hour Hunt Finds Oswego Boy," p. 3-A.
22. Kennedy, "How Dark the Woods," pp. 1-A, 5-A.
23. Lyons and Truzzi, *The Blue Sense,* p. 61.
24. Kennedy, "How Dark the Woods," pp. 1-A, 5-A.
25. Lyons and Truzzi, *The Blue Sense,* p. 71.
26. Kennedy, "How Dark the Woods," pp. 1-A, 5-A.
27. Lyons and Truzzi, *The Blue Sense,* p. 227.
28. Colin Wilson, *The Psychic Detectives* (New York: Mercury House, 1985).
29. Ibid., p. 202.

9

A Product of the Media: Greta Alexander

Ward Lucas

Illinois psychic Greta Alexander owes a great deal to the news media. For nearly two decades, friendly reporters have followed her career as a soothsayer, nurtured her mediumistic exploits on the pages of the nation's newspapers, and lovingly caressed her into national prominence. Repeatedly they have ignored her multitude of psychic failures and stroked the thin details of her sparse successes until she has become, literally and figuratively, larger than life. In fact, a review of credulous news articles and headlines across the nation shows that Greta Alexander is perhaps one of the most prominent and seemingly successful "psychic detectives" in the country. Her apparent accomplishments at helping police locate murder victims, find missing children, and solve crimes is nearly unparalleled in the psychic world.

From the *Decatur Herald* a headline blares, "Psychic Leads Searchers to Man Lost On Ginseng Hunt."[1] From United Press International, "Psychic Helps Find Missing Man."[2] An Associated Press story trumpets, "Psychic's Description of Missing Man and Death Scene Proves Accurate."[3] Still another story about the discovery of the body of murder victim Mary Cousett carries the following lead sentence, "Information provided by a psychic led officials to the skeletal remains of a woman from Alton, Illinois."[4] Even in news articles purporting to contain a skeptical theme, the bias of obviously believing writers seeps in. One such example reads, "Even though a psychic steered police to the body of a murder victim, Madison County's chief law enforcement official says consorting with people who dabble in the occult and witchcraft is wrong."[5]

In his exhaustive analysis of some of the nation's better known psychics, even Dr. Marcello Truzzi, a knowledgeable sociology professor at Eastern Michigan University, appears to be enamored of the blizzard of favorable headlines that swirls around Greta Alexander's ample shoulders. In his book, *The Blue Sense,* co-authored by fiction writer Arthur Lyons, Truzzi cites some of the numerous news stories about Alexander's successes. While professing some skepticism, he decidedly leans in the direction of belief in her efficacy as a psychic crime solver. While Truzzi appears to beg the question of whether psychic ability actually exists, he still concludes that ". . . use of the blue sense [psychic ability] may only give us a . . . small advantage [in crime solving] but it perhaps remains better than nothing."[6]

In interviews with the media Truzzi takes an even more generous stance toward the relationship between Greta Alexander and law enforcement. He told the *Chicago Tribune*: "She seems to have an unusually good track record in terms of finding bodies in water. . . . I am comfortable in recommending Greta because I don't feel she is going to rip anybody off."[7]

As Greta Alexander's fame as a psychic crime-buster continues to grow, the number of headlines increases along with her legions of fans. Each day, the Illinois psychic fields a growing number of calls from desperate homicide investigators anxious to clear their desks of unsolved cases. In recent years the more favorable headlines and news accounts have made their way into press releases which she freely hands out to reporters. But a deeper review of the stories behind the headlines shows an intriguing pattern of distortion and intentional or inadvertent manipulation of the facts by the midwest media.

The problem with analyzing Greta Alexander's alleged abilities through newspaper story leads and headlines is that reporters are just as gullible as police officers. While reporters pretend to approach each story with skepticism, in reality their skills at critical analysis are often atrophied. A good working definition of news is "deviant behavior" or "that which deviates from the norm." A story about a psychic finding a missing homicide victim is deviant enough to please editors and readers and therefore has a greater chance of publication. But when that same reporter makes a few extra phone calls and discovers conclusive evidence that a psychic had nothing to do with the solution to a crime, the story's so-called "sex appeal" or "deviancy factor" decreases and the story's headline value drops. Only the reporter with an overwhelming desire to seek the truth has the ability to overcome the headline value of sensational surface facts and seek those facts buried below the surface.

Elizabeth Bettendorf, a reporter for the *State Journal-Register* in Springfield, Illinois, explains her coverage of Alexander in this way: "Greta Alexander is such a colorful character, such a cult figure in this area, I can't afford not to cover her. She makes good copy." Bettendorf, however, is one of the few reporters in the nation's heartland who has included a fair amount of sidebar coverage of the skeptical viewpoint. Far from detracting from her 1991 feature article on Alexander, the reporter's presentation of some of Alexander's detractors made the psychic's story all the more interesting.[8] Yet, balanced coverage like that presented by Bettendorf is rare in the news media.

A 1991 feature-length article in the *Chicago Tribune*'s "Sunday Tempo" presents the more common method of covering Greta Alexander. The writer, Wes Smith, presents case after case of alleged psychic miracles wrought by Alexander, apparently based only on the claims of Alexander herself. The skeptical viewpoint is not presented at all. In fact, Smith notes that Greta refers to skeptics as "yahoos and pipsqueaks," and he echoes her terms in his own reference to her detractors. The *Tribune* writer claims, "Alexander has made believers of hundreds of skeptics, police and pipsqueaks among them, through jaw-dropping displays of her abilities."[9]

Then, Smith discusses the Mary Cousett murder case (in which Alexander supposedly located the missing body psychically), and cites as his authority Marcello Truzzi's book, *The Blue Sense*. The writer of the *Tribune* article apparently didn't make a single call to anyone involved in the Cousett case to see if Alexander did, in fact, locate the body. Had he done so, he might have discovered that Alexander's success in the case was highly suspect or even nonexistent. He might have found that police officers who initially gave glowing accounts of Alexander's "accuracy" had since decided they were probably hoodwinked by the psychic's pronouncements. In short, the *Tribune* article was erroneous. It was based on previous erroneous information in Truzzi's book, which in turn was based on even older erroneous information in regional newspapers. And the legend of Alexander psychically locating a missing murder victim continued to take form.

GRETA ALEXANDER: LARGER THAN LIFE

Greta Alexander is a colorful and imposing character, a mountain of flesh and fabric. Alexander confesses to having a life-long weight problem, yet even that advance knowledge is hardly enough to prepare the newcomer for her commanding size and presence. Her salt-and-pepper hair is piled up into a perpetual beehive, and her iridescent muumuus swathe her enormous frame in blinding color. When Greta speaks, the room falls into awed silence.

By age 60, she had achieved a great deal in her community. Thousands of people seek her psychic advice each year, begging for paranormal insight into the future. Some of those clients include such Hollywood glitterati as Debbie Reynolds and soap opera star Ruth Warrick. Once, Warrick even appeared with Greta on the Geraldo Rivera show. Greta gets forty dollars for each half-hour session with a client. Her four assistants handle the mounds of mail that arrive each day. So many people call her seeking psychic advice that the waiting period for a session is sometimes seven months to a year.[10] She only accepts phone calls for appointments on one day of the week. Officials of Illinois Bell have told reporters that they know when Alexander is taking calls because of the thousands of calls that surge through the telephone circuits.

Alexander's house, a 150-year-old farmhouse in Delavan, Illinois, is cluttered with religious artifacts, ceramic cherubs, and pictures of Jesus. She proudly shows off her chandeliers to visiting reporters. Greta has a second office in Springfield, and the income from her psychic readings is substantial. A 900-number telephone hookup collects even more money, as callers from around the country listen to a taped message of inspiration and hope. Her 24-room home has been expanded to include an indoor swimming pool which she uses to work off the tensions of too many requests for psychic aid.

But the side of Alexander's persona that has endeared her to the people of Southern Illinois is her charity. A portion of her income is used to support her "House of Hope," a five-bedroom home that shelters needy families who have relatives in Illinois hospitals. In several barns on her property she collects used clothing and goods which are periodically donated to the poor. Her doors are occasionally opened to troubled teenagers who have no place to stay. Greta Alexander is more than a cult figure; she is an icon, a beloved rural legend. The wise skeptic keeps his thoughts about Greta to himself in downstate Illinois.

Three decades ago, Greta Alexander lived on the edge of poverty, making a paltry living plucking feathers from chickens. In those days, she was paid twenty-five cents for each bird she stripped of plumage. But according to her story, Alexander became psychic after a freak accident in 1961. She was lying in bed one day, watching a thunderstorm. At the time, she was pregnant with her fifth child. A bolt of what she described as "cold lightning" came through the window, set fire to the bed, and wrapped her body in the Venetian blinds that had been torn from the window. In that instant, she was imbued with psychic powers that allowed her to peer into the future and view distant events. She claimed she could answer the phone before it rang, and see future developments in the lives of other people.

Alexander believes that two spirits or guardian angels named Raoul and Isaiah guide her on her psychic journeys into the netherworld. They're "her boys," as she calls them, and they deliver to her the prophecies which she, in turn, hands to her paying clients. She even provides reporters with a precise physical description of "her boys." Raoul is tall and dark-complected. He's a snappy dresser who wears suits and occasionally chides Greta for her appearance. Isaiah, on the other hand, is more like the classical version of his Old Testament namesake, complete with flowing robes and a subservient manner.

The visitor to Alexander's home or office is asked to prepare an inkprint of his or her hand, and the psychic studiously examines the palmprint in semi-darkness. From the inked lines, the Delavan psychic divines a variety of facts and visions. Health, love-life, and money troubles are all discussed in great detail with each client. No tape recorders are allowed in the sessions. Greta explains that the whirring of the motor is distracting to her psychic antennae. Besides, she explains that nine times out of ten the client's tape recorder fails to function anyway, apparently because of the energy fields generated by her mind during the reading.

While Alexander's private readings for clients have brought her a significant amount of income, it's her work with police investigators that has brought her nationwide fame. She bemoans the fact that she makes nothing from helping police solve criminal cases and find missing bodies, but she says she can't refuse a police agency's call for help when a serious crime is going unsolved. She receives up to five phone calls a week from law enforcement officers. One of those pleas for help became her most acclaimed case. It generated a multitude of headlines, magazine articles, and TV appearances, and was used to introduce Marcello Truzzi's book. Yet, beneath the surface is a suspicious set of circumstances, and a police investigator who says he was bamboozled by Greta Alexander.

MISSING BODIES AND THE COPS

The Mary Cousett case was a frustrating one for police. It was especially puzzling for Detective William Fitzgerald, who headed the investigation.

The Alton woman disappeared April 25, 1983. Police suspected almost immediately she had been murdered and they arrested her boyfriend, Stanley Holliday. The suspect confessed to police he had dumped the body somewhere along Route 121 next to the Mackinaw River, but he was vague about the exact location. Police knew that if Holliday was telling the truth, the body would have to be along a twenty-mile stretch where the river paralleled the highway. For months they combed the fields and banks along the river without success. Finally they were informed by prosecutors that they had just three more days to locate the body, or Holliday would have to be freed. The officers organized one last search.

Unbeknownst to Detective Fitzgerald, a member of the Tazewell County State Attorney's office called Greta Alexander to ask her to get involved in the case. The Delavan psychic began spewing forth images and predictions about how Cousett's body would be found, where it would be found, and how the searchers might recognize the right area when they came to it. She even drew a circle on a map, next to the river, and said the body would be within that circle. Searchers did not go to the area Alexander circled, but they convened at a spot along the river they had planned to search again anyway. Within three hours the body was found.

This discovery was a stunning one. Telephone lines in downstate Illinois were burning up with the news that a psychic had gotten involved in the search and located the body. News articles about the psychic's predictions hit the wires. The story that follows was typical of most of the wire accounts:

ALTON, ILLINOIS (UPI)—Information provided by a psychic led officials to the skeletal remains of a woman from Alton, Ill., police said.

"I was skeptical to begin with," Alton Detective William Fitzgerald said Tuesday, "but I guess I'm going to have to be a believer, now."

Fitzgerald said Greta Alexander, a psychic from Delavan, Ill., provided 22 clues that led authorities to the body of Mary L. Cousett, 27, believed to have been murdered in April. The body was discovered Saturday in an area south of Peoria.

Fitzgerald said Ms. Alexander predicted the location of the body, its condition and the way it would be found. He said she even predicted it would be found by a man "with a bad hand" and that the initial "S" would be important to the discovery.

Fitzgerald said the body was found by Steve Trew, an auxiliary policeman in Tazewell County.[11]

Over the years, skeptical investigators have siphoned through details of hundreds of psychic anecdotes like the one in Alton. Yet, not a single provable case of true psychic ability has been established. If, indeed, Greta

Alexander had finally been able to solve a police case through psychic means, then she had overturned some of the most fundamental and significant scientific principles in the universe. Unfortunately for true believers, details of the Alexander/Cousett case began to fall apart as soon as they were subjected to scrutiny.

Soon after the Cousett case hit the wires, Detective Fitzgerald provided this writer with a list of 24 psychic clues that came out of Greta Alexander's psychic reading. At the time, Fitzgerald confessed to being astonished at their accuracy. He admitted that Alexander may have made scores of additional pronouncements, but the ones he recalled specifically are as follows:

1) The area where the body is has already been searched.

2) A man with funny-looking boots walked right past the body during a previous search.

3) The man with the boots had a dog.

4) A man with a crippled hand will find the body.

5) There are three roads.

6) The initial "S" will play an important role.

7) The initial "B" is around the victim's body.

8) The body would not be found in the state where she was born.

9) Grabner's farm would play a part.

10) There would be tree cuttings near the body.

11) The road splits near the body.

12) The road near the body is bumpy.

13) The body will be off the main highway.

14) A leg or a foot on the body will be missing.

15) The head will not be with the body.

16) The body will be near a bridge.

17) The body was dragged from the place where the victim was killed.

18) Only part of the body will be showing.

19) Cars stopping nearby will be important.

20) The body will be down an embankment.

21) A faded sign will be important.

22) The body will be across a road, down from the river.

23) Mountains or hills are nearby.

24) A church will play an important part.

Assuming that members of a search party fervently believed the psychic was accurately seeing the body's location, an analysis of the clues shows that only a few of them could reasonably lead police to the murder scene. Investigators would, of course, search the circled area. They would attempt to find Grabner's farm and see if they could locate a church, some mountains or hills, a bridge and a conjunction of three roads nearby, perhaps near a faded stop sign.

The problem was, the name Grabner didn't correspond with any known people in that part of Illinois. And along this stretch of highway, there are a number of churches, bridges, and road conjunctions. All the other predictions were so vague they could reasonably apply to virtually any portion of the twenty-mile stretch of Route 121. So the searchers, rather than spend precious time trying to study the psychic's predictions, convened their search at a previously chosen location. It turned out to be the right location, not because of Alexander's help, but because of an apparent coincidence.

News of the discovery of Mary Cousett's body spread rapidly through the search party, and as police roped off the murder scene the searchers congregated nearby. Suddenly, members of the group began reviewing Alexander's predictions. The first thing that hit them was that Officer Steve Trew, the one who found the body, had an injured finger. His first initial, of course, was *S*. The bones of the victim were, indeed, scattered, just as Alexander had said. Then they began going down the list of Alexander's other clues. There was a bridge off in the distance. There wasn't a church nearby, but there was a church camp about a half mile to a mile down the road. There were also piles of salt on the highway about a quarter mile away which seemed to match the "mountains or hills" prediction. The excitement grew as they assessed the seeming accuracy of the psychic's prophecies.

Many of Alexander's predictions were also completely wrong. There was no Grabner's Farm. There were no tree cuttings near the body. The road nearby was not bumpy. The only cars that traveled nearby were on a main highway and did not stop there at all. The only signs nearby were not faded. And the circle Alexander drew on the map missed Cousett's body by a good distance.* Yet these "psychic misses" seemed to lose their significance as the "hits" were reflected upon.

Detective William Fitzgerald was bombarded with phone calls about the case. In the months to come he told his story repeatedly, expressing increasing amazement at the fact that Alexander had predicted a man with a crippled hand would find the body. Fitzgerald's name was repeatedly cited by the media as the authority on whom their stories about Greta Alexander's psychic abilities were based.

As hundreds of phone calls continued to pour in to the Alton Police Department, Fitzgerald began to have gnawing doubts about whether Greta Alexander's involvement actually had anything to do with the discovery of Mary Cousett's body. As with any competent police detective, his mind refused to let details of the case rest. Over and over he reflected on the two dozen predictions. Slowly, he began to realize their lack of significance in actually leading searchers to the murder scene.

Greta Alexander's predictions, like those of all psychics, seem to fall into four different categories: extremely general statements that have a very wide application, self-fulfilling prophecies, and an occasional wild guess with very specific characteristics; the fourth category involves predictions that are patently false, but contain enough flexibility that they can be instantly modified and corrected when confronted with an objection.

The first category, the vague or general statement, might include a prediction such as, "I see the letter 'B' all around him." The prediction is essentially meaningless, since there are thousands of "B" words that could logically apply. It could refer to brown clothing, or brown soil, or blue water, or branches, or the first initial of a county. It could refer to bridges, or brush, or any of a myriad of words one could pull from pages of a dictionary.

The second category, self-fulfilling prophecy, is interesting because it involves the mental process which governs the way human beings think. Humans are nature's ultimate problem-solvers because their minds are capable of sifting through and processing millions of details as a problem

---

*Statements from various witnesses vary on how far away from the body the circle was drawn. Initial interviews done within weeks after the story broke indicate the circle on the map was approximately twenty miles from the location where Cousett's body was found. In later interviews, Detective (now Sargeant) William Fitzgerald said he didn't remember exactly how far off the circle was drawn.

is being resolved. The mind solves mysteries by "filling in the blank spaces" with the easiest possible answers first. If the easiest answers fail to provide a solution, the mind accepts increasingly complex possibilities until the problem is eventually resolved.

Under certain circumstances, however, this problem-solving skill can be subverted. The average person seems to be endowed with a certain amount of skepticism. However, that skepticism can be converted to an attitude of "suspension of disbelief" if the person comes under the influence of a charismatic and seemingly powerful individual. When a new belief system is proffered by a colorful salesperson who seems to have some personal magnetism and skills of persuasion, a large number of people can be swayed to suspend their disbelief. Psychics like Greta Alexander are extremely charismatic people with good verbal skills and aggressive, persuasive personalities.

When the average person allows his disbelief or skepticism to be suspended, he no longer solves problems by searching for the easiest possible solutions. Instead, he accepts tenets of the new belief system regardless of how illogical and complex they may be. Instead of trying out easy solutions when presented with a problem, he allows his charismatic companion to "fill in the blank spaces" with unsupportable answers.

Self-fulfilling prophecy takes advantage of this whole process. With his disbelief in suspension, the susceptible person accepts a prophecy without questioning the motive of the prophet. Then, instead of challenging the legitimacy of the prediction itself, he searches for ways to make it come true. Once the prophecy is apparently fulfilled, he stops looking for more logical solutions. In the Mary Cousett case, a number of Alexander's statements seemed to follow this formula.

Some of the self-fulfilling prophecies given to Detective Fitzgerald included the statement about "three roads." After the discovery of the body, searchers might have looked around and discovered that there were, indeed, three roads visible. A fourth road off in the distance would undoubtedly be ignored. The same thing applies to the predictions about the road splitting "near" the body, and a bridge "near" the body. After the body was found, searchers might logically look around until they found a bridge and a road splitting, regardless of how far away they were. As for the prediction about the church, there weren't any nearby. But searchers might give undue significance to a nearby church camp, or a church bus, or the fact that the victim might have recently come from church. None of these prophecies, however, would have any significance prior to the discovery of the victim's body. They would become important only afterward, and therefore would play no role in the discovery itself.

The third category of clairvoyant prediction can be a dangerous one for the person doing the prophesying. Wild guesses have to be used in just the right proportion for a psychic like Alexander to maintain credibility with her clients. Much like a recipe where a slight amount of salt improves the broth but too much is actually destructive, dangerous guesses are almost always wrong and tend to confuse the client. Like the trapeze artist who fails twice before the third and final climax, a psychic builds credibility with an occasional failure. But those rare occasions where a wild prediction comes true can elevate a psychic from a store-front palm reader to a millionaire with massive power and influence.

The fourth category involves prophecy which can be rapidly altered when confronted with an objection. Greta Alexander makes frequent use of this type of prediction. If she says, "I see a road" and is told that none exists, she could then say something like, "Well, it looks like a road from a distance, because it's flat and it's sometimes used as a trail by livestock or other animals." Or if she sees gold flowers where none exist she could back out of the erroneous statement by saying, "Well, I still see the color gold. It's evening and the sun is setting and it's reflecting off the foliage."

A good example of her use of the rapidly altered prophecy was recorded in the *Chicago Tribune* in 1986, after Alexander appeared on stage at the Illinois State Fair in Springfield. She asked a woman in the audience if she had back problems. (Most people above the age of 30 do suffer back pain.) But the woman replied, "No." Shifting gears, Alexander drove her psychic bulldozer over the volunteer by saying, "Well, my back hurts with you, so watch for kidney and bladder infections."[12]

Another strategy Alexander appears to use to ameliorate the damage caused by erroneous guesses is to give the type of guess that can be rapidly re-categorized as circumstances see fit. Therefore, the wild guess at the name "Grabner" could be altered to actually mean "Wagner" or "Abner" if she was lucky enough to encounter such a circumstance. Or by using "the man with the crippled hand," she might also be credited with a "psychic hit" if the man who found the body had a gimpy leg or some other physical deformity. In this manner, a wild guess actually becomes a self-fulfilling guess.

Although Detective William Fitzgerald (now Sergeant Fitzgerald) may not have contemplated Alexander's predictions in the Cousett case in such painstaking detail, he was bothered by the fact that the discovery might not have been so paranormal after all. He began to doubt whether the statements he originally gave the media were accurate. He questioned whether the psychic predictions made by Alexander were as specific and miraculous as he had once believed.

Against this backdrop of increasing doubt, Fitzgerald made a startling discovery. He found that, prior to his talking with Alexander, she had been given precise information about the Cousett case by other investigators in Tazewell County. The information included the suspect's confession in which the twenty-mile stretch of Route 121 was mentioned as the dumping ground for the body. And it was in this same general area that Alexander had later drawn the circle on the map.

In an interview with this writer in December 1991, Sergeant Fitzgerald had the following reflections about the case:

> I found out later that before we even talked to Greta Alexander, the people up in Peoria had already talked to her. I didn't know that at the time. It was their Sheriff's Department in Tazewell County. You just find these things out later, after the fact.
>
> I started looking into psychics, and trying to prove and disprove the twenty-four points on our list. You know, when she talked about water, well there's always water somewhere. And when she talked about the head being removed from the body, you know, when a body's been there for a period of time an animal always drags the bones off.
>
> When she talked about the hills or mountains of some type, you know at that time of year, you're getting lots of piles of salt placed along that road.
>
> The circle on the map, see that's the point I'm trying to get at. In the suspect's statement, he said he had dropped the body right along that area, so Greta Alexander already had that previous information to my understanding. You know, that's the thing that frosted me, I'll never forget it. She had that previous information that we didn't know she had.
>
> The one thing I'll say, as far as the investigation was concerned, we knew if we didn't find that body, they were going to dismiss the charge on a Monday. Getting Greta involved and getting publicity involved, I ended up having somewhere between fifty and seventy-five volunteers up there searching. We'd have eventually found that body, but it sure would have taken us a lot longer without those volunteers.
>
> The thing that still bothers me, though, is the man with the crippled hand. I could disprove everything except the hand. It still blows my mind.[13]

Sergeant Fitzgerald's post-mortem of the Cousett case is fascinating, in that he took it upon himself to critically analyze his own previous beliefs about Alexander's abilities. Most people enamored with psychics will rationalize away contradictory information forever. Despite the fact that the easiest and most popular course is to accept the existence of psychic phenomena, Sergeant Fitzgerald swam against the apparent tide of public opinion. He decided for himself that Greta Alexander's success in the search for Cousett's body was dubious at best.

With regard to the one prediction out of twenty-four that still "blows" Fitzgerald's mind, there's an easy answer. It was a coincidence. Alexander's prediction that a man with a crippled hand would find the body was nothing more than a good cold reader at work. Psychics often talk about body deformities in their readings, and with good reason. Ask any group of people how many have a scar on their left knee, and an overwhelming percentage will respond in the affirmative. Ask the same group how many are concerned about the health of someone close to them, possibly someone who is taking a medication that comes in a small white tablet, and the vast majority will admit to having such a concern. Psychics invariably use high-percentage predictions like these to supply the bulk of their readings. Erroneous predictions are quickly forgotten. But the rare coincidental "hit" often turns into media coverage and a skyrocketing income for the psychic.

The more readings a psychic does, the more the odds favor the occasional "hit."[14] Greta Alexander does lots of readings for police agencies. In fact, she says she gets so many calls from police officers that it interferes with her regular cash business. All a psychic need do is score one or two major "hits" in a career, and gullible members of the press will remain loyal forever. A good example of that loyalty is Wes Smith's *Chicago Tribune* article of June 9, 1991, which again recounts Alexander's "miraculous" discovery of the Cousett body. A single phone call to Sergeant Fitzgerald would have overturned Alexander's psychic claims to the case. By the time the *Tribune* article was researched and written, Sergeant Fitzgerald had long since become a relatively hardened skeptic.

Greta Alexander discounts skeptics who critically assess the usefulness of her "psychic ability" in the Cousett case. Questions about her involvement meet with a vague explanation of how she obtains her "visions." In one interview, she admitted she did have some advance information about the suspect in the killing of Mary Cousett, and where he went immediately after the murder. But she said she didn't recall how much information was provided. She claimed it probably wasn't "significant" information.[15]

Even if one were to accept the proposition that Greta Alexander actually did have a "psychic revelation" in her viewing of the man with the crippled hand, a troubling question remains. Did the crippled hand prediction have anything to do with leading police to the body? The answer, of course, is no. The search was going to be conducted anyway. The search area had already been selected. The crippled hand prediction, as astounding as it seemed at the time, was discovered to be accurate only after the events of that day had already unfolded. Yet it is the single prediction now being held out by some as justifying the use of psychics in police investigations.

THE PRESS CORPS AT WORK

One of Greta Alexander's more recent cases generated even more favorable headlines than the Cousett case. But once again, a closer examination shows that legions of reporters made the unforgivable error of not verifying basic facts. The following news item best sums up the case:

> EFFINGHAM, ILL. (UPI)—A psychic helped police Saturday find a missing 74-year-old man who fell down in a bean field during a ginseng hunting expedition and couldn't get up.
>
> Authorities summoned Greta Alexander after they turned up nothing Wednesday, Thursday and Friday in their quest for Rex Carpenter.
>
> Alexander, employed by law enforcement agencies in similar circumstances previously, reviewed a list of the towns in the area of the search in rural central Illinois.
>
> "You're looking in the wrong area," she told authorities, according to a state trooper.
>
> The psychic suggested police scour another area. They did, and found Carpenter around 9 A.M. He was a bit dehydrated but listed in good condition.
>
> Asked about Alexander's contribution to the hunt, Sheriff Larry Mulvey said he doesn't understand how that sort of thing works, but that "she gave us very valuable information and provided several ideas that worked out."[16]

The story on the psychic discovery of Rex Carpenter made fascinating reading. Its conclusion challenged known laws of physics and science. Like other favorable news coverage which Greta Alexander frequently enjoys, it was also patently false.

Rex Carpenter vanished on a Wednesday evening in Jasper County. The date was September 4, 1991. His wife, Ruth, had dropped him off in an area several miles from town to hunt for ginseng, a Chinese herb that grows wild in wooded areas of southern Illinois. His instructions were to walk southeast across a field, and she planned to pick him up a half mile away in two or three hours.

Carpenter suffered from Parkinson's disease, a degenerative muscle disease that causes tremors and loss of motor control. The elderly man was dressed in a plaid shirt and bib overalls, and he carried a green raincoat and a shovel.

At the appointed time, Ruth arrived at the spot where her husband was to meet her, but he was not there. After searching for a couple of hours, she called Jasper County Sheriff Larry Mulvey. The sheriff immediately mobilized a search party and they began looking for Carpenter. As the hours went by, more and more volunteers showed up to do their part. Thursday came and went, still with no sign of the missing man. Sheriff Mulvey contacted other police agencies, including the Illinois State Patrol in Effingham. Trooper Ed Hoopingarner was one of those who joined the search.

Trooper Hoopingarner had learned of Greta Alexander on a television talk show and offered to call her into the Rex Carpenter case. He and Sheriff Mulvey had used the psychic just two months earlier in an unsuccessful search for another missing man. The other disappearance, coincidentally, was less than a mile from the spot where Carpenter vanished, so Alexander was already somewhat familiar with the area.

Jasper County is a relatively flat farming community, where about ten thousand people live and work. The land is a colorful patchwork of farms and woodlands marked by occasional country roads; small creeks; and shallow, wooded ravines. The ravines, at most, are five to fifteen feet deep. The county's main income comes from agriculture, including grains, beans, and corn. Since the September weather was still quite warm, most of the crops had not yet been harvested. The searchers rightly figured that Carpenter was not in good enough physical shape to walk very far, so the search was concentrated in an area about four miles square.

By Friday afternoon, the searchers had still not located Carpenter, so Trooper Hoopingarner made his call to Greta Alexander. His first contact with the psychic was at 3:15 in the afternoon. Hoopingarner did not record his conversation with Alexander, but from memory he provided this writer with the following list of her predictions:

1) Carpenter was still alive.

2) The missing man was near a road which came to a dead end.

3) A horse with four white feet that had a foal was important.

4) There were gold flowers around Rex Carpenter.

5) Carpenter was in a waterway.

6) Carpenter was in a ravine, and had trouble getting up the slippery bank.

7) She could see woods.

8) She saw fresh choppings of wood, like a beaver would cut.

9) Along the edge of the woods, there were prairie flowers or short weeds.

10) Way off in the distance there was a tower of some kind, with high-tension lines.

11) She heard a "click, click, click" sound.

12) She could see Carpenter's leg jumping, like he had suffered a stroke.

13) She could see a handkerchief or a piece of clothing that would be found.

14) There was a secondary road that ran right past Carpenter.

15) The road stops, but if you went through, you'd have to go around.

16) She told Hoopingarner he would have to "go around to where the draw goes through."

17) Rex Carpenter has walked farther than everyone thinks.

18) Carpenter's family is panicking more than Carpenter himself is.

19) Carpenter has something on his head.

20) Carpenter was getting tired and physically exhausted.

21) She saw a man of about 6'3" or 6'4", with a full head of white hair, and a square chin.

22) She again mentioned the ravine and said, "Go down that ravine, and you'll find him."

23) She said, "If you don't find him by Sunday, it'll be too late."

For someone who believed in psychics, hearing these very specific-sounding predictions must have given new energy to the search crew. At about 4:50 that same afternoon, Trooper Hoopingarner made a second call to Greta Alexander, and this time patched the phone call through to Floyd Ernest, who was in a pickup truck driving along the many secondary roads that criss-crossed the search area. Several hundred feet above, a private plane circled the searchers while staying in touch with Ernest by radio. (Alexander repeatedly referred to the plane as a helicopter.)

During this three-way conversation, Greta Alexander tried to psychically direct the aircraft to the very spot where Carpenter was lying. Repeatedly, she mentioned the ravine and said, "Go down that ravine, and you'll find him." When Floyd Ernest protested that there wasn't really a ravine in the area, she replied, "Well it's a draw. I say draw, because that's what Carpenter would have called it." Ernest admitted that there was a slightly depressed area which hadn't yet been searched. During this conference call, according to Ernest, Greta made some additional predictions:

24) Carpenter was between two steel towers.

25) There was "green stuff" around.

26) There were yellow flowers.

27) There was some green in the low spots.

Following his participation in the conference call, Ernest didn't talk to any of the other searchers, but went home. Presumably, Trooper Hoopingarner or Sheriff Mulvey talked to other members of the search party, because rumors about the use of a psychic began spreading. A list of the specific predictions was never circulated, but some of the searchers became aware of some vague statements like the yellow flowers, a ravine, and the weeds at the edge of the woods.

Meanwhile, at about 7:30 that evening, one of the searchers, Albert Fitzmaurice, came across a set of tracks and some strange indentations in the soil about a quarter mile from the spot where Carpenter had vanished more than forty-eight hours earlier. The unusual tracks had been spotted the previous evening by another searcher who discounted their significance and failed to tell anyone about them.

Fitzmaurice, however, immediately recognized the indentations as marks made by a shovel being used as a walking stick. He remembered that Carpenter had taken a shovel on his ginseng hunt. He realized that he was, indeed, looking at Carpenter's trail and alerted Sheriff Mulvey. But it was growing dark and the searchers were afraid they would destroy the faint set of tracks in the dirt. The sheriff asked most of the searchers to go home, and he asked a small number of men who had coon hunting lights to continue through the night. Again, their efforts proved fruitless.

The next morning at daybreak, Fitzmaurice returned to the search area and again attempted to follow the tracks he had spotted the previous night. The trail disappeared into a grassy area, so Fitzmaurice walked to the other side of the field in an effort to pick up the trail once again. About a quarter mile away, he again found the indentations made by the shovel and followed them several hundred yards further into a bean field. Because the tracks were two days old and extremely faint, Fitzmaurice summoned Sheriff Mulvey and Royal Carpenter, the missing man's son.

While the sheriff went to his patrol car to drive to the other side of the bean field, Fitzmaurice and Carpenter walked into the bean field, carefully following the trail of shovel marks. Within just a few minutes, they saw Carpenter's green raincoat, and then found him face down in the field just a few feet away. It was more than a mile from the spot where Greta Alexander had tried to direct the airplane the previous evening. Carpenter was lying between the bean plants, about fifteen rows into the field. He was alive, although dehydrated, and was rushed to the hospital. The seventy-four-year-old man survived his ordeal in relatively good shape.

Some of the searchers, and subsequently the media in downstate Illinois, went berserk with details of the discovery. The leaves in the beanfield were gold and ready for harvest. This, they reasoned, must be the "gold flowers" Greta Alexander foresaw. Since Carpenter was found lying in a three-inch-deep furrow between the rows of bean plants, some stories indicated that the prediction about the "depression" or "ravine" must have been accurate. Then one of the three hundred searchers realized that he had a mare with four white stockings and a foal at home. This too, suddenly took on tremendous significance. The clicking sound predicted by Alexander was interpreted to mean one of the many oil wells in the area. Since it was also harvest time, there were numerous combines operating across the countryside. The power lines and towers were never really located, but a distant church steeple sufficed.

As the news of the psychic's participation in the hunt spread, few people asked the searchers who actually found Carpenter about their thoughts on the discovery. The ones who spoke to this writer were somewhat disgusted by the hoopla surrounding Alexander's "psychic visions" in the days that followed.

Albert Fitzmaurice admits that he might have heard one or two of the rumors about Alexander's predictions, but all he remembers hearing is that Carpenter was "down over an embankment by a steep bluff." He didn't give the rumors any credence. In fact, had he spent his time looking in ravines or over bluffs, he might never have found the shovel marks, since the marks were in a flat beanfield, nowhere near a ravine. He also says he never heard the story about the gold flowers. Besides, he says, in a farming community like this, there are gold flowers everywhere.

Royal Carpenter, the missing man's son, says he tried to duck all the reporters after the discovery. When he talked to this writer, he scoffed at suggestions that Greta Alexander had anything to do with finding Carpenter. "As far as I'm concerned, psychics are of no use whatsoever.

Everything written about my father was exaggerated beyond belief. During the search, I was hearing so many rumors I just ignored them all. The general consensus here is that the newspapers were full of baloney. Everything that came out of Decatur [*The Decatur Herald*] was wrong."

Even Floyd Ernest, who was part of the three-way conference call with Greta Alexander, judged her more harshly than the eager Illinois media. "She was of very little value," Ernest said. "The biggest thing it did, when you've searched for three days, it makes you wake up. She did say you're not looking far enough and I'll give her that.

"But she said Carpenter was between two steel towers. There was nothing like that around. She said there were motors running, but there are lots of those around. She said he was down in a draw, but after you farm a field, you rim out a ditch. Every field's got dozens of those. She said there was green stuff around, yellow flowers, green in the low spots, it just wasn't there. We don't feel like she helped us at all. The good publicity Greta Alexander got, it didn't come from us. It had to have come from her."

When asked what kind of percentage of accuracy he would ascribe to Greta's numerous predictions, Ernest replied, "Twenty percent. No more. I don't know how she gets such good publicity."

Greta was given a much higher percentage grade by State Trooper Ed Hoopingarner who originally called her into the search. He assigned her an accuracy percentage of about fifty percent. But he agreed that was just like flipping a coin. He says he doesn't believe in psychics and doesn't disbelieve, but he would consider using Alexander again if he was in a bind on a police search.

Still, Greta Alexander was credited by the media with a rock-solid success at finding Rex Carpenter. In the *Effingham Daily News,* reporter Nora Bentley described Greta Alexander as "a woman with an unusual ability." She wrote:

Alexander is a psychic, who was able to help find Carpenter with "pictures" she saw in her mind.

"I said this is the way I feel, and I started giving him some directions. He [Carpenter] was walking through my head," Alexander said of what she did after being given basic information over the phone.

She also was "patched" through to people searching in a helicopter, and this enabled her to see what the people on the ground were seeing, Alexander said.

In the visions she was having of Carpenter, Alexander said she could see his footprints, and this is what allowed her to lead the searchers to him.

Carpenter was found lying face down in a soybean field near Rose Hill where he had fallen and was unable to get up. Searchers had been looking in the fields and woods near Falmouth where Carpenter's wife had dropped him off.[17]

An article that appeared in the *Decatur Herald* was just as credulous and inaccurate. It appeared under the headline, "Psychic Leads Searchers to Man Lost on Ginseng Hunt."

Carpenter was found in a soybean field after authorities consulted psychic Greta Alexander of Delavan when two days of a massive search had proven fruitless. About 325 volunteers searched fields and woods near Falmouth on Friday, but Alexander told authorities to look instead in the Rose Hill area.

Jasper County Sheriff Larry W. Mulvey said Alexander "gave us valuable information" that helped lead searchers to Carpenter.[18]

The news articles on Greta Alexander weren't even close to reality. Rose Hill is about four miles due north of Falmouth on State Route 130. Carpenter vanished from a spot almost two miles east of Route 130, equidistant from both communities. The news stories that said searchers were concentrating their search in the Falmouth area were therefore patently wrong. In addition, Carpenter's trail showed he consistently walked north-east, away from Rose Hill, never toward it.

In any event, the Rose Hill clue was extremely misleading to the searchers. Albert Fitzmaurice explained it best: "If Greta said we were looking in the wrong area, look instead in the Rose Hill area, that was completely meaningless to anyone who knows this area at all. It just wouldn't have meant anything to anyone who lives here."

Despite the fact that Greta Alexander only had a four-square-mile area within which to work, she steered searchers in precisely the wrong direction, away from Carpenter's location, more than a mile from the spot where he was lying, waiting for help. Still, the southern Illinois papers continued their stream of articles praising Greta Alexander's "accuracy." From an editorial in the *Newton Press-Mentor:*

Through the Carpenter family, a known and proven psychic, Greta Alexander, was consulted and assisted with projections regarding Mr. Carpenter's whereabouts.[19]

With a newspaper endorsing her on the editorial page as a "known and proven psychic," Greta Alexander couldn't have purchased better advertising. From the front page of the *Sunday Herald and Review* came a hint about the effectiveness of Alexander's vague and self-fulfilling prophecies which can be rapidly modified to correct errors:

> A week ago Alexander helped the Jasper County Sheriff's Office find Rex Carpenter, 74, of Rose Hill, 68 hours after he failed to return from a ginseng hunt. The department contacted her for help.
>
> "My hand started trembling, and I said, 'His hand is shaking,' " Alexander recalled. "They said, 'Yes, he has Parkinson's Disease.' Then I knew I was right."[20]

Here, Greta Alexander makes an obviously vague statement about Carpenter's hand shaking. Of course it's shaking! He's 74 years old, he's lost, hungry, tired, cold, perhaps a little frightened. Besides, no one would know if his hand was shaking or not. But because of the elderly man's disease, Greta is credited with a direct psychic hit!

Finally, disgusted with all the erroneous, distorted, self-delusion in the newspapers, the man who found Rex Carpenter, Albert Fitzmaurice, felt called upon to write a letter to the editor of one of the local papers:

> I cannot force myself to believe all the articles I have been reading in your newspaper about the psychic's involvement in finding Mr. Rex Carpenter here in Jasper County a few weeks ago. Personally, I think too much credit has been given Greta Alexander, the psychic.
>
> Let's give God some credit; He is the one who was leading the search, not the psychic.[21]

Unfortunately, history has proven that truth rarely prevails over belief in the paranormal. The myriad of deceptive articles about Greta Alexander are now part of the public record. Researchers for decades to come will be able to look back, harvest the headlines, and reach conclusions about Alexander's so-called "psychic abilities."

If a psychic actually had led police to Carpenter's body, the miracle would have been a stunning one that overturned all the laws of logic, reason, science, physics, and probability. Such an astounding event should have warranted more investigation by the media.

CHEATING THE COPS

Even if those directly connected with the discovery of Rex Carpenter were disgusted by media claims that the psychic was useful, there seems to be general agreement about a single point. When they heard that a psychic believed Carpenter was still alive, it gave them new energy. Floyd Ernest said, "It woke us up." Sheriff Mulvey said, "It perked us up and sort of gave us a second life to think he might still be alive."

A troubling question, therefore, involves cases where the psychic claims the subject of the search is already dead. Does that demoralize and rob a search party of energy? That very scenario happened just two months earlier when Greta Alexander was called into the first Jasper County search by Sheriff Mulvey and Trooper Hoopingarner.

The missing man was 52-year-old Robert Lucas, who vanished in this same area of Jasper County in July. The only clue the sheriff's department had was that his vehicle was found abandoned in a cemetery near his parents' home. Lucas was an occasional fisherman, and there was some thought that he might have gone fishing in one of the local streams. Trooper Hoopingarner recalls that the psychic said the man was already dead, and that his body was in the Embarras (pronounced Ambraw) River. Some of her many statements as recalled by Hoopingarner are as follows:

1) The current has moved his body downstream.

2) There's an old piece of farm equipment in the river, and the body is just downstream from that.

3) On the opposite side of the stream from the spot where you'll find his body, the cows come down to drink and the river is curved.

4) There's some kind of target practice or shooting going on nearby.

5) The name Wynette, or Lynette, is important.

6) When the sun starts down, if Lucas could see the bridge over the river he could see the sun.

7) I see a real new shiny black vehicle.

8) Lucas fell down a bank in the water and he's cussing and carrying on and saying, "Those sons of bitches aren't going to take this away from me."

9) There's a pole leaning over the water. (When told by Hoopingarner that they couldn't find a pole she replied, "Well, it's a tree stripped of bark.")

10) Lucas is dead because I see the sign of the cross.

11) I see an older style bridge that has been rehabilitated.

12) I hear a bell ringing.

13) I can see a corn crib without a roof.

14) There are two little islands and an old fence lying there.

15) I can hear a buzz saw.

16) Lucas is still under the water stuck under a crevice of rocks.

17) Just upstream from his body is a spot to camp, where there's a tent.

18) I can hear an Indian warhoop that sounds like, woowoowoo.

19) There's a house where part of the roof slants more than the other.

20) I see some kind of a carcass, like a deer or a cow. (When told they found no carcass, she replied, "If it's not there now, it will be in a day or so.")

Members of Sheriff Mulvey's department spent many hours floating the Embarras River looking for Lucas's body. They were initially impressed, because some of Alexander's predictions seemed to have the ring of truth. They learned that many years earlier, an Indian had lived in one of the homes along the river. Lucas, indeed, possessed a newer model black Chevy S-10 pickup truck. It was several payments behind and was about to be repossessed. The searchers felt that Greta must have heard Lucas "cussing out" the finance company that was about to reclaim the vehicle. And after much searching, they did finally find a tree hanging over the river that seemed to have lost some bark. They even found a house with lots of gables, and decided it must be the one in her prediction. But finding the specific location to which Greta Alexander seemed to be pointing them was impossible.

Had Lucas' body never been discovered, Sheriff Mulvey and Trooper Hoopingarner might have believed forever that they were just a few feet away from the body during their various expeditions down the river. However, in early November 1991 they found Lucas' remains. His body was a mere half mile from his abandoned pickup truck, a full three and a half miles away from the Embarras River. He was nowhere near a significant body of water.

In retrospect, very few of Alexander's predictions were even remotely close to the truth. A number of questions immediately come to mind: Didn't logic dictate that Lucas would most likely be found somewhere near the pickup truck he abandoned? Would the case have had a different outcome if the sheriff's attention not been improperly diverted to a location many miles away? Would Lucas have been located much sooner, perhaps even as he was lying on the ground, waiting for help, as Rex Carpenter had been? And where were the reporters? Why didn't they report Greta Alexander's patently false predictions in the Lucas case? Why did they only report her predictions in the Carpenter case, which had a successful ending?

In case after case around the country, the use of psychics like Greta Alexander has negatively impacted police investigations. Occasionally, psychic involvement interferes to the point that investigations are literally led astray.

One such case happened in Idaho Springs, Colorado, in August 1983. Fourteen-year-old Beth Miller vanished while jogging through her town. Members of the tiny police department were inundated with hundreds of calls from psychics. Rather than being diverted or ignored, each tip was carefully logged and taken seriously. The investigators, inexperienced in complex criminal investigation, even began proactively seeking psychic advice from well-known tabloid mystics.*

Shortly after the teenager's disappearance, posters appeared in the windows of businesses throughout the state. Each poster contained a detailed description of a man who had supposedly abducted the girl. The description, according to the poster, had been supplied by four psychics who claimed she was still alive. The likelihood that the description was accurate was remote, and may even have diverted attention away from the real suspect. In fact, an erroneous description may have given the real suspect confidence that investigators were not on his trail.

Some in Colorado law enforcement privately complained that a basic homicide investigation in the Miller case was never done, because so much time was devoted to interviewing psychics. Nine years after the Miller girl's disappearance, a member of the Colorado Bureau of Investigation (CBI) revealed that his agency was never asked by Idaho Springs to participate

---

*One investigator who worked on the case was familiar with Greta Alexander. But he couldn't recall the level of her involvement (if any) in the Beth Miller investigation.

in the investigation, despite the fact that the CBI maintains a staff of investigators and a well-equipped crime lab.

Police officers, for the most part, are sadly unequipped to confront the paranormal. They are goal-oriented and generally have scant interest in how a case is solved. It matters little whether a homicide case is solved through a confession, a witness, an accidental discovery or a psychic. All that counts in the end is whether a suspect is prosecuted and justice served. Police officers take classes in analyzing clues, but classes in parapsychology are rarely, if ever, part of the curriculum.

Reporters, on the other hand, are occupationally better equipped to sift through the chicanery that inevitably accompanies psychic stories. A reporter's goal, theoretically, is to present a reader, viewer, or listener with the truth, regardless of whether that truth creates ill will. Ethical reporters should not distort their stories in an effort to be popular or sell newspapers. If a majority of the public believes in the existence of psychic ability, as most polls seem to indicate, a reporter has a responsibility to offer an argument based on honest research. He should not attempt to uphold the popular belief system if it is, indeed, scientifically unsupportable. His responsibility, rather, is to investigate, and interview, and test, and sort through the evidence and present the truth, whatever that truth may be.

A police officer who uses psychics may adversely impact his case or slow down the investigation process. But his crime is one of gullibility, not of a violation of integrity. It's different for reporters. A reporter who perpetuates a myth, whether through carelessness, laziness, or gullibility, is guilty of a higher crime. Not only does he cheat himself and his readers, but he, like the psychic, cheats the very police officers whose activity he covers. By reporting distorted and erroneous details of the involvement of psychics in police work, he helps create an atmosphere in which the use of psychics by police continues to gain acceptance. Other police agencies may read that reporter's account of a psychic's work and attempt to avail themselves of the same assistance. The reporter, in other words, is the primary person responsible for generating malignant urban legends.

Until the day when science proves there is such a thing as psychic ability, the use of clairvoyants in police cases is not "better than nothing," as some writers have suggested. It is not benign. Instead, it overrules and suppresses logic in investigatory situations where logic may be the key ingredient needed to solve a crime and achieve justice. It is negative, and adversely impacts the public good.

NOTES

1. *Decatur Herald,* September 9, 1991.
2. United Press International, Effingham, Illinois, September 13, 1991.
3. The Associated Press, Harrisburg, Illinois, November 6, 1985.
4. United Press International, Alton, Illinois, November 16, 1983.
5. The Associated Press, Edwardsville, Illinois, November 18, 1983.
6. Arthur Lyons and Marcello Truzzi, *The Blue Sense: Psychic Detectives and Crime* (New York: The Mysterious Press, 1991), p. 254.
7. Wes Smith, "Seeing Things," *Chicago Tribune,* June 9, 1991.
8. Elizabeth Bettendorf, "Sixth Sense, Greta Alexander's Psychic Mission," *Heartland-The State Journal Register,* March 15, 1991.
9. Wes Smith, *Chicago Tribune,* "Tempo," June 9, 1991, p. 10.
10. Ginny Lee, United Press International, "Greta Alexander Turns Psychic Power to Law Enforcement," January 28, 1984.
11. United Press International, Alton, Illinois, November 16, 1983.
12. Robert Blau, *Chicago Tribune,* August 18, 1986.
13. Telephone interview conducted with Sgt. William Fitzgerald on December 3, 1991.
14. Perhaps the best and most readable treatise on the concept of "coincidence" is the book *Innumeracy: Mathematical Illiteracy and Its Consequences* by John Allen Paulos (Vintage Books, 1990). The author discusses with delightful clarity how poorly most people understand the frequency of coincidental occurrences. With devastating logic, Paulos demonstrates how "miraculous" coincidences are really quite normal occurrences, well within the probability curve. The supposedly psychic guesses of self-professed clairvoyants like Greta Alexander, while surprising to the uneducated, are really a perfect demonstration of the magic of random chance. For someone like Alexander to escape the laws of probability and random chance, her psychic "hits" would have to be much more frequent than her record has demonstrated. Two or three psychic "hits" can make a career for someone like Alexander. But they do not mean those hits were the product of actual psychic ability.
15. Telephone interview conducted on November 13, 1992.
16. "Psychic Helps Find Missing Man," United Press International, Effingham, Illinois, September 7, 1991.
17. Nora Bentley, "Psychic: Carpenter Was Walking in My Head," *Effingham Daily News,* September 11, 1991.
18. Ron Ingram, *Decatur Herald and Review,* September 8, 1991.
19. Don Hecke, *Newton Press-Mentor,* September 16, 1991.
20. Jeffrey Bils, *Decatur Herald and Review,* September 15, 1991.
21. Albert Fitzmaurice, Letter to the Editor, *Effingham Daily News,* September 20, 1991.

10

A Psychic Detective Bureau:
Some Additional Claimants

Joe Nickell

While the preceding chapters have permitted an extended look at a few well-known "psychic" crimebusters, there are many others who invite mention. Here, several more such claimants are briefly presented and their reputed powers are reviewed.

One sensational historic case was the alleged psychic uncovering of Jack the Ripper by Robert James Lees, a British medium. Unfortunately, the case has slipped into legend, there being many conflicting versions of the tale. For example, while dining with friends Lees reportedly received a vision that another murder had just been committed, and he went immediately to Scotland Yard, where he learned that news of the slaying had not yet arrived. When the news did come presently, the police were supposedly so astonished by Lees' knowledge that they took him to the scene. Thereupon, he led the police—much as a bloodhound might have done—across London to the home of a prominent physician. Subsequently, according to the legend, the doctor was certified as insane and secretly committed to an asylum.[1]

Actually, however, according to Alan Lang: "Mary Jane Kelly, the final Ripper victim, was definitely alive at 2:30 A.M. on Friday, November 30, and on medical evidence, probably killed between 3:30 and 4:00 A.M., somewhat late for Lees to be dining. Furthermore, the body was only discovered at 10:45 A.M." Moreover, Lees was not involved in the investigation as alleged. According to his own diary, he did not go to the police until October 2, following the penultimate slaying, and the police considered him "a fool and a lunatic." Lang concluded, "Sometime after the events, Lees claimed that he had cornered the Ripper, a claim that, like the one that he was 'Queen Victoria's personal psychic,' is based solely on his unsupported word."[2]

Another intriguing British case involved the celebrated mystery writer Agatha Christie. When her sensational disappearance in 1926 made head-lines across Britain, fellow writer Sir Arthur Conan Doyle, creator of Sherlock Holmes, enlisted the aid of a psychic. Unfortunately, Conan Doyle did not trouble to provide the man's name, but in a letter to the *Morning Post* Conan Doyle stated:

> In this case, I obtained a glove of Mrs. Christie's, and asked an excel-lent psychometrist for an opinion. I gave him no clue at all as to what I wanted or to whom the article belonged. He never saw it until I laid it on the table at the moment of consultation, and there was nothing to connect either it or me with the Christie case. The date was Sunday last. He at once got the name of Agatha. "There is trouble connected with this article. The person who owns it is half dazed and half purposeful. She is not dead as many think. She is alive. You will hear of her, I think, next Wednesday."[3]

When Miss Christie was located a few days later, Conan Doyle judged the psychic's pronouncements a success. But were they? The headlines and a woman's glove obviously indicated the subject was Miss Christie—especially when the inquiry was being made by a fellow mystery writer. As to her being "half dazed"—a supposed hit since she claimed amnesia —that could easily have been suggested by her personal traumas and hysterical behavior just before her disappearance. (Her mother had died and her philandering husband had asked for a divorce.) Conan Doyle did admit that the psychic made one error, in having had "an impres-sion of water," but actually he made another: Miss Christie was found on Tuesday night rather than on the predicted Wednesday. But so credulous was Conan Doyle that he rationalized the error, noting that "it was actually Wednesday when the news reached us." He also admitted that there had been a "good deal" of other information in the reading "which was outside my knowledge,"[4] and so the psychic's already weak showing might have been even worse. All in all, the case does little more than underscore the problems with such anecdotal reporting.

Before the arrest of the notorious "Yorkshire Ripper" in 1981, that case was "a bonanza for the UK psychics and for the sensational news-papers as well," according to psychic investigator James Randi.[5] Britain's most famous psychic at the time, Doris Stokes, was asked by the *Sunday People* to divine the Ripper's appearance. Under her guidance, a newspaper staff artist produced a "psychic portrait"—actually a vague sketch that was of no more use to investigators than Stokes' feeling that the Ripper was named Johnny or Ronnie. (His name was Peter Sutcliffe.) The *Daily Star* followed suit by engaging an unknown medium to provide psychic drawings of the Ripper's alleged relatives and friends, even supposedly of his auto mechanic! Comments Randi, "Needless to say, all this information was not only useless but totally wrong."[6] As a spokesman for the West Yorkshire Police concluded:

> Many people contacted us during the Ripper inquiry. Many of them were mediums or people professing to have psychic powers. However, nothing that any of these people told us has any bearing on the outcome of the case. We certainly did not discuss our investigations with them.[7]

The police spokesman's sweeping statement presumably includes British medium Nella Jones, who was mentioned in the introduction as an example of one who failed a test of alleged psychic powers. In her book, *Ghost of a Chance,* she claims that some eighteen months before Peter Sutcliffe was arrested she provided police with a psychic portrait of the murderer, together with the name "Peter" and Sutcliffe's address! But authors Lyons and Truzzi observe:

> There are discrepancies between the psychic's claims and the facts, however. Although the house number she says she gave for the Ripper—6—was correct, the name of the street was not. Her sketch of the killer, moreover, bears no resemblance to Sutcliffe. Still, she did come up with the name Peter. Unfortunately, her pronouncements were never published in advance, so that one only has Jones's account to go by.[8]

Equally abysmal for British psychics has been their track record in the case of Suzy Lamplugh, who disappeared in 1986. Again Randi:

> Investigators were told by one psychic—who, I was told, lost the way while trying to visit Suzy's mother!—that Putney Bridge was somehow involved in the mystery, but that notion proved useless to them. Psychic Doris Stokes said that Suzy was alive, as did most of the psychics early on in the case; but then, when it began to appear unsolvable, they began to say that she was dead.

He continues:

> How many psychics offered their ideas for locating Suzy? Some four hundred of them. And what has been the result? Nothing at all. In response to the psychics' instructions, much digging and probing has taken place, but to no avail. When we spoke to a friend of the Lamplugh family, she told us that an area the size of Chelsea Harbour could have been dug up by now with all the excavating that was done in response to the psychics' urgings. She showed us two heavy suitcases filled with letters from all those psychics who had offered ideas to solve the case. None were of any use.[9]

American psychics seem to fare little better. Take John Catchings, for example, a Texan described as "one of the best-known psychic detectives in the country,"[10] one with a reputed talent for finding dead bodies. On Valentine's Day 1981, a family of five disappeared while boating on Lake Dallas (north of the city), and since the weather did not appear to be a factor, foul play was suspected. Eventually, out of desperation, Catchings was brought in, based on his reputation for assisting other Texas law enforcement agencies. He immediately captured the media's attention by making overflights of the area in a news station's helicopter, but he accomplished little else. According to psychic investigator Dan Korem: "He *missed on every clue* he gave police, but the myth was propagated that he did provide positive assistance." Adds Korem: "Again, as in most cases, the local press didn't follow up on his failures. The net result was that people remembered the headline stating he was brought into the case."[11]

Another case involving Catchings was an unsolved murder. Mary Cook Spencer had disappeared from her Lusby, Maryland, home in 1984, and two years later her parents engaged Catchings to help search for her body. He afterward brought in what he calls his "psychic detective squad" for assistance. Sergeant L. C. Stinett of the Maryland State Police worked with Catchings but—while he appreciated his efforts—states that he does not believe Catchings has psychic ability:

> I think that by him being in the area, one thing we gained was we were allowed to perform an additional search of the area, which may not have been allowed without him coming. But as far as them having psychic ability, I didn't believe in that bunk. I believe they do no more than use good common sense, good logic.
>
> I've never seen a psychic go out on a case without previously going over the case and having knowledge of the case. I think some of them are very intelligent and would make very good police detectives. But I don't think they have psychic ability any more than you or I have.

> Some of them are complete hoaxes. Some of them send someone in advance to pick up little tidbits on the case that they can drop later. Now, John Catchings didn't do that.

Nevertheless, Stinett believes he learned something from Catchings' methodology:

> Whenever there was a low spot or a high spot in the woods, he directed us to dig. One of the things he taught us is that when somebody buries a body, you have to do something with the ground to hide it. If it's a recent burial, the ground will be disturbed. If it's old, the ground will sink. Also, it's hard to put leaves and sticks over the grave to make the ground look normal. So you will have a pile of brush over the grave or a pile of trash. That's what I learned from John Catchings.[12]

And Dan Korem reports:

> Virtually every law enforcement officer and reporter I have interviewed admits that Catchings has no powers. I asked one officer how Catchings seemed to hit on one clue in a case involving the disappearance of an attractive young woman. He said that Catchings *was given* that information in confidence by police, and he leaked it to the press. The officer kept quiet, not wanting to explain how stupidly the information was divulged.[13]

In another instance, reportedly "Catchings and a local police officer have been investigated by the Texas Rangers to determine if they had moved a body" (apparently to make the spot where it was found conform to Catchings' predictions).[14]

Korem mentions another homicide investigation (unrelated to Catchings) in which the police actually invented the story that a psychic had supplied the essential clues. Korem explains that the purpose of the fake story was to conceal the true source. The murderer's former cellmate was the tipster, and the "psychic" cover story was a shrewd means of protecting his identity.[15]

Another instance of using a make-believe psychic took place in Beloit, Wisconsin, in 1981. In response to an unsolved double homicide at a Radio Shack outlet, Beloit Police Chief John Mizerka announced that he was employing a psychic to re-search the crime scene as well as bringing in sophisticated equipment to search for trace evidence. Actually the story was a ruse. Mizerka thought—wrongly as it turned out—that it might somehow prompt the killer to return to the scene of the crime.[16]

Apparently, sometimes the alleged psychic may exist but the law enforcement agency itself may prove elusive. Walter F. Rowe, a professor in the Department of Forensic Sciences at the George Washington University in Washington, D.C., describes just such an instance, one concerning Dutch psychic detective Marinus Dykshorn. States Rowe:

> He is credited [in a book called *Psychic Criminology*] . . . with having aided the North Carolina State Police in four murder cases. Unfortunately, there is no such organization as the North Carolina State Police. Detective Bill Doubty of the North Carolina *State Bureau of Investigation* (who has been with the bureau twenty years) has never heard of a psychic named Dykshorn; furthermore, to the best of his knowledge the bureau has never requested the aid of a psychic.[17]

Although, as we have seen repeatedly, where psychics are concerned there is often less than meets the eye, sometimes there may instead be much, much more. Consider the case of Brett Cadorette, who volunteered to police details from his psychic visions of the attempted murder of a Staten Island, New York, woman. The sexually abused victim had had her throat slashed, but when Cadorette described her clutching in her hand a clump of hair the police were especially intrigued: that fact had not been made public! Police did not buy the "psychic vision" claim and instead made Cadorette their prime suspect. He was eventually convicted of the crime.[18]

Then there is the case of Etta Louise Smith, whose one-time "vision" of a murder victim's body led to her arrest by Los Angeles police, although she was subsequently "vindicated" by a Los Angeles Superior Court jury. Her alleged vision was of the location of the body of a missing nurse, Melanie Uribe, at an area in rural Lopez Canyon. Indeed, after Mrs. Smith had gone to the police and pinpointed the location on a map, she decided to drive to the site with two of her children. They had located the body and were en route to a telephone when she met the arriving police! Later questioned about her precise knowledge, and failing a lie detector test, she was jailed for four days on suspicion of having some connection with the crime or criminals. The latter were three black men, and the fact that Mrs. Smith (who is white) had close ties with blacks in her neighborhood fueled the suspicion. Mrs. Smith subsequently sued the police for the trauma she had suffered, asking $750,000 in damages. She won her case but the jury, some of whom were apparently suspicious of Mrs. Smith's "psychic" vision, awarded her a mere $26,184—sufficient to reimburse her for lost wages and attorney's fees, but providing little for pain and suffering.[19]

Actually, forensic analyst John F. Fischer and I have been looking into this noteworthy case and believe one can be skeptical of Mrs. Smith's psychic powers without suspecting her of being an accessory. Recall the case mentioned above by Korem, in which an informant's identity was protected by a psychic cover story. Is it not possible that an acquaintance of Mrs. Smith, privy to information about the crime, sought her help in revealing the information? Could Mrs. Smith not merely have been protecting her source? The possibility gains credibility from the fact that the killers were uncovered because one of them "had bragged about the murder to residents of his Pacoima neighborhood" and, at the time, Smith lived in Pacoima! Interestingly, as Smith went searching for the nurse's body, her psychic powers seemed to wane, and it was one of her children who actually spied the white-clad corpse.[20]

A case reminiscent of Etta Smith's supposedly psychic vision is one that took place in 1987. On January 7, an alleged clairvoyant named Normand G. Joyal entered the police department in Holliston, Massachusetts, and stated he had discovered a corpse in the septic system at the rear of a shopping center. He claimed a vision had led him to a set of six manhole covers and, by praying over each, he said he could "see" a body beneath one. As Joyal had directed, police and fire officials retrieved from the septic tank the body of a sixteen-year-old boy who had disappeared two months before, apparently by falling in the tank.

However, an investigation by C. Eugene Emory, Jr., science writer for the *Providence Journal*, recalls a remarkably different set of events.[21] Emory found that, days earlier, Joyal had made inquiries about the shopping center, and had come to suspect that—as others had theorized—the body might be found in the septic system. In any case he had lifted the wrong manhole cover and seemed ready to give up the search when the building inspector (whom Joyal had asked to accompany him) insisted on trying the remaining covers. The next three were stuck shut, but the fifth was only covered by a sheet of metal. It was the inspector who peered into the tank and discovered the floating corpse. He then went for his boss and Joyal went to the police station to report his "psychic" discovery. Gene Emory checked out nine other alleged successes by Joyal and concluded that he "has no verifiable successes among past cases." Emory adds, "Yet they were often reported in the press because . . . the reporters didn't check out Joyal's extraordinary claims."[22]

Another psychic vision, albeit a somewhat mundane one, reportedly provided a breakthrough in the case of the stabbing death of D. Scott Rogo, a widely published author and lecturer on the paranormal. After Rogo's tragic death on August 16, 1990, a suspect was identified, but police were unable to find evidence that clearly linked him to the crime scene. Then a psychic, Armand Marcotte, who was brought into the case by Rogo's friends, allegedly had a vision of a glass bearing some fingerprints. As a consequence, the police rechecked all the fingerprints lifted at the scene and did make a positive match with the suspect's prints.[23]

Marcotte reportedly "works *exclusively* with police departments,"[24] but at least one such department has found his "flamboyant" personality troublesome: The Pomona, California, Police Department had to quit using him because, as Lieutenant Kurt Longfellow explained, "He was like a sideshow."[25] In the Rogo case, Marcotte made his psychic forecast by using both meditation and astrology. His reading was taped. In it he said that "there *should be* empty glasses around the place" (emphasis added) and that "they have fingerprints on them—I'm sure they do." Thus one gets the impression that all Marcotte really accomplished was to reason that the presence of fingerprints on a glass was a logical likelihood; his real accomplishment seems to be that he permitted the police to review the evidence that they already had. As Rogo's father, Jack Rogo, stated:

> I'd much rather believe this was solved as the result of good and honest investigation. I keep away from the psychic stuff. I also had a psychic that said they were going to solve it in two weeks—and that was three weeks after the killing. We are not disbelievers, but I don't believe everything that goes on.[26]

It was indeed solid police work that prevailed in the case of the "Hillside Strangler," notwithstanding the claims of a California dowser named Verne McGuire. He told a credulous writer for the *Ridgecrest Daily Independent* that at first the authorities refused to listen to him, but finally he and some fellow dowsers

> got the Los Angeles police and sheriff's department, the Marshal Service and the Federal Bureau of Investigation. They told us that if we knew where the Hillside Strangler was, we must be involved with him. To prove we weren't involved, we had to find him in such a way that it was impossible we could be involved, so we moved in with some cops. Then he killed again. Because he would now be on the run, we thought this was the best time to look for him.[27]

McGuire went on to say that they plied their dowsing pendulums over a map of the area, and actually succeeded in locating the Strangler. They sent police to the site where he was discovered sitting in his car at a service station. In the car's trunk police found clothing and a purse belonging to one of the Strangler's victims. After he was arrested, McGuire said, "He knew they had him. We were vindicated."[28]

Actually, the facts are quite different. Not only were the U.S. Marshal's office and the FBI not involved in the investigation, but the Hillside Strangler proved to be not a single person but a pair of killers working together. According to the Los Angeles police,

> McGuire's statements concerning the "Hillside Strangler" case and his involvement are in conflict with what occurred. One of the suspects was arrested in Bellingham, Washington, and the second was arrested at his place of business in the city of Glendale. No clothing belonging to any of the victims was ever found.[29]

Investigator James Randi writes of the case:

> Electrical engineer David J. Simmons, a reader of the *Ridgecrest Daily Independent,* was enraged at the statement made by McGuire in that newspaper. Simmons made a few single telephone calls that discovered the misrepresentation, and submitted his findings to the editor of the newspaper. What happened? Nothing. The newspaper already had its wide-eyed story, and the editor apparently thought that his readers did not deserve the truth.
>
> The original story told by McGuire has made the rounds on the gee-whiz circuit, and I had it thrown up to me some months before at a lecture I gave in Florida. Not having Simmons's research data at that time—since it had never been published—I was forced to admit that I simply didn't know any of the facts about the case. Another win for the media who pander to a credulous public.[30]

Another serial killer, Ted Bundy, has also attracted the claims of psychics. Washington, D.C., psychic Ann Gehman has claimed that, while earlier living in Florida, she was involved in the Bundy case, specifically working on the disappearance of Kimberly Leach, Bundy's last victim. She claims she described Bundy and his car and told investigators he was using stolen credit cards. She also said she worked with several investigators including an FBI agent. But as Walter Rowe writes:

> As for her claim to have worked with an FBI agent in the Ted Bundy case, the FBI does not solicit information from psychics (in fact, psychics are classified as unreliable sources). While it may be true that she provided police with information in the Ted Bundy case, her information

certainly did not aid in either the apprehension of Bundy or the recovery of the body of Kimberly Leach. Gehman is not mentioned in either Ann Rule's *Strangler beside Me* or Stephen Michaud and Hugh Aynsworth's *Only Living Witness,* two detailed accounts of Ted Bundy's criminal career. Bundy was apprehended when a police officer spotted the stolen car he was driving coming out of a restaurant parking lot late one evening. Curious to identify the driver of the car, the officer followed Bundy and radioed in a routine check on the license of Bundy's car. When the officer learned that the license plate was stolen, he gave chase and ultimately subdued Bundy after a struggle.

Rowe continues:

> The recovery of Leach's body was the result of good forensic work, not psychic detection. According to Ann Rule, "when the Dodge van [in which Kimberly had been abducted] was processed, criminalists had taken samples of soil, leaves, and bark found inside and caught in its under-carriage. Botanists and soil experts had identified the dirt as coming from somewhere close to a north Florida river."
>
> The discovery of a pile of Winston cigarette butts near the entrance to Suwanee River State Park had focused police attention on the state park and its environs as a possible search area. The ashtray of Bundy's stolen car had also contained Winston cigarettes. A careful ground search of the forests surrounding the park uncovered Leach's body under an abandoned shed. The absence of any references in Rule's book to psychics helping police apprehend Bundy or find his last victim is significant because Rule professes to believe in ESP and elsewhere in the book relates the (unsuccessful) attempts of psychics to aid police in solving the murders Bundy committed in the Pacific Northwest.[31]

Another Florida case that attracted psychic claimants was that of a young woman named Tiffany Sessions, who had disappeared a number of years before while jogging in Gainesville. On November 1, 1991, New York "psychic detective" John Monti held a press conference to announce that he intended to solve the Sessions case. Three days later Monti appeared on a Tampa Bay TV program with Sessions' mother, who explained that although she had previously been disappointed by psychics, she now felt success was at hand. She and Monti were to travel to Gainesville and spend November 6 and 7 in a search for Tiffany. Unfortunately those days came and went with the disappearance remaining as unsolved as ever.[32]

In other words, Monti had been no more successful than he had been in another case that year. In May 1991, five-year-old Timothy Wiltsey had disappeared from a carnival in Sayreville, New Jersey, and about a week later John Monti arrived on the scene. Monti claimed to have a vision of a woman kidnapping the child and driving off with him in a white car to an apartment complex. But when Monti failed to locate the child he blamed the mother, alleging that she did not really want to find the boy. "I can do so much as a psychic," Monti maintained, "but I'm not going to tell parents what to do with their kids. . . ."[33] Psychic investigator Gary P. Posner followed up on Monti's failed efforts by inquiring of the South Amboy, New Jersey, Police Department. Detective Sergeant Ray Durski told Posner:

> He gave us about four different locations that we checked out. He had strong feelings that the boy had been in an abandoned building on our main thoroughfare. We went through the entire building and found no articles of clothing that he suggested we might find. The following day he suggested an area near a railroad track where he had strong feelings that there was someone who had committed suicide, and that he could be in that wooded area. We searched that area and there was nothing there also. He then contacted our South Amboy First Aid Department and gave them strong feelings that we could possibly find a body in a landfill area adjacent to the waterfront. Then they conducted a search with over 100 people and they found nothing there. After that, he came back again, and he stated that he sees the boy running away from the mother's house in the direction of the railroad tracks. Of course we checked that area, too, and came up with nothing.[34]

More recently, Monti was mentioned in a recounting of psychics' failed predictions for the year 1991. Along with forecasts by various psychics— e.g., that California would slip into the ocean, the pope would encounter a crazed camel, and the like—came John Monti's prediction that a former U.S. president would die and that an assassination attempt on then Soviet President Gorbachev would be foiled by an American tourist. Monti's premonitory visions were included in the San Francisco Bay Area Skeptics' eighth annual list of failed psychic predictions that gained tabloid headlines without actually making news.[35]

Jeane Dixon also made the list—with both failed visions and predictions that were rather obvious. Many people still believe that Miss Dixon once scored a psychic-detective coup—not by solving a crime but by forecasting a sensational one: the assassination of President John F. Kennedy. Actually, however, she merely claimed that a president elected in 1960 would die in office—an assertion based on certain astrological notions. But she nullified that forecast in 1960, when she publicly predicted that Richard M. Nixon would be elected president.[36]

Numerous psychics, astrologers, fortune tellers, and the like also predicted the assassination of Ronald Reagan—based on the same astrological notions that Jeane Dixon applied to the 1960 election. But while most soothsayers merely gave vague renderings of the stock prediction, California psychic Tamara Rand provided astonishingly accurate information regarding John Hinckley's attempted assassination of President Reagan on March 30, 1981. Reportedly, on a January 6 radio talk show Rand (real name Naomi Randall) predicted that Reagan would experience a "thud" in the chest toward the end of March, that there would be shots fired "all over the place," and that the attempted assassin would be fair-haired and have a name "something like Humbly—maybe Jack." Unfortunately, the astonishing accuracy was due not to psychic powers but to a deliberately concocted hoax. The tape was made the day *after* the assassination attempt, not three months earlier as claimed. The talk-show host, Dick Maurice, and his producer, Gary Greco, had been approached by Rand, who said, "This could make me the Jeane Dixon of the eighties."[37]

Whereas Tamara Rand's "prediction" seemed too good to be true (as indeed it was), some allegedly psychic visions are at the other end of the spectrum. For example, when an elderly woman wandered away from a Marble Falls, Texas, nursing home in mid-1981, and a search of the area proved fruitless, the woman's daughters consulted a psychic in Lubbock. The psychic suggested several areas which law enforcement officers agreed to search, and eventually they located the woman's body face down in a creek. However, when asked whether the site matched information the psychic provided, the county sheriff gave an equivocal "possibly," adding that the area was one that had been searched earlier. In fact, observed the sheriff's chief deputy, "the creek was the target area of the search." Indeed, the body might have been discovered earlier, since the psychic had also visualized a large building, and sheriff's deputies spent considerable time searching the local VFW hall and town school buildings.[38]

Even less successful was another unnamed psychic who was enlisted in a 1988 Alabama case. Inspired by reports that $280 million in drug money was once buried at a farm belonging to an accused drug dealer, a former FBI informant obtained a photograph of the property from the FBI, consulted a psychic, and soon dug up a vault. "Alas for the credibility of psychics," however, a judge would later say of the discovery, "the vault which was discovered was not at a point designated by the psychic." Its successful location was actually due to the use of a metal detector. And, unfortunately in light of the man's efforts, when opened the vault contained nothing but kitty litter.[39]

Of course, psychics can sometimes achieve both success and failure—

the latter providing an interesting perspective on the former. Take the Green River, Washington, serial killings, for example. Psychic Barbara Kubik-Patten, a 43-year-old grandmother, found the remains of one victim in 1984, allegedly by psychic means, although eighteen previous remains were discovered by police search teams and by ordinary citizens, and a dog found one set of remains. In fact, the nineteenth victim had been discovered only a short distance from where Kubik-Patten discovered the twentieth victim. Then the following year came a second discovery of Kubik-Patten, one that suggested her methodology might have more to do with persistence in searching likely dumping sites than with genuine psychic ability. Her second find turned out to be the remains of a large dog. Remarked the *Northwest Skeptics Newsletter,* "Apparently the psychic vibrations of Ms. Kubik-Patten are a little out of tune."[40]

Sometimes psychics are worse than merely ineffectual; they can cause a serious drain on law enforcement resources, as Monti did in New Jersey. Consider also the case of five-year-old Jason Foreman, who disappeared from near his Peace Dale, Rhode Island, home on May 18, 1975. The publicity engendered by a widespread search drew pronouncements from up to 50 alleged psychics. Some, accompanied by television cameramen, had police re-search places that had already been gone over. Recalled Detective Sergeant William Robertson: "After we had gone through the Peace Dale mill complex with a fine-tooth comb, a psychic would come up to us and say, 'I was driving by the mill and I got vibrations of a boy trapped alive inside.' You'd have to pull ten to fifteen people off the search because you couldn't disregard it."

Other psychics visualized the child in the vicinity of a sand-and-gravel area; still others imagined him in a nearby pond. "It got so bad," said the detective, "we had to drain the pond down to three feet of water to dispel the psychics." Two days of draining yielded nothing.

"Another fellow sent us tape-recordings of someone under hypnosis. [He had a vision of a gray car and part of a Rhode Island license plate.] When he was asked about it, he wasn't able to see any digits, just the letters SF," Robertson said. "You had to listen to the tape for two hours to get the information; then you had to turn around and send two guys to the [motor vehicle] registry to go through 999 registrations to see if there's a gray car with the license plate SF."

Why did police follow up such tips? Explained the detective: "After the first 24 hours, you start to grab at straws [and also] police have to protect themselves. You have to ask, 'Suppose the psychic snatched the boy?' By not going back and searching where they say, you might miss something."[41]

One psychic—William J. Finch, who said he was a former Erie, Pennsylvania, police chief—even implicated the innocent owner of a local gas station in the boy's disappearance. The psychic, who had never visited the area but who had obtained newspaper clippings about the case, persisted even after he was assured the man was not a suspect. Fortunately for the man, almost seven years after the disappearance the boy's bones were discovered in a box in the bedroom of another man. Of the suspicion that had been wrongly directed at him, the innocent man said: "It doesn't bother me now. But if the case wasn't solved, I would have been quite upset." Ironically, the reason the man's service station had been mentioned in news accounts was that he had allowed the police to use it as a field operations center during the search for the missing boy.[42]

In light of such cases, the authors of a 1987 article in *Police Review* calculated the potential loss caused by psychics:

A typical costing for the use of mediums on a murder has been applied to [a certain] case. If a police decision had been implemented to "follow up" the 600 unsolicited responses from mediums it would take an average of six man hours per medium for officers to visit or contact them and assess their information. A further two hours is required for the administrative and evaluative effort of the control room team. Thus 3,600 detective man hours and 1,200 control room man hours, a total of 4,800 man hours would have been expended. Taking an average fixed cost of £7 ($12.41) per man hour this exercise would have cost £34,000 ($60,299) from the inquiry budget.[43]

The Dallas Police Department's homicide chief stated in 1986:

Not one time, one clue, or one piece of evidence or information from a psychic ever helped our investigations. Our experience has been that the only thing psychics do . . . is to take advantage of the emotions of the families [of the victims].[44]

Lieutenant T. C. Swan, head of the homicide section of the Fort Worth Police Department, agrees:

It creates a circus atmosphere. They [psychics] call you on sensational cases, not on cases where some wino is stomped to death in some back alley.

And a lot of time, they give false hopes to survivors who are desperate. These are the most vulnerable people. When it comes to reality, psychics offer nothing but generalities. We don't base our investigations on psychics.[45]

Many more cases and more psychics could be studied, but there would never be an end to the claims. And after all, as psychic investigator Melvin Harris pointedly observes: "Unfortunately, while a lie can be coined in minutes, months may be taken up in exposing that lie. And therein lies the difficulty of grappling with accounts of psychic detection."[46] Nevertheless, we have taken a long and serious look at the alleged successes of many prominent psychic detectives. In the following chapter, psychology professor James E. Alcock summarizes the results of our individual efforts and draws some conclusions about the efficacy of psychic sleuthing.

NOTES

1. Alan Lang, "Jack the Ripper & the Psychic Detective," *The Skeptic* (Summer 1989): 40–42; Arthur Lyons and Marcello Truzzi, *The Blue Sense: Psychic Detectives and Crime* (New York: The Mysterious Press, 1991), pp. 19–20.

2. Lang, "Jack the Ripper & the Psychic Detective," p. 41.

3. From the full letter quoted in Edward T. Woodhall, *Crime and the Supernatural* (London: John Long, 1935), pp. 33–34.

4. Ibid.

5. James Randi, *James Randi: Psychic Investigator* (London: Boxtree Ltd., 1991), p. 92.

6. Ibid.

7. Bob Baxter, chief press officer for the West Yorkshire Police, quoted in Randi, *James Randi: Psychic Investigator* p. 92.

8. Lyons and Truzzi, *The Blue Sense,* p. 82.

9. Randi, *James Randi: Psychic Investigator* p. 93.

10. Dan Korem, *Powers: Testing the Psychic & Supernatural* (Downers Grove, Ill.: InterVarsity Press, 1988), p. 66.

11. Ibid., pp. 66–67.

12. From *Dallas Morning News* (April 29, 1984), quoted in Korem, *Powers,* pp. 67–68.

13. Korem, *Powers,* p. 67.

14. Walter F. Rowe, "Skeptic's Response: Psychic Detectives," *NCAS Skeptical Eye* (Fall 1991): 7.

15. Korem, *Powers,* p. 68.

16. Lyons and Truzzi, *The Blue Sense,* p. 235.

17. Rowe, "Skeptic's Response," p. 7. The book referred to is Whitney S. Hibbard and Raymond W. Worring, *Psychic Criminology* (Springfield, Ill.: Charles C. Thomas, 1982).

18. Rowe, "Skeptic's Response," p. 8.

19. Richard Varenchik, "L.A. Court Vindicates Psychic Vision," *FATE* (August 1987): 42–48.

20. Jan Klunder, "Woman Whose 'Vision' Led to Murder Victim Sues over Arrest," *Los Angeles Times* (March 19, 1987): section 2, pp. 1, 6; Varenchik, "L.A. Court Vindicates Psychic Vision," pp. 44–45.

21. C. Eugene Emory, "An Investigation of Psychic Crimebusting," *Skeptical Inquirer* 12, no. 4 (Summer 1988): 403–410.

22. Ibid., p. 410.

23. Jaxon Van Derbeken, "Psychic's Clue Points to Suspect," *Los Angeles Daily News* (April 7, 1991).

24. Lyons and Truzzi, *The Blue Sense,* p. 90.

25. Ibid., p. 230.

26. Jack Rogo, quoted in Derbeken, "Psychic's Clue Points to Suspect."

27. Quoted in Randi, *James Randi: Psychic Investigator* p. 49.

28. Ibid.

29. Ibid., p. 50.

30. Ibid.

31. Rowe, "Skeptic's Response," p. 9.

32. Gary P. Posner, " 'Psychic Detective' John Monti Searches for Tiffany Sessions," *Tampa Bay Skeptics Report* 4, no. 3 (Winter 1991–92): 1, 5.

33. Ibid., p. 1.

34. Ibid.

35. "Skeptics Scoff at Psychics' Failed Visions of How '91 Might Have Been," *The Star-Ledger* (Newark, N.J.) (January 1, 1992).

36. Curtis D. MacDougall, *Superstition and the Press* (Buffalo, N.Y.: Prometheus Books, 1983), p. 35.

37. Ibid., p. 67; Kendrick Frazier and James Randi, "Predictions after the Fact: Lessons of the Tamara Rand Hoax," *Skeptical Inquirer* 6, no. 1 (Fall 1981): 4–7; Lyons and Truzzi, *The Blue Sense,* pp. 129–30.

38. Kay Powers, "Psychic Enlisted to Seek Missing Nursing Patient," *Austin American Statesman* (July 8, 1981); "Searchers Find Woman's Body in Marble Falls," *Austin American Statesman* (July 9, 1981).

39. Amy Todd Geisel, "Psychic Used to Hunt Drug Money Vault," *News-Sentinel* (December 8, 1988).

40. Brief news item in the *Northwest Skeptics Newsletter* (July 1984): 2, and (February 1985): 2.

41. Quoted by C. Eugene Emory, "When Psychics Falsely Accuse," *Skeptical Inquirer* 12, no. 4 (Summer 1988): 406.

42. Ibid., pp. 406–407.

43. Michael Riley and David Thompson, "Hearing Voices of Reason?" *Police Review* (January 16, 1987): 121–22.

44. Quoted in Jane Martin (Fort Worth *Star-Telegram*), "Are Psychics a Help or a Hindrance?" *Sunday News* (August 24, 1986).

45. Ibid.

46. Melvin Harris, *Investigating the Unexplained* (Buffalo, N.Y.: Prometheus Books, 1986), p. 36.

11

Afterword:
An Analysis of Psychic Sleuths' Claims

James E. Alcock

You have been presented with a collection of the best that psychic sleuthdom has to offer. What do you, the reader, conclude? Have you been persuaded that these leading psychic detectives have no special talents, no extraordinary powers of divination, nothing useful to offer to forensic inquiry? Or do you believe that these obviously skeptical writers have been too severe, too demanding of hard evidence in a domain characterized by feeling and intuition, too eager to disregard the opinions of those police officers, albeit few in number, who attest to the powers and the usefulness of one or another of these psychics?

Just what is a *psychic sleuth,* anyway? *Sleuth,* according to the Oxford English Dictionary, originally referred to the trail left by a person or animal, and specially trained *sleuthhounds* were used to track down people on the run. From sleuthhound, the verb *to sleuth* gradually developed in reference to the act of following a fugitive's trail. Eventually this begat the noun *sleuth,* used as a label for a person who could use his or her skills to find someone who had disappeared or to discover who had committed a crime.

As for the adjective *psychic,* that term is used in reference to supposed mental abilities which transcend time, space, and the known laws of matter and energy, and which provide the psychically gifted individual with information about objects or other people's thoughts without the use of

172

the ordinary sensory channels. It is only when an individual produces information which would seem impossible to obtain by normal means that the term *psychic* is invoked. It should be noted that, to date, the scientific community does not accept the reality of putative psychic phenomena. This is largely because there has never been any demonstration of psychic phenomena that has been replicable by neutral scientists. Insofar as people's reports of psychic experiences are concerned, there are many normal, if not always obvious, ways in which phenomena can occur which *seem* to an individual to be psychic, even if, as most scientists believe, truly psychic phenomena do not exist.[1]

To qualify as a *psychic sleuth* then, one should be able to solve crimes or find missing people, and to accomplish this in a manner which involves more than ordinary reasoning and the normal sensory channels. In other words, before there is any need to debate the presence or absence of psychic ability, we need to know that the "psychic sleuth" can actually solve, or help solve, crimes. The information presented by the authors of the preceding chapters indicates that even the term *sleuth*—let alone the adjective *psychic*—should not be applied to the individuals whom they have discussed, for despite the vaunted claims, careful examination reveals no successful crime-solving but instead only tangled webs of misinformation, generalization, opportunistic credit-taking, and, in some instances, probable deceit. Since they have not been found to be successful sleuths, there seems little to be gained by debating whether or not they are *psychic* sleuths.

EVALUATING CLAIMS

Every one of us is regularly engaged in the process of evaluating claims of one sort or another: This beer promises smoother taste. That skin cream offers escape from the wrinkling ravages of time. This politician promises to work to bring about lower taxes. That politician argues that we must pay higher taxes in order to be able to protect the environment. This automobile brings the art of vehicle manufacture to near perfection. Tests show that that vehicle may catch fire if rear-ended. Take up jogging, for it's good for your heart; don't take up jogging, it's bad for your knees. Scientists advise the drinking of two ounces of alcohol each day to protect your heart and circulatory system. Other scientists recommend the drinking of red wine because it cuts cholesterol while white wine does not. Still other scientists advise us not to drink alcohol at all, for it damages the liver and may interfere with the body's ability to resist cancer.

If we are to avoid sinking into neurotic indecision, each one of us comes to some decision, however tentative, about each such claim we read in the newspapers or hear about on television or radio. Sometimes we may decide simply to leave the question in abeyance, either because the subject is unimportant to us, or because we recognize that the information is insufficient to allow a reasonable opinion. But most of the time we make decisions on the fly, accepting this tidbit, rejecting that one. Indeed, we all have little voices inside our heads that proclaim "That's nonsense" or "Wow, that's amazing" when we are faced with dramatic claims. We assign events, or accounts of events, to the "nonsense" or the "amazing" category very quickly, usually without conscious awareness of the decision-making process and the diverse factors that lead to the quick decision. For most readers of this book, the latest tabloid headline about aliens amongst us, or about another Elvis-spotting, will evoke the "nonsense" response, and even if we pass the time while waiting our turn at the super-market checkout by reading the account, we will shake our heads in dismay at the silliness of it all. However, what about a headline in a monthly magazine digest that proclaims, "Fatty foods can be good for your health": Is the "nonsense" response just as automatic, or do our fascination antennae go up, as we flip through the magazine to find hoped-for justification for eating French fries and hamburgers?

Just about everyone is capable of making sound, rational decisions about issues in some circumstances. Needless to say, everyone is also prone to making unsound decisions in other circumstances. The skeptic who is careful not to go beyond the data in evaluating a psychic's claims may well be foolishly taken in in some other area of his or her life: buying stock on the basis of a friend's "inside information"; getting into a romantic involvement despite clear evidence that the other person is likely to be unfaithful or incompatible as a partner; foolishly trying to swim across the lake that he or she could easily swim across—twenty-five years ago; or smoking cigarettes despite mounting evidence of the associated dangers.

Our minds work to make sense of the world, and to provide a considerable degree of consistency amongst our various beliefs and feelings and actions. It is easy for our own considered opinions to seem eminently reasonable and those of others whose beliefs we do not share to seem unreasonable or even foolish. The safety of nuclear generating stations, the existence of bodies of crashed aliens at an air force base in Texas, the dangers of the dwindling ozone layer, the discovery of a "gene for homosexuality," the salubrious qualities of evening primrose oil, the wonders of Prozac, the sinister spreading of Satanic cults, the breakthrough in the treatment of autistic children through "facilitated communication"—

one can find educated and normally reasonable people who will mount a spirited attack on, or defense of, each of these propositions.

Before going any farther along, consider a psychic detective who is not very well known and who has escaped mention so far in this book—the late Anderson Kirby of Winnipeg, Manitoba, who died in 1968 at the age of seventy-four. According to people who studied his apparently remarkable skills, he was instrumental in helping police all over Western Canada to solve crimes that had seemed unsolvable. He was consulted regularly by the Winnipeg Police Department, as well as by the Royal Canadian Mounted Police.

Kirby, when involved in a criminal investigation, would enter a sort of trance and, in a strange voice, give out details about where the police should search for a murderer or for a victim's body. According to newspaper reports, the information he provided was often quite specific, and very useful to the police.

One of his many apparent triumphs was the solving of a murder that had bedeviled police for twelve years. According to a newspaper account, a leading Winnipeg businessman, one Harley Crockford, had left home one morning in 1933 to go to his office and was never seen again. His automobile was found a few days later, the window on the driver's side smashed. The front seat was soaked in blood, but the police had no way of determining whether or not it was Crockford's. Although he had made a number of enemies in the business community, there were no clues as to who may have been responsible for Crockford's apparent demise.

Kirby was not consulted directly about the Crockford case. However, twelve years later, in 1945, Kirby was called in by the chief of police in Winnipeg to try to help find a missing child who, it was feared, may have been killed. Kirby was asked to try to locate the body. Rather than going into a trance as he usually did, Kirby held a pendulum over a map of Winnipeg, closed his eyes, and began to hum, almost inaudibly. A few minutes later, the pendulum dropped against the map, and Kirby opened his eyes and demanded a survey map of the area corresponding to the spot touched by the pendulum. Such a map was obtained, showing in detail that particular part of the city. The procedure was repeated, and again the pendulum fell against a point on the map, and Kirby told the police to go to that place and start digging. The map was detailed enough to pinpoint a backyard. Apparently there was some heated debate amongst members of the police force about the wisdom of trying to obtain a court order to dig up private property on the basis of a psychic's claims, but such was done. To the surprise of everyone, a body was found—not that of the missing child, but rather what proved to be the skeletal remains of Harley Crockford. The owner of the property, who had once worked for Crockford until he was fired, subsequently confessed to his murder. Note that although Kirby apparently helped solve the Crockford crime, he absolutely failed to provide any information about the missing child, who, as it turns out, was subsequently found alive.

Kirby became something of a local celebrity following this event, and other police departments began to contact him in the hope that he could help them in a similar way. Again, according to newspaper reports, Kirby's apparent powers were subjected to extensive scientific testing at the University of Manitoba, and it was finally concluded that, while the scientists hesitated to label him a "psychic," his abilities baffled them and they could find no normal explanation for them. Kirby might have been more widely known had he not tried to keep such a low profile. He asked only that his expenses be covered, and accepted no payment for his work, believing his ability to be a gift from God intended to enable him to help others.

How *is* the thoughtful reader to react to such an account? This is not a trivial matter: Think for a moment about your reaction to the story. Do you find the account fascinating? Does it seem to offer reason to believe that there is something to psychic sleuth claims after all? Or did you react with skepticism and attempt to poke holes in the story as you read it through? You might try to explain it away, for example, on the basis that the newspaper reports might be in error, or that the reporters were gulled, or that Kirby may have been an acquaintance of Crockford's murderer, and having seen a suspicious mound in the murderer's backyard, used his reputation as a psychic to alert the police to the possibility that there was a body in the garden. However, there is nothing in the account above to support any of those speculations.

Regardless of how you reacted, your reaction probably had less to do with the information itself than you may realize. Had this been an account of an investigator who used DNA evidence to identify a murderer, most of us would have accepted the account at face value, whether or not we know anything about DNA identification techniques, or their reliability, or even what the letters DNA stand for. DNA testing seems to come straight from the heartland of science, and to the layperson there is little controversy about it. On the other hand, had the crime been solved through handwriting analysis—someone supposedly had divined the personality and probable occupation of the murderer by analyzing the handwriting in a grocery list found on the floor of the victim's car, and this information enabled the police somehow to track the murderer down— many of us would immediately don our skeptical hats and view the account with more jaundice than in the DNA case. Others who are less skeptical about handwriting analysis might take the account at face value, and indeed see it as support for the validity and efficacy of such analysis.

Thus, as mentioned earlier, we quickly categorize information in terms of its general credibility, and as a consequence then apply harsher or gentler standards of evaluation to it. For those who believe in psychic powers, there is nothing particularly unreasonable about the Kirby account. For those who do not, the automatic presumption is that things did not happen as they were described in the newspapers, and that those who took Kirby's abilities to be psychic were in error. Of course, the most reasonable action with respect to the Kirby story might be to consider it to be just what it is, an anecdote which may or may not be accurate. However, it is difficult for most of us to live with such ambiguity. After all, in a very real sense, all news reports are anecdotes, and if we believe none of them, then we will have a difficult time sorting out what is going on in the world around us. As for making an effort to confirm or deny the accuracy of the account, most readers would have neither the time nor the inclination nor the training and skills to carry out their own inquiry into Kirby's accomplishments. (Think of the time and effort that went into the analyses reported in the preceding chapters.) Even if they wanted to do so, what could they do apart from consulting the newspaper's archives, for it would likely be extremely difficult, all these many years later, to find anyone who actually knew Kirby or who was involved in the investigations in which he provided information. In lieu of first-hand analysis of the data, the individual is left to the analysis performed by others. And that analysis is likely to be accepted or rejected as a function of one's prior beliefs about psychics in general and psychic sleuths in particular. Ultimately, then, the reader's conclusion about the likelihood that Kirby had psychic powers depends on factors that go beyond the information given in the account.

Whether or not we react rationally, whether or not we are welcoming or cautious, about new information, and—in terms of the current discussion—whether we are likely to reject psychic sleuth claims out-of-hand, or give them the benefit of the doubt, depends on a number of factors, including the following:

1) Prior Beliefs

We evaluate claims partly in terms of their consistency with what we already believe to be true. It is not just data that lead us to one conclusion or another. Reasonable people can evaluate the same evidence and come to different conclusions, not because one has more or less perspicacity or rationality than the other, but because they approach the data in different ways, with different *a priori* beliefs and expectations, and perhaps different criteria, or different thresholds, for deciding that the data at hand warrant a particular interpretation.

Some beliefs are so fundamental that they resist the influence of contrary information. These have been referred to as "primitive beliefs."[2] For example, it would be extremely difficult to persuade most people that human beings can jump up from the ground and fly. (However, it is not impossible to alter such beliefs. Consider, for example, those Transcendental Meditation devotees who apparently believe that they can learn to levitate. Their primitive beliefs have been altered dramatically by the Maharishi's theology.) Whether or not we accept, at a deep, "primitive" level, the existence of psychic forces is extremely important in terms of our evaluation of claims of psychic sleuths. Surveys show that most people do believe in the existence of psychic processes such as extrasensory perception (ESP). If one accepts that ESP exists, then it is not such a leap to accept that some people can use their ESP to find the bodies of murder victims or to determine the identities of their killers. After all, this is no different in principle from the belief that ESP can be used to divine the site of illness, the location of buried oil or water, and so on. If, on the other hand, we do not believe in psychic phenomena, then it is very difficult to accept the proposition that some people can use psychic powers to help solve crimes, and we are likely to demand more evidence of such powers than if the claim were made that some less controversial technique, such as DNA analysis, had been used.

There is another aspect of prior belief that is important. As I have discussed at length elsewhere,[3] children grow up generally having learned two distinct generalized systems of belief, which Frank[4] has referred to as the "scientific-humanist" system, characterized by a belief in only one level of reality that is to be approached through logical analysis, and the "transcendental" system, typified by religious beliefs and spiritual concepts. Children, who are not born with a logical approach to understanding the world, most often learn, as they acquire logic, *not* to apply logical analysis to the realm of religion, spirits, bogeymen, or things that go bump in the night. Religious belief is generally encouraged on the basis of faith, not reason, and psychic and other beliefs are generally linked to intuition and emotion and are often seen by their very nature as defying logical analysis. Adults who continue to hold to such different orientations to data, one based on logical understanding and the other on intuition and faith, are very prone to turning off their logic when confronted with phenomena or claims that seem to pertain to the transcendental realm.

2) Source of Information

The source of information is often an important guide which we use to evaluate probable truth, and we may accept or reject information on the basis of who said it or where it was written. For example, about fifteen years ago, I read in the *Globe and Mail,* one of Canada's best newspapers, that an endocrinologist from Harvard University had addressed a medical conference in Toronto and stated that male and female nipple and breast structures are so similar that should a normal male allow an infant to suckle at his nipple over a period of a few weeks, he will actually begin to produce milk. Had I read this in the *National Enquirer* while waiting in the supermarket checkout line, I would have quickly dismissed the assertion as no more believable than the accounts of crashed aliens and the like. Yet, this was a report in a reputable newspaper quoting an apparently reputable specialist from Harvard. Even now, I am not entirely sure about what to believe about the possibility of male lactation, but obviously the claim—no doubt because of where it appeared and to whom it was attributed—has stayed with me to this day. Similarly, while we might be wary of the claims of self-styled psychic sleuths, we are more likely to perk up our ears and take more seriously the pronouncements of chiefs of police in this regard, even though they themselves are not expert in evaluating psychic claims and can be victims of deception or self-delusion. Had the Kirby account appeared in the *Skeptical Inquirer,* it might have raised more interest among skeptics than were it to have appeared in the *National Enquirer.*

3) Emotional Needs and Anxiety Reduction

Our beliefs can soothe our anxieties and improve our well-being, just as they can also make us fearful. Whether or not we accept that there is an increasing danger to us all because of a shrinking ozone layer will influence the extent to which we enjoy summer pleasures such as lying in the sun. The individual who loves sunbathing may be more drawn to opinions which suggest that the ozone crisis is overblown and that all that is being observed is cyclical fluctuation that has always occurred: Nothing is happening, nothing to worry about.

Depending on which belief makes us the least uncomfortable, the least anxious, that belief will often be the one we come to adopt. The cigarette smoker may give emphasis in her evaluation of smoking to the suggestive evidence that some people are genetically more prone to developing lung cancer than others, and given that her parents and grandparents all smoked and did not die of cancer, her chances of avoiding it seem pretty good. Her friend may avoid smoking because she has placed more importance on the newspaper reports stating that scientists now overwhelmingly believe that tobacco smoke is a cause of lung cancer. Which of these two people is the more reasonable? If you choose the latter, then on what grounds? Do you have any evidence at hand to persuade you that smoking is bad for your health? Most of us do not have such evidence. We have come to believe that this is true because we have been bombarded with reports in the media that tell us that this is so. Few of us go to the medical literature, and we would probably have a hard time understanding such literature even if we did. Yet, most readers—the nonsmokers especially—are likely to be almost certain, as I am, that tobacco consumption is a cause of cancer. Note, however, that a few centuries ago, almost everyone believed that there were witches among them, poisoning wells, causing crops to wither and farm animals to die. Such a belief looks foolish to us now, but the evidence available to the average person—word of mouth in those days—presented no less solid a case for witches than do newspaper accounts today demonstrate the dangers of smoking.

Psychic belief in general assuages the anxieties of many people with regard to their existence and the likelihood of the survival of their personalities following physical death.[5] Psychic sleuths can also serve to reduce anxiety to some degree, and this explains part of their appeal. They usually work in circumstances which have generated specific anxiety for many people—the parents of a missing child are willing to try anything in order to find him or her; the neighbors who are worried about the possibility of a maniac being on the loose and who might pose a danger to their families; and the police, who are under great pressure to solve the mystery of the disappearance. Anxiety and stress tend to make us less critical in our evaluations of claims, and more willing to grasp at straws to resolve a frightening mystery. Such an emotional context makes it all the more likely that so-called psychic sleuths will be listened to and taken more seriously than if they were offering their services in calmer circumstances.

Given their anxiety, many people will bend over backward to help the psychic succeed, even to the extent of unknowingly shading their interpretation of what the psychic says to make it fit more closely with the situation at hand. The hopes, the expectations that go along with working with a psychic also lead people later to justify the psychic's involvement by unwittingly twisting things a little in order to find correspondence between what the psychic said and the subsequent events—where the body is discovered and so on. The reader has been exposed to ample evidence of this in earlier chapters.

4) Personal Experience

Many, many people have experienced what they take to have been some sort of psychic phenomenon, and the memory of such an experience makes it all the more believable that some people possess psychic powers and can use them in detective work. It matters little that such experiences most likely are the product of misinterpretation of events. They *seemed* to be psychic, they *felt* psychic, and there is little that will change the person's mind once this categorization has been made. This is as true of a police officer who is impressed by the pronouncements of a psychic sleuth as it is of a person who is impressed by a palm reading. Such experiences are powerful, but they do not necessarily mean that the individual witnessed a genuine psychic phenomenon. We are all prone to many sorts of errors and cognitive biases when we evaluate information, and we are all the more likely to make such errors when in anxious or stressful situations.

We are the products of millions of years of evolution. Our nervous systems have been honed by the exigencies of living not for the capacity to find truth, but rather for the capacity to survive and reproduce. It matters little that the rabbit from time to time perceives danger and runs even when there is no danger. Better this than waiting around to obtain enough evidence to rule out the possibility that the movement in the grass was only the wind. The rabbit that seeks truth, the rabbit that evaluates competing hypotheses as to the cause of a particular sound or movement in the grass, is all the sooner dispatched to the great heavenly hutch than is the rabbit that runs at the first sign of possible danger.

Our nervous systems are set up so as to enable us to learn quickly what goes with what. We automatically try to find patterns in what we see, what we hear, what we experience in general. Eat some unusual food, and feel sick an hour later—it is difficult not to attribute the latter to the former, and most of us will do exactly that, even though we may quite often be wrong. Take an aspirin when you feel a pounding headache, and when the headache subsides a short while later, it is difficult not to attribute this easing of pain to the pill, and one is left never knowing whether the headache was about to go away on its own anyway. It is almost automatic to interpret the sequence of events, aspirin—pain relief, as a causal one. Dream a dream about a fire, and witness a conflagration the following day, and it is very difficult to avoid the feeling that the dream presaged the fire. And what is important to note is that even if one is fully aware of the fact that this may be the result of coincidence or other factors (e.g., one heard a fire siren during the night, which triggered the dream; in the morning, one witnessed the still-burning building on the way to work), the *feeling* is difficult to dismiss. That feeling is not something that we can by virtue of our rationality simply turn off, and it is such a feeling that leads many people to reject their rational misgivings, if they have them, and accept the notion of, in this example, the presaging of the fire.

The same applies to psychic sleuths. If the psychic mentions a bridge, water, a tall structure, and lots of noise, and if the body is found under a roller coaster, our brains may immediately see a connection between the roller coaster and the predicted "tall structure" and "lots of noise." The fact that neither the bridge nor water were present is ignored. This could even be taken to be almost a direct hit, unless one stops to realize that this is an instance of what Lucas (Chapter 9) referred to as "retro-fitting." The description of bridge/water/tall structure/lots of noise could be applied to many, many situations. This sort of thing occurs frequently in psychic sleuthing. Recall, for example, the numbers that Allison and Kerr generated in some of their cases (see Dennett, Chapter 2; Taylor and Dennett, Chapter 7), and note particularly the reinterpretation of the meaning of these numbers by some people—after the bodies were found—that led them to conclude that the psychic had actually had something important to say.

So, personal experience with a psychic sleuth, while it might be suggestive enough to promote more careful investigation, should never qualify as solid evidence that the claimed psychic powers are genuine.

SCIENTIFIC APPROACH TO PROTECTING AGAINST ERRORS

Because our brains are so good at finding patterns and correspondences that seem meaningful, even when they are not, it is difficult for anyone to avoid faulty conclusions about the significance of such patterns in at least some situations. Scientific methods have evolved partly because of the need to minimize the likelihood of such faulty interpretations. Science is a method of discovery, a socially evolved method to discover truth as best we can while protecting ourselves from error—those errors thrust upon us by our nervous system's search for patterns and meaning, and by our culture's generalized but sometimes erroneous beliefs about the way the world works.

When we talk about evaluating psychic sleuths under "controlled conditions," this often raises the objection that such wonderful powers cannot be produced on demand, and in any case are not likely to manifest themselves unless the psychic is comfortable and relaxed and not under suspicious scrutiny. That all may be true. However, the desire to evaluate psychic powers under "controlled conditions" is not intended to cast aspersions on the claims of the psychic, but rather to try to make sure that whatever ability we attribute to the psychic is actually so. As Nickell discussed in the opening chapter, when Klyver and Reiser carried out a controlled study of so-called psychic sleuths' abilities to provide useful information about crimes, the researchers did not only look at the information produced by a sample of psychics, for it could be difficult to evaluate any useful information in terms of whether or not it was a lucky guess. They also put a sample of college students and a sample of homicide detectives through the same procedure. This made it relatively easy to evaluate the influence of so-called psychic abilities, which turned out to be nil.

While we cannot all go about conducting controlled experiments, we can *think* in terms of control groups. Thomas Gray,[6] a psychologist at Concordia University in Montreal, has written much about the importance of what he refers to as control-group type of thinking. For example, he points out that it makes no sense to try to evaluate the crash rate of a particular fighter aircraft in terms of whether or not it is extreme, unless one is aware of the average crash rate for other similar fighter aircraft. In other words, one needs a "control group" to provide a base rate against which to compare.

We may be impressed with the accounts provided by people during "past life regressions," but if we are control-group thinkers, we will immediately hold our impression in abeyance until we can find out whether people simply *pretending* to be in a past life trance are any less impressive in their reports. When we think about a psychic detective's pronouncements, we need to stop and think about how impressive the correspondence between pronouncement and reality is, compared to what acknowledged nonpsychics could produce. The control-group thinker will suspend judgment until such information (such as that provided by Klyver and Reiser mentioned earlier) is available.

I recall once visiting a friend in a major North American city, and reading that a particular brand of European wine had been found to have a high level of asbestos fibers, apparently as a result of having been filtered through asbestos, once a common practice. My psychologist friend chided me about jumping to the conclusion that this wine should be avoided, and said that ordinary tap water might be just as asbestos laden. "Where is your control group?" he asked. I took this to be a rather whimsical defense of his favorite wine, but to my surprise, a newspaper report a few days later gave the results of an analysis of the local tap water, and indeed the asbestos fiber count was higher! So, control-group thinking is important in all areas of our lives.

When we think about the performance of a particular psychic sleuth, instead of trying to figure out whether or not the jumble of information that was provided was actually more than one would expect through guessing, it is sometimes helpful to think of the individual's production in comparison with what someone *trying to pass himself or herself off as a psychic sleuth* might do. In that case, we would be pushed to think about how the latter might use readily available information to make his or her suggestions seem more precise. We might consider ways in which a pretender could obtain some pertinent information that might not be generally available, by quizzing the very police he or she sets out to help, for example. We might take claims of past successes less seriously if we think of what the pretend psychic might say.

One more example of how control-group thinking can illuminate psychic claims in some instances: In the course that I teach on anomalistic psychology, I present the following true scenario (with the permission of the person who gave me the letter described below; I have changed the details slightly to provide greater anonymity).

A woman came to see me in great distress, literally clutching an envelope in her hand. Before asking me to read the letter, she sketched out for me the following situation in which she found herself. She was separated from her husband, and their three children lived with her, although no formal custody arrangement had been decreed in court. The separation had been initiated two years earlier at her insistence due to severe emotional abuse on the part of her husband. In recent months, her husband, now living with another woman, had begun insisting that their seven-year-old son come to live with him, a possibility which she rejected because of her fears that her husband's violent temper would be visited upon the boy.

A few weeks earlier, the boy had been diagnosed by a school psychologist as having a learning disability and was to be placed in a remedial classroom. This news provoked her husband to accuse her of emotional abuse of the child. She said that she had been able to handle her husband's tirades, since she was used to his manner of dealing with things, until she had received a letter from her mother, who was now living in Berlin.

After having provided this background, I then read to the class the actual letter (names deleted) in which the woman's mother takes great pains to explain that by writing, she only wants to bring good news about the boy, even though the news may be somewhat difficult for her daughter to take. She relates how she took the child's picture to a well-known German psychic, and telling him only that the child had been diagnosed as being learning-disabled, and that the parents were separated, he concentrated on the picture, and then broke into a broad smile and announced that. . . .

I stop at that point, and ask each student to pretend that he or she is the psychic, a psychic whose reputation and income depend on the appearance of success. I ask them to write down what they might, in the psychic's place, announce to the woman's mother.

What invariably happens is that most of the students choose to say that the child is not learning-disabled, but merely emotionally troubled. (Principle of providing good news.) The separation has upset him greatly. Some typically go on to suggest that the mother is using the little boy as a substitute for the father, taking out her anger toward her husband in various ways, because boy and father resemble one another. "If only the mother would solve her own emotional problems, then the boy would be fine and would not need remedial education." "If she truly loves her son, then she should take steps to make sure that this situation does not continue."

The psychic had said almost exactly that. The woman's mother was overwhelmed by the psychic's performance, even though she gave no reason in the letter for such an emotional reaction. The woman herself was devastated, for the psychic seemed to confirm what her husband had been saying, that the boy would be much better off with him (even though neither psychic nor student actually drew that conclusion).

The point for the students is, of course, that if we try to imagine what we might say if we were pretending to be a psychic, then apparent insights on the part of a psychic appear much less impressive, and we can better see how easy it is to seem to be psychic.

SO YOU WANT TO BE A PSYCHIC SLEUTH . . .

When we watch a good magician, we are fooled, and often fooled with such cleverness that we are amazed and baffled. Yet, we do not approach the magician's performance with the view that either we can find a reasonable explanation for the effects or it must be truly magical, in other words, "psychic." We use a third category, and that is the category of events which we do not understand but which we know to be the deliberate productions of the magician using perfectly natural, but not obvious, means. When considering the psychic sleuth, however, for many people there are only two relevant categories: either one can readily provide prosaic explanations for the effects produced by the psychic sleuth, or these effects must be due to psychic powers. The third category, effects produced in a natural way by the individual but by means unknown or unrecognized by us, is usually missing.

To help build up such a third category, it helps to think about what we would do if we were motivated to try to pass ourselves off as psychic sleuths. How would we go about it? Once we have decided that, perhaps we will recognize in the so-called psychic sleuths some of the same actions.

Here are some suggestions about how to become a psychic sleuth:

1) Gather As Much Background Information As You Can about the Crime or Disappearance You Plan to "Solve"

As Nickell pointed out early in the book (Chapter 1), there is often considerable information about a crime available to the psychic. Absorb what is offered in the news media. Pick up what you can from the police. Pay attention to rumors, for they sometimes are based in fact. Using whatever information one can glean, one can make better guesses about where bodies may be found or about characteristics of the perpetrators.

2) Use the Techniques of a Cold Reader

A cold reader is a person who apparently can tell a stranger all sorts of details about him- or herself, without the latter having apparently divulged such information. As Nickell discussed, again in Chapter 1, in part the cold reader must be sensitive to information that is at hand, and in part the reader can respond to the situation as it unfolds. This is similar to what Lucas (Chapter 9) described as the "rapidly changing hypothesis"—you must be flexible and change or reinterpret your pronouncements to accommodate incoming information. As do cold readers, it would be wise to offer up a number of generalities (e.g., "I see water and a sidewalk") as well as a few specifics (e.g., "I see the number 7") which by chance may prove to be associated in some way with the crime or disappearance. A chance "direct hit" is most impressive. Use multiple end points so that the same characteristics you cite may later be fitted to a number of different situations. For example, "I see the boy's limp body, eyes closed" is a statement that could be later interpreted in various ways. If the missing boy is found dead, then you "clearly" foresaw that. If the boy is found alive, he had perhaps fallen asleep from fatigue. Provide lots of information—all the more likelihood of a chance correspondence. (Note that in the Klyver and Reiser study [see again Nickell, Chapter 1] the psychic sleuths, while no more accurate than the college students or homicide detectives they were being compared with, produced ten times as much useless information.)

3) Claim to Have Extensive Psychic Powers and Use Some of the Trappings Associated with Such Powers— Trances, Pendulums, Seeing Auras, and So On

The psychic sleuths discussed in this book do not suggest that they are using "intuition" or that they are making lucky guesses. They claim outright psychic ability, often far beyond the realm of psychic sleuthing. For example, Hurkos declared (Gordon, Chapter 2) that he was "a psychic, sensitive to people and events that concern them," and said that he had a full range of ESP gifts. Allison (Dennett, Chapter 4) described her abilities in terms of a psychic gift bestowed by God. Ward presents himself as expert in biorhythms, auras, astrology, chiromancy, and psychometry (Lippard, Chapter 6).

4) Seek Publicity

The psychic detectives in this book for the most part are excellent at obtaining and managing publicity. Hurkos, as Gordon points out in Chapter 2, was a master at publicity garnering. Allison has her own publicity agent (Dennett, Chapter 4). Renier has a promotional packet entitled "Book a Spellbinder . . ." (Posner, Chapter 5). Ward has a publicist and uses a flyer that describes him as a psychic investigator of crimes, and as skilled in hypnosis, psychometry, and chiromancy (Lippard, Chapter 6).

For publicity's sake, go to the police and offer your services, and even if you are not well-received you can claim to have been involved in the investigation.

5) Attribute Your Ability to a Gift from God

This will win respect by association and allay criticism in some quarters. Several of the sleuths discussed in this book, including Hurkos, Allison, Ward, and Kerr, do exactly that, while some others, Renier and Alexander, lean toward New Age religion and claim to have spiritual Entities that guide them.

6) Claim Credit for Having Solved Other, Sensational Crimes

Most of the psychic detectives in this book claim credit for having solved or helped solve crimes when careful scrutiny shows that they did not: Hurkos took credit for helping solve the Boston Strangler murders, even though he fingered the wrong man (Gordon, Chapter 2). Allison took credit for having helped solve the Atlanta child murders (Dennett, Chapter

4). Verne McGuire claimed to have used dowsing to find the California Hillside Strangler (Nickell, Chapter 10). That these claims have been found to be specious is not important for the publicity.

7) Suggest that Your Abilities Have Been Validated by Scientists

If anyone presses you for details, either become very vague, or throw about a few names of researchers, and leave it at that, in the hope that no one will follow up on them anyway. Most of the psychic detectives in this book claim to have been scientifically validated. Even though Rhine denied it, Hurkos claimed to have been tested, and his powers validated, by him as well as other scientific authorities (Gordon, Chapter 2). Croiset was "scientifically validated" by his mentor Tenhaeff, who benefited greatly from Croiset's success (Peterson, Chapter 3). Allison claimed to have been tested at Duke University, although Dennett (Chapter 4) was unable to obtain verification of this. Renier suggests that she is accepted by scientists insofar as she claims to be "working with scientists" (Posner, Chapter 5).

8) Do Not Actually Submit Yourself to Scientific Testing, or If You Do, Choose the Researchers Carefully

You have nothing to gain and a lot to lose. Do like Ward: simply refuse to undergo any scientific tests (Lippard, Chapter 6). Croiset, while submitting to tests by parapsychologists all over Europe, declined twice to submit to testing by J. B. Rhine, the dean of experimental parapsychologists (Peterson, Chapter 3).

9) Learn to Be Adept at Reinterpreting Your Pronouncements after the Fact to Make Them More "Predictive" of What Was Found

The various chapters in this book give ample evidence of "retrofitting" (see Lucas, Chapter 9) either by the psychics themselves or by people around them who are eager to find truth in their pronouncements.

Think again about Anderson Kirby. The account about him showed evidence of just about every one of these stratagems. That does not mean that he consciously chose to manipulate, any more than we can conclude that all the people discussed in this book are conscious manipulators. However, sincere people can be as much a victim to self-delusion as they are to being deceived by others. It is not beyond belief that some of these "psychic sleuths" may be very sincere, and may honestly believe that they have the powers that they, and their supporters, say they have.

A FINAL WORD

The authors of the preceding chapters have done an excellent job of demonstrating how accounts of psychic sleuths' accomplishments wither when exposed to careful investigation and analysis. We must be careful not to accept at face value further narratives about these or other psychic sleuths. Media accounts often mislead—reporters, too, can be taken in deliberately or fall prey to self-deception. We should all follow *Hyman's Categorical Imperative,* named after Ray Hyman, whom I have so often heard enunciate this point: "*Do not try to explain something until you are sure the there is something to be explained.*" Be it someone's anecdote or a newspaper account, the most we should make of a report of a psychic sleuth is that we are dealing with an anecdote. If we are interested, we must look more deeply into the matter before even considering the need to posit a psychic explanation.

Anderson Kirby is my invention. Before being too annoyed at that, recall just what your reaction—emotional and intellectual—was when you first read the account. Did you employ the Hyman Imperative, or did you succumb to trying to explain the story away, or did you yield to fascination with the possibility that the man was genuinely psychic? That reaction of yours is a guide to how you probably react in general to such accounts. Full marks if you followed the Hyman Imperative. Learn from it if you did not.

Finally, so long as any of us get a shiver down the spine listening to a ghost story—even if we do not believe in ghosts—so long as individuals seek a reason for our existence or an escape from anxiety about death, and so long as we continue to fall prey to our brain's wonderful capacity to find meaningful patterns even when there is no meaning, there will be belief in psychic phenomena. And so long as there is belief in psychic phenomena, the psychic sleuth will have appeal. It is the task of books like this to try to ensure that rationality and not emotion, reality and not myth, are brought to the arena of criminal investigation.

NOTES

1. J. E. Alcock, *Parapsychology: Science or Magic?* (Oxford: Pergamon Press, 1981); J. E. Alcock, *Science and Supernature* (Buffalo, N.Y.: Prometheus Books, 1990).

2. M. Rokeach, *Beliefs, Attitudes, and Values* (San Francisco: Jossey-Bass, 1968).

3. Alcock, *Parapsychology: Science or Magic?*

4. J. T. Frank, "Nature and Function of Belief Systems," *American Psychologist* 32: 555–59.

5. Alcock, *Parapsychology: Science or Magic?*

6. T. Gray, "Gender Differences in Belief in Unsubstantiated Phenomena," *Canadian Journal of Behavioural Science* 22 (1990): 181–90.

Appendices

Appendix A

An Evaluation of the Use of Psychics in the Investigation of Major Crimes*

Martin Reiser, Louise Ludwig,
Susan Saxe, and Claire Wagner

In the past, there have been numerous anecdotal reports of major crimes being solved by information provided by "sensitives," individuals deemed to have psychic ability.[1] Attempts to verify these reports with the police agencies mentioned have been unsuccessful to date.

The Los Angeles Police Department (LAPD) psychology staff has in the past worked with two psychics individually on two unrelated homicide cases. In these two instances, information elicited from the psychics proved to be of no value in concretely assisting case investigators.

More recently, a highly publicized series of rape-murders in Los Angeles, the "Hillside Strangler" cases, have resulted in numerous offers of assistance to the LAPD by psychics and others claiming to have extrasensory perception capabilities. In the interest of possible increased effectiveness, and the saving of time, manpower, and funds, it was decided to design a research study

*This article originally appeared under the same title in *Journal of Police Science and Administration* 7, no. 1 (1979): 18–25. Reprinted by permission.

At the time this article was published, Dr. Reiser was director, Dr. Saxe staff psychologist, and Ms. Wagner research assistant, Behavioral Science Services Section, Los Angeles Police Department; Dr. Ludwig was associate professor of psychology at Los Angeles City College.

Appreciation is acknowledged for valuable assistance by Lieutenant Ronald Lewis and Investigator John Edwards, Los Angeles Police Department.

to investigate the feasibility of utilizing psychic information to aid in the identification and apprehension of suspects in major crime cases.

PURPOSE

In collaboration with an academic psychologist, who is also a researcher of psychic phenomena, a double-blind design was established in order to minimize experimenter bias. The purpose was not to address the question of the existence of ESP or paranormal phenomena generally, but only to confront the narrower issue of the usefulness of this kind of information in the solution of major crimes at this police agency at this time.

POPULATION

Twelve psychics participated in this project. Eight of the group are considered to be professional psychics as they either partially or wholly earn their living by means of fees for their psychic services. Four of the group are considered nonprofessional psychics. The participants were selected by the second author, an academic psychologist, from among those considered to be the most reputable and able in the Los Angeles area who were willing to participate.

APPROACH

Four crimes, two solved and two unsolved, were selected by an investigator not involved in the research. No information about the crimes was given to the project staff or to the academic consultant. Of the unsolved cases, one contained a detailed description of the suspect and the crime itself, and no suspect information was available in the other. Physical evidence from each of the four crimes was placed in sealed, numbered envelopes. Each psychic interviewed individually was first asked to elicit information from the sealed envelopes. Responses were tape recorded. Then the psychic was asked to open each envelope, and again react to the unconcealed evidence. These responses were also recorded verbatim.

Neither the participants (psychics) nor the psychologist-experimenter had any prior knowledge of any of the cases or the evidence. This prevented the experimenter from unconsciously "sending" or influencing the participants in a prejudged way.

Data were grouped into the following categories which corresponded with the information recorded on the original crime reports: crime(s) committed, victim(s), suspect(s), physical description(s), and crime location(s). Other information elicited from the participants, but which could not in each case be verified, included accessories to the crime, lifestyle of the victim and/or suspect, and psychological traits of the victim and/or suspect. However, as only approximately 50 percent of the information provided by the psychics was verifiable, the study focused on these verifiable criteria indicators.

In many instances the psychics did not comment on all categories, and often they did not specify in which category specific information applied. Further, some of the participants were extremely verbose, while others provided only very sketchy responses.

The following response provided by one participant illustrates the type of information which the researchers had to evaluate against known facts:

> I get a man, black. I hear screaming, screaming. I'm running up stairs and down. My head . . . someone bounces my head on the wall or floor. I see trees—a park? In the city, but green. Did this person live there? What does the number "2" mean? I get a bad, bloody taste in my mouth. The names "John" or "Joseph" or something like that. I am running on the street like a crazy. This is a *very* serious crime. I can't hold the envelope in my hand.

This response, though briefer than some, is representative in content of numerous responses of other psychics.

Factors said to influence psychic responses include the following: a psychic may generate relatively accurate information on one case, but be totally incorrect on another; correct information may be generated only in parts of each case; all information from some psychics may be incorrect; a psychic may have picked up correct information about one case, but may have reported it for another case (displacement); a psychic may be more accurate on one day as opposed to another; and personal motivation or involvement may be required on the part of some psychics to provide accurate responses.

RESULTS

Crime No. 1 was a robbery-homicide involving a 30-year-old Caucasian female victim. The suspect is still at large. The evidence given to the psychics in this case was a brown and yellow metal cigarette lighter. Six psychics correctly identified the sex of the victim; five, the ethnic identification of the victim; and five, the type of crime. Out of a possible 21 key indicators, two psychics correctly identified 4 of the indicators. The average correct response rate for all of the psychics was the identification of two known criteria. Statistically, this is not better than chance. (See Table 1.)

Crime No. 2 was a robbery-homicide involving an 89-year-old male victim. The suspect is in custody. The evidence presented to the psychics included a pair of brown, loafer-style shoes with tassles and an eyeglass lens. Out of the possible 33 key indicators known, the average correct response rate was 1.8, ranging from a low of 0 to a high of 3 correct responses. Six psychics correctly identified the type of crime, and seven, the sex of the suspect. (See Table 2.)

Crime No. 3 involved the murder of a young mother who was returning to her car with her husband and their two small children, while the suspect was attempting to steal their car. Although the suspect is still at large, a detailed description supplied by eyewitnesses was available. The psychics were given evidence consisting of a red purse and red wallet. Out of the possible 28 verifiable responses, the average correct response rate was 2.3 with a low of 1 and a high of 5 correct responses. Six psychics correctly identified the sex of the victim, and seven correctly identified the type of crime and the sex of the suspect. (See Table 3.)

Crime No. 4 involved the murder of a woman. The suspect is in custody. Evidence made available to the psychics included a woman's wallet, some miscellaneous papers and a seven-inch screwdriver. Out of a possible 29 verifiable responses, the average correct response rate was 2.7 with a low of 0 and a high of 6 correct responses. Nine psychics correctly identified the sex of the victim; eight, the sex of the suspect; and four, the type of crime. (See Table 4.)

In Crime No. 1, where no verifiable information was available on the suspect, a comparison was made between the responses of the participants to determine how much they agreed. These responses are illustrated in Table 5. Ten of the psychics believed the suspect was male, two thought he was Caucasian, two believed he was black, and two believed him to be six feet tall. This degree of agreement corresponded with the degree of agreement on the verifiable items and except for the sex of the suspect is considered no better than chance.

On verifiable items not specifically mentioned above, there was little or no consistency among responses.

DISCUSSION

The research data do not support the contention that psychics can provide significant additional information leading to the solution of major crimes. The area of greatest accuracy had to do with the sex of the suspect and sex of the victim. Some degree of accuracy was also detected in the type of crime committed. A common thread ran through many of the psychics' responses. The most commonly repeated conception of these crimes was that the victim was a female prostitute murdered by a male, with drug involvement either by the victim, the suspect, or both.

Many of the psychics believed these cases might have been connected with the "Hillside Strangler," a highly publicized case in the news at the time this study was conducted. However, none of the crimes involved in the study was related to that case.

Two specific responses are worth noting. Regarding Crime No. 2, involving an 89-year-old church historian as the victim, one psychic believed that this crime occurred around a church and reiterated his feelings of the importance a church played in this crime.

In Crime No. 3, wherein a homicide resulted from an attempted auto theft, none of the psychics identified the attempted auto theft as part of the crime. However, two psychics believed an automobile played a significant role in the crime. The victim was accompanied by her two children when she was murdered. Three psychics mentioned children in connection with this crime. While the above two instances were interesting, they did not contribute any specific information which would be helpful to investigators in solving the crimes.

Overall, little, if any, information was elicited from the twelve psychic participants that would provide material helpful in the investigation of the major crimes in question. There was a low rate of inter-psychic congruence and accuracy among the responses elicited in this research. We are forced to conclude, based on our results, that the usefulness of psychics as an aid in criminal investigation has not been validated.

While our experience with psychics to date has been essentially unproductive, further research in this area would be desirable.

An augmented replication of this study is planned using two control groups, one consisting of experienced investigators and the other of "nonpsychic" persons. This will permit cross-comparison of response patterns on a hierarchy of variably sophisticated subjects.

In half of the cases, all known relevant information about the crimes, except that relating to the suspect, would be given to the subjects to test the effect of focus and associative congruence on information yield.

Other major crimes, in addition to homicide, will be added to the information pad to determine if affective intensity-reactivity is a factor in eliciting useful information.

Because much information reported by subjects does not readily fit into established categories for purposes of analysis, case investigators will later be asked to examine the data for possible connections with their total background of experience with the crimes in question. This may aid in closing gaps inevitable in real-life research.

We hope to report the results of this project in the near future.

NOTE

1. Paul Tabori, *Crime and the Occult* (1974); Norma Browning, *The Psychic World of Peter Hurkos* (1970); Gerold Frank, *The Boston Strangler* (1966); Fred Archer, *Crime and the Psychic World* (1969).

Table 1

Psychic "Hits" for Crime No. 1

Psychic Number	VICTIM'S NAME	Crime Location	Address	Sex	Descent	Age	Hair	Eyes	Height	Weight	Build	Complexion	Clothing Worn	Cause of Death	Occupation	Date Occurred	Time Occurred	Property Taken	Modus Operandi	Weapon	Crime	TOTALS
1																						0
2				x	x				x												x	4
3																						0
4				x																		1
5-A					x													x				2
6-A					x																x	2
7-A				x	x	x																3
8																				x	x	2
9-A				x	x		x														x	4
10				x			x															2
11				x																		1
12																			x	x	x	3
TOTALS				6	5	1	2		1									1	1	2	5	

A=Nonprofessional psychic.

Table 2

Psychic "Hits" for Crime No. 2

Psychic Number	VICTIM'S NAME	Crime Location	Address	Sex	Descent	Age	Hair	Eyes	Height	Weight	Build	Complexion	Clothing Worn	Cause of Death	Occupation	Date Occurred	Time Occurred	Property Taken	Modus Operandi	Weapon	SUSPECT'S NAME	Crime	Address	Sex	Descent	Age	Hair	Eyes	Weight	Height	Physical Oddities	Occupation	Clothing Worn	TOTALS
1																						x	x											2
2																								x	x							x		3
3																																		0
4																							x	x	x									3
5-A																								x										1
6-A																							x											1
7-A			x																				x											2
8																							x											1
9-A																								x								x		2
10																								x										1
11																																		0
12																							x	x										2
TOTALS			1																				6	7	2							2			

A=Nonprofessional psychic.

Table 3

Psychic "Hits" for Crime No. 3

Psychic Number	VICTIM'S NAME	Crime Location	Address	Sex	Descent	Age	Hair	Eyes	Height	Weight	Build	Complexion	Clothing Worn	Cause of Death	Occupation	Date Occurred	Time Occurred	Property Taken	Modus Operandi	Weapon	SUSPECT'S SEX	Crime	Car	Descent	Age	Hair	Eyes	Weight	Height	TOTALS
1			x																		x				x					3
2																						x								1
3					x																									1
4																					x	x								2
5-A			x	x													x				x		x							5
6-A			x																		x	x								3
7-A			x																		x	x								3
8			x																											1
9-A																						x								1
10																					x	x								2
11			x																		x									2
12																						x	x					x		3
TOTALS			6	1	1												1				7	7	2		1			1		

A=Nonprofessional psychic.

Table 4

Psychic "Hits" for Crime No. 4

Psychic Number	VICTIM'S NAME	Crime Location	Address	Sex	Descent	Age	Hair	Eyes	Height	Weight	Build	Complexion	Clothing Worn	Cause of Death	Occupation	Date Occurred	Time Occurred	Modus Operandi	Weapon	SUSPECT'S NAME	Crime	Address	Sex	Descent	Age	Hair	Eyes	Weight	Height	TOTALS
1				x																	x									2
2			x	x																	x									3
3																														0
4				x										x							x	x	x							5
5-A				x	x	x																	x							4
6-A				x				x						x							x		x					x		6
7-A				x																			x							2
8				x																			x	x						3
9-A				x														x					x						x	4
10																														0
11				x																			x							2
12																							x							1
TOTALS			1	9	1	1		1						2				1			4	1	8	1				1	1	

A=Nonprofessional psychic.

Table 5

Psychic Responses regarding Suspect for Crime No. 1

Psychic Number	Suspect's Name	Address	Sex	Descent	Age	Hair	Eyes	Weight	Height	Physical Oddities	Occupation	Clothing Worn
1			Male	Blk								
2	Ralon Charles		Male	Blk	Early 30s					Scar on r. cheek		
3												
4			Male									
5-A			Male									
6-A			Male									
7-A			Male	Cauc.					6'			Tattoo Beard
8	Pete Micky Nickl		Male				Blue					Mustache Limps
9-A	John James		Male	Cauc.	Late 30s-early 40s	Brn			5'10"			
10			Male				Blue					
11												
12			Male						6'			L. hand: parts of 4th & 5th finger missing

A=Nonprofessional psychic.

Appendix B

A Comparison of Psychics, Detectives, and Students in the Investigation of Major Crimes*

Martin Reiser with Nels Klyver

There has been a great deal of controversy surrounding the use of "sensitives" or individuals who claim to possess extrasensory abilities in the area of criminal investigation. Many media reports have stated that police departments have made widespread use of psychics in major crime investigations and have also described impressive successes resulting from their collaboration with police. However, attempts by the Los Angeles Police Department (LAPD) psychology staff to substantiate these claims have met with only limited success. Contrary to some statements, the LAPD has not employed psychics in criminal investigations. The same situation appears to be true for most police departments contacted. In several well publicized major cases where inviduals who claimed psychic powers *volunteered* information to the Department about the crime, the information has not proven useful to the investigation. Similarly, a comprehensive analysis of psychic claims in solving major crimes by Hansel (1966) revealed little correspondence between media reports and later objective documentation.

Although the LAPD has not used psychics in crime investigation,

*This is reprinted by permission from Martin Reiser, *Police Psychology: Collected Papers* (Los Angeles: Lehi Publishing Co., 1982), pp. 260–67.

Special acknowledgment is given to Detective Philip Sartuche and Staff Psychologist Susan Saxe, Ph.D.

apart from two research studies, the Behavioral Science Services staff of LAPD has received several first-hand accounts of reported success with psychics from several other departments.

In one case, for example, an investigator reported that a psychic had provided him with highly specific and useful information in two major crime investigations. By his estimate, 90 percent of the information provided by the psychic was "accurate" but only 15–20 percent was investigatively useful. In several cases with other departments (cf. Newport Beach Police Department), investigators have told us that psychics were, in their judgment, able to provide a great deal of accurate information about cases under investigation but that none of it was helpful in the identification of suspects.

Reiser et al. (1979) conducted an experimental test of psychics' ability to aid in criminal investigation by having 12 identified psychics examine selected physical evidence from each of four different major crimes that had occurred in Los Angeles. The information generated by the psychics in this study, although quite extensive, was judged to be no better than chance and was of little investigative value.

On the other hand, a more optimistic view of law enforcement's use of psychics was published recently by the California Department of Justice (1978). Eleven officers who had used psychics were interviewed and the document contends that eight of the officers reported successful experiences. Based on this finding, investigators were encouraged to seek out psychics in difficult cases. The report provides detailed instructions on how to contact a psychic, how to set up conducive working conditions, and describes the kinds of information that may be expected. The report concludes that "a talented psychic can assist by helping to locate the geographic area of a missing person, narrow the number of leads to be concentrated on, highlight information that has been overlooked, and provide information previously overlooked by the investigator."

RATIONALE FOR THE STUDY

Because of the controversy about the usefulness of psychics in crime investigations, it was desirable to attempt a replication of Reiser's (1979) study. Since there was difficulty in assigning clearly derived probabilities to the data produced by the psychics in the previous (1979) study, in the present study it was decided to utilize two additional comparison groups which could provide empirical reference points. The use of control groups would also help clarify whether individuals not identified as psychic can produce investigatively useful data.

METHOD

Subjects

Two teams of "sensitives" (identified by non-LAPD psychologists), four in one group and eight in the other, participated in the study. In addition, two comparison (control) groups were used. The first group consisted of eleven college student volunteers who were representative of the general student population. The second comparison group was composed of twelve homicide detectives who volunteered to participate in the project.

Procedure

Four actual crime cases (murders), two solved and two unsolved, were selected for the study by a detective supervisor not directly involved in the research. A "double blind" procedure was followed. Thus, no information other than selected physical evidence was made available to either the experimenters or the subjects until after the data had been collected, summarized, and tabulated.

Case information was available in all four cases for victim data and in two cases for suspect data. One piece of physical evidence from each crime was sealed in an envelope: underwear, a red felt hat, a T-shirt, and a necktie.

The two non-psychic groups were instructed to take each piece of evidence and attempt to intuit or guess characteristics of both the victim and suspect in each crime.

The psychics worked in two teams. Each team followed a procedure it thought would maximize success. Thus, one team worked individually in a darkened room, closed their eyes, and dictated impressions they felt they were "receiving" from the evidence. The other team also worked individually, but wrote, rather than dictated, their responses.

RESULTS

Overview of Data

The data produced by the three groups differed markedly in character and in quantity. Most of the psychics generated lengthy discourses with dramatic and confident-sounding statements. Their accounts were also characterized by many direct perception statements of the form "I now see such and such." The average length of each of the psychics' responses resulted in 1½ typewritten pages, single spaced.

The following example was typical of the responses made by the psychics:

"I see some kind of hospital, operating room. The impression I get is that the doctors are trying to save this person. The impressions I get is from bullet wounds, and I'm getting three bullets. One seems to be in the left shoulder, one in the bottom right side of the stomach area, and one up on the chest area. Three bullets."

"But stronger than the bullets I get this operating room. The doctors just leaning over the person. Trying to save his life. But being unable to. I see this very clearly."

"I am getting a last name like Robuck or Roe . . . something. Roeb . . . something. I keep seeing stripes, maybe either this person was a convict or the person who murdered him has been caught now and is serving time behind bars. I keep seeing prison outfits and uniforms and bars."

"Last name of Price. Having something to do with the murder. Used to be a problem with the right wrist. The outside part of the right wrist seems to be damaged. I keep getting the number 62. I don't know if it's part of some other number, but I keep seeing the 62 very clearly."

"Something about a goose. I have no idea what connection this has with anything. I keep seeing this big goose. I'm getting something about New Mexico or Mexico. August 9th, there's something very, very significant about August 9th. I keep seeing it over and over again. Either the criminal was apprehended or this is the criminal's birthday. But something about August 9th."

"Plays tennis. I'm having respiratory problems now and having a lot of trouble breathing. Gasping for breath. Flintstone glasses around. This may imply that there may be children around."

"I see some large, kind of white, beige-ish building. It's an apartment building but it's old, I'd say it could be 40 years old, maybe more. Lot of windows, maybe six floors. Very long. Something important about this building. Maybe where the killer was living. It's old though. Old elevators, old building."

"Getting pain all across my stomach now. Riddled with pain now from one side to the other. I'm seeing an unclear image now. It's either someone with a cowboy's hat on or a fireman's hat. I'm getting an older car, in the '60s, a large sedan, but I can't figure out what it is. Large, old, and dirty."

"The problem breathing is quite severe. Terrible problems breathing. I'm getting a license plate now, BBR 609. The two Bs I can see clearly, the last letter I can't see. It's either an R or . . . I'm not sure."

In contrast to the psychics' statements, the detective group produced very terse and highly qualified statements. They clearly felt uncomfortable with the instruction set which asked them to rely on intuition and feelings. The length of their responses resulted in an average of ¼ of a typewritten page.

The following protocol conveys the general character of the detective responses:

"Victim probably homosexual killed by a homosexual lover during a lover's fight."

"Suspect—male, 6-0, 215 lbs, very strong, homosexual."

The student group appeared to feel slightly more at ease with the task than did the detectives. They also produced data which resulted in an average of ¼ of a typewritten page. Their statements tended to be lists of information without any of the dramatic and apparently sensory-derived descriptions that characterized the psychics' data.

The following statements convey the general quality of the student group's data:

"Suspect is a male, a very close friend of the victim. In the Hollywood area."

"Person was of medium height, fair hair, blond or light brown. I see a door with a lot of light—a back door or service porch door . . . a lot of light with no curtains."

"The victim was acquainted with suspect . . . not close friend, but he knew him."

"There was not much of a struggle, perhaps the victim was caught off-guard."

The murderer was a much younger person, early twenties, dark complexion, olive skin, dark hair. Mod looking."

The data generated by each subject were classified into 20 response categories and an additional miscellaneous category. These categories are shown in Table I. Approximately 50 percent of the data produced by the students could not be used in the study because there was no way to verify the information.

Analysis of Results

Since the psychic group produced approximately 10 times as much information as either of the two comparison groups, it is more likely by chance alone that their data would produce more "hits." Despite this statistical advantage, the psychics were unable to produce information that was significantly better than the two comparison groups. (Table II displays total number of accurate statements made by each group.) It is important to note that *no* information that would have been especially useful investigatively such as first and last names, license plate numbers, apartment house locations, etc., was accurately produced by *any* of the subjects. Table III summarizes the rank order by frequency of data categories that were produced by each group. Statistically, the data fit a pattern that could be expected by chance.

The data provided no support for the belief that the identified "sensitives" could produce investigatively useful information. Additionally, the data also failed to show that the psychics could produce *any* information relating to the cases beyond a chance level of expectancy.

Evidence from this study is consistent with the findings of Reiser's earlier study. Extending the results of these studies would indicate that the use of psychics in the investigation of major crimes is unlikely to produce investigatively useful information. Perhaps the compelling manner in which self-identified "psychics" tend to present their information may account for some of the positive beliefs about psychic abilities in law enforcement. Possibly, individuals listening to the productions of "psychics" are persuaded more by the dramatic character of the information produced rather than by its objective merit. However, it is recognized that the samples utilized in this study are limited and may not be generalizable to all psychics or to all cases.

If an investigator wants to use a psychic, it would be highly desirable to set up an independent verification procedure where an objective observer could record the events. This procedure might aid other police departments to judge for themselves the cost effectiveness of using psychics in major crime cases.

TABLE I

Categories Scored from Raw Data

1. Sex
2. Ethnic group or descent
3. Age
4. Hair color and texture
5. Eye color
6. Height
7. Weight
8. Overall build
9. Residence (victim)
10. Residence (suspect)
11. Car type
12. License of car
13. Occupation
14. Clothes worn
15. Marital status
16. Distinguishing physical characteristics
17. First and last names
18. Cause of death
19. Date and time of occurrence
20. Other relevant information

TABLE II

Total Number of Accurate Statements for Each Group

	Information about Victims (summed over 4 cases)	Information about Suspects (summed over 2 cases)
Psychics (N=12)	26	8
Detectives (N=12)	18	9
Students (N=11)	27	12

% Difference between the three groups is not statistically significant.
Chi-Square (X^2)=.798

TABLE III

**Rank Order of Most Frequently Occurring Categories
of Information Produced by All Three Groups**

	Category	Frequency
1.	Sex	28
2.	Ethnic descent	22
3.	Build	13
4.	Weight	11
5.	Age	10
6.	Eyes	6
7.	Hair	6
8.	Cause of death	4

REFERENCES

Hansel, C. E. M. *ESP: A Scientific Evaluation.* New York: Scribners, 1966.
Reiser, M., et al. An Evaluation of the Use of Psychics in the Investigation of Major Crimes. *Journal of Police Science and Administration* 7 (1979): 18–25.
Criminal Information Bulletin. California Department of Justice, February 1979.

Appendix C

Psychics! Do Police Departments Really Use Them?*

Jane Ayers Sweat and Mark W. Durm

"Clairvoyant Crime Busters," "Cops Amazed by Crime-Busting Psychic," "Can Psychics See What Detectives Can't?" These are titles of just a few of the articles published in recent years proclaiming the ability of self-described "psychics" to help police. But do so-called psychics really help? To what extent are they even used? To answer these questions the authors of this study undertook an investigation of the police departments in the 50 largest cities in the United States.

People in America are frequently exposed to the belief that "psychics" aid police investigations. The mass media promote this view. An example of a magazine doing so would be the *McCall's* article "Clairvoyant Crime Busters." (Wolkomir and Wolkomir 1987). The article gives details about individual psychics and their supposed crime-solving abilities. Psychics Dorothy Allison and John Catchings are mentioned often. Even the possibility of an "ESP gene" is discussed because John Catchings and his mother are allegedly both psychic! The article also states that, although the psychic gives information to the police, it is the policeman's job to ascertain what the information means.

An earlier *McCall's* exclusive, "Can Psychics See What Detectives

---

*This article appeared originally in *Skeptical Inquirer* 17, no. 2 (Winter 1993): 148–58. Reprinted by permission.

Can't?" (Ralston 1983), says that "many" psychics help investigate various crimes and that some police departments see this psychic assistance as a "legitimate investigative tool." This article also acclaims Dorothy Allison and says that she has to know only where and at what time the crime was committed in order to solve the crime, and that she can do it even by phone!

A *Weekly World News* article, "Cops Amazed by Crime-Busting Psychic" (Alexander 1988), focused on diviner Carol Pate. This article contends that she has helped solve at least 65 murders and a hundred other crimes around the country.

West, the *San Jose Mercury News* Sunday magazine, ran a piece titled "Sylvia Sells Sooth by the Seer" (Holub 1988) about San Jose psychic Sylvia Brown and how she had helped find 20 missing children but never charged a fee. The article says she helped police but preferred to remain anonymous.

Such articles continue. A 1992 article in *Woman's Day* (Duncan 1992) asks in its title, "Can Psychics Solve Crimes?" It answers affirmatively, and uncritically: "Yes, say these two women [Noreen Renier and Nancy Czetli] who are hired to do it every day—with uncanny success."

There are also many books that proclaim psychic power. A recent example of this genre is Arthur Lyons and Marcello Truzzi's (1991) *The Blue Sense: Psychic Detectives and Crime* (reviewed in *SI,* Fall 1991). The uniqueness of this book is that the authors give the impression of objectivity in their investigation of psychic detection. This veil of objectivity is thin, however, and the reader soon realizes that Lyons and Truzzi are subtle proponents of "the blue sense"—that intuitive sense that cops and psychics have that goes beyond what they can hear, see, or smell. Another book proposing psychic power is Colin Wilson's *The Psychic Detectives* (1987). In it he discusses people like Peter Hurkos, Nelson Palmer, Gerard Croiset, and Edgar Cayce. First, Wilson contends that phenomena must be real if they are reported again and again. Second, he says that skeptics doubt because of "everyday consciousness." Wilson also claims that there is "abundant evidence" to prove that psychic powers will "operate on demand" (p. 251). He says that dozens of psychics have proved their powers under rigorous laboratory settings and that those who refuse to accept this evidence are not just unconvinced by the demonstration, but find "the whole idea deeply disturbing and disagreeable." Why does Wilson believe all this? He says that clairvoyants get information from "probably the right brain." This information is then picked up by the left brain. Where, then, does the right brain get its information? Wilson says it comes from either the subjective mind, the subliminal self, or the unconscious. These, he believes, come from "some sort of record that already exists in nature" (p. 252).

Not all articles and books extol psychics' abilities to aid police. Several are very poignant in their disclaimers. *Newsweek* (Morganthau and Smith 1980) described Dorothy Allison's trip to Atlanta in 1980 to help in the case that later became known as the "Atlanta Child Murders Case." The city of Atlanta had invited Allison to participate. *Newsweek* reported, "Her much publicized snooping broke no new ground and the mother of one missing boy complained that the seer never returned her only photograph of her son."

Henry Gordon, in his book *ExtraSensory Deception* (1987), also discussed Allison's visit to Atlanta. Gordon reported that an Atlanta police official said she gave police 42 names of the possible killer, but that they were all wrong. Gordon remarked, "She rode around in a big limousine . . . for three days, then went home" (pp. 142–43).

In the same book Gordon quotes Harold Graham, Ontario Provincial Police Commissioner (41 years with the Ontario Police) as saying, "A psychic never to my knowledge has solved a case" (p. 141). Gordon remarks that psychic detectives "operate on a fixed formula." The formula usually involves their providing such generalities as several different locations and unconnected details, and when a case is finally solved, the psychic can probably then find one or two of his or her guesses that seem to fit the facts of the case.

Another book that tells of psychic assistance in police investigations is *The Dungeon Master: The Disappearance of James Dallas Egbert III,* by William Dear (1984). Dear, a private investigator, wrote about how he solved the Egbert case. He says hundreds of psychics called him about the case during his investigation. He writes: "I always talk to psychics, though. They generally seem sincere to me, though none has ever helped me on a case" (p. 49).

In the book *Careless Whispers: The Lake Waco Murders,* Carlton Stowers describes how psychic John Catchings took part in the case. Stowers writes: "All in all, however, Catchings's visit was a disappointment. He provided nothing specific, only a few impressions which he admitted reservations about" (p. 195).

Martin Reiser, director of the Behavioral Sciences Services Section of the Los Angeles Police Department, has done two major studies on the value of psychics' information to police investigations. The first study, in 1979, was titled "An Evaluation of the Use of Psychics in the Investigation of Major Crimes." Twelve psychics participated in the double-blind experiment. Two solved crimes and two unsolved crimes were selected by an investigator not involved in the research. The results: little, if any, information was gained from the psychics that would help in the investigation of the crimes.

In 1980, Reiser conducted the second study, called "A Comparison of Psychics, Detectives, and Students in the Investigation of Major Crimes." Once again, a double-blind was used. The sample included 12 psychics, 11 college students, and 12 homicide detectives. Four cases, two solved and two unsolved, were chosen by a detective supervisor not directly involved in the research. The psychic group produced about ten times as much information as either one of the other groups. Even with this advantage, the psychics did *not* produce any *better* information than the other two groups. The psychics did not produce any information relating to the cases beyond a chance level of expectancy. Reiser suggested that if an investigator wants to use a psychic, it would be best to set up some verification procedure where an objective observer could record all events.

Ward Lucas, in his investigative article "Police Use of Psychics: A Waste of Resources and Tax Money," published in the *Campus Law Enforcement Journal* (1985), described an experiment similar to the research conducted by Martin Reiser. In 1984 an investigative team at KUSA-TV in Denver took well-known psychics and presented them with six solved and unsolved cases from local police departments. Original evidence was also used. Each psychic was allowed to establish what he or she considered to be fair conditions. Later, the same cases were given to students and they made guesses. Each group scored according to chance. Says Lucas: "We may as well have opened fortune cookies to derive solutions to our criminal cases" (p. 16).

Results indicate that opinion is divided on how useful psychics are to the police. There are those who argue they help and others who argue they hinder. But who better to ask than the police departments themselves.

Thus, we undertook the present study.

PRESENT STUDY

Based upon the 1980 U.S. Census records, the police departments from the 50 largest U.S. cities were surveyed. (See Table 1.) A questionnaire was sent to the chief of police in each city. Either the chief or his designee could respond. Those personnel who did respond included eight deputy chiefs, five homicide unit commanders, five lieutenants, four chiefs of detectives, four detectives, three inspectors, two captains, two sergeants, and one deputy police administrator, among others. All 50 cities replied, although Philadelphia and Washington, D.C., declined to answer.

A five-item questionnaire was used, and either yes or no answers were to be circled by the respondent. Room was also provided for any comments the respondent wished to make. (See Figure 1.) It should be stated that there could possibly be an "underrater bias" among respondents since identification with psychics among police could have negative connotations. It is believed by the authors, however, that in this particular study this effect was minimal, if it occurred at all. This belief was due to the conviction with which the comments were made. In the following analysis, the questions and responses were analyzed individually.

Question 1: In the past has your police department used psychics or does the department presently use them in solving investigations?

Of the 48 respondents, 31 answered no, and 17 answered yes. As stated before, Philadelphia and Washington, D.C., declined to answer. Therefore, approximately 65 percent do not use and have never used psychics.

Below are some comments on Question 1 from the respondents, arranged alphabetically by city:

Chicago: Edward S. Wodnicki, Chief of Detectives, said that he, but not the department, had used a psychic on two occasions. "This was on my own volition and does not reflect policy of the Chicago Police Department."

Cleveland: David P. McNea, Deputy Chief, said his department "does not solicit the aid of psychics in solving investigations."

Detroit: James E. Kleiner, Inspector, Commanding Officer, Goals and Standards Section, said his department "has not and does not solicit psychics."

Los Angeles: W. O. Gartland, Commanding Officer, Robbery-Homicide Division, said: "The Los Angeles Police Department does not use psychics as an investigative tool, although we are often contacted by them."

Nashville: Myra W. Thompson, Sergeant, Planning and Research, said its department has used a psychic "once only."

San Francisco: Larry Gurnett, Deputy Chief of Investigation, said: "Psychics have volunteered information or the victims' families seek that service and the information received is then given to us to evaluate for follow-up investigation."

Seattle: Roy Calvin Skagen, Asst. Chief: " 'Used' is a misleading word, perhaps. We have 'listened' to psychics when they contact us . . . usually at the request of a family member of a missing homicide victim. We do it as a courtesy and to show openness to explore any possibility when regular leads run dry. Success rate when we listen and look at a location indicated is *zero.*"

FIGURE 1

Questionnaire

Please Circle

yes no 1. In the past has your police department used psychics or does the department presently use them in solving investigations? If yes, please answer questions 2 through 5.

    2. If so, in which of the following categories?

        Homicide   ____

        Missing Persons   ____

        Kidnapping   ____

        Locating Stolen Property   ____

        Other   ____

            Specify _____

yes no 3. Does your police department presently handle information received from a psychic any differently than information from an ordinary source?

yes no 4. a. If your department has used psychics, was the information received more helpful in solving the case than other information received?

        b. What kind of information was it and how was it used?

_____

_____

yes no 5. Do you personally consider information from a psychic more valuable than information received from a regular source?

Respondent's Position (Voluntary) _____

Question 2: If so, in which of the following categories?

Homicide	_____
Missing Persons	_____
Kidnapping	_____
Sexual Assault	_____
Burglary	_____
Locating Stolen Property	_____
Other	_____

Psychics had been used in 17 of the departments. They were used in 15 homicides, one missing-persons cases, one kidnapping, one burglary, and 1 assault case.

Question 3: Does your police department presently handle information received from a psychic any different than information from an ordinary source.

Of the 40 cities responding to this question, 33 answered no and 7 answered yes.

Question 4: (a) If your department has used psychics, was the information received more helpful in solving the case than other information received? (b) What kind of information was it and how was it used?

Of the 26 who answered this question, all answered no.

Below are the comments (4b), again arranged alphabetically by city:

Albuquerque: Richard Hughes, Lieutenant, said the information received concerned "attempts to locate bodies." He added, "We have had no real success with one."

Atlanta: W. J. Taylor, Deputy Chief Field Operations Division, said: "The Atlanta Bureau of Police Services does not as a general policy utilize psychics during criminal investigations." He added that, in 1980, psychic Dorothy Allison was called upon as police investigated the murders and disappearances of 30 black males in Atlanta. He said that Allison stayed in Atlanta for three days "visiting crime scenes, after which she provided investigators bits and pieces of information that proved to be of no value to the investigation." Said Taylor: "Personally, I think our invitation to her was a mistake. Her visit was highly publicized by both the local and national media. As a result we received thousands of psychic readings from across the country. This flood of letters placed a tremendous burden on my investigators because each letter had to

TABLE 1

Responses of Police Departments of the 50 Largest Cities in America
(Y = Yes, N = No, C = Comment, K = Kidnapping, B = Burglary, SA = Sexual Assault, H = Homicide, MP = Missing Person.)

City	Question 1	Question 2	Question 3	Question 4a	Question 4b	Question 5
*Albuquerque	Y	H, MP	N	N	C	N, C
*Atlanta	Y	H	N	N	C	N
*Austin	N, C	–	Y	N	C	N, C
*Baltimore	N	–	–	–	–	–
Birmingham	N	–	–	–	–	–
*Boston	Y	H	N	N	C	C
Buffalo	N	–	N	–	–	N
Charlotte	Y	–	N	–	–	N
*Chicago	Y, C	H, B	N	N	C	N, C
Cincinnati	N	–	N	N	–	N
*Cleveland	N, C	–	–	–	–	C
Columbus	N	–	N	–	–	N
Dallas	N	–	N	–	–	N
Denver	N	–	N	–	–	N
*Detroit	N, C	–	–	–	–	–
El Paso	Y	H	Y	N	C	C
*Fort Worth	N	–	N	–	–	N, C
Honolulu	Y, C	H, MP	N	N	C	N
Houston	N	–	N	N	–	N
Indianapolis	N	–	N	N	–	N
Jacksonville	N	–	N	–	–	N
Kansas City	N	–	N	–	–	N
Long Beach	N	–	N	N	–	N
*Los Angeles	N, C	–	–	–	–	C
Louisville	N	–	N	–	–	N
*Memphis	N	–	N	N	C	N
*Miami	N	–	N	N	–	N
Milwaukee	N	–	–	–	–	–
Minneapolis	N	–	N	–	–	N
*Nashville	Y, C	MP	N	N	C	N
New Orleans	N	–	N	–	–	N
New York City	Y	H, MP	N	N	–	N
Newark	Y	MP	N	N	C	N
Oakland	N	–	N	–	–	N
Oklahoma City	N, C	–	N	N	–	N
*Omaha	Y, C	H, MP	N	N	C	N
Philadelphia	(Declined to answer.)					
Phoenix	N	–	Y	–	–	N
Pittsburgh	N	–	N	N	–	N
*Portland, Ore.	Y	H, MP	Y	N	C	N, C
*Saint Louis	Y	H	N	N	–	N
San Antonio	N	–	–	–	–	N
San Diego	Y	H	Y	N	C	N
*San Francisco	Y, C	H, MP, SA	N	N	C	N
San Jose	N, C	H, MP	N	N	C	N
*Seattle	Y, C	H	Y	N	C	N
Toledo	N	–	N	–	–	N
Tucson	Y	H, MP, K	Y	N	C	N, C
Tulsa	N	–	–	–	–	N
Washington, D.C.	(Declined to answer.)					

*Respondent gave persmission to be quoted.

be read and analyzed. In the final analysis none of the information provided a linkage to the killer."

Austin: Mike Belvin: "Information received has been voluntary, unreliable, and useless to our investigation."

Boston: Patrick J. Brady, Detective, said: "Peter Hurkos, a psychic from Holland, was used in the Boston Strangler case."

Chicago: Edward S. Wodnicki, Chief of Detectives, said he personally has used a psychic twice. "In both instances the information was general. In regard to the burglary, the psychic was accurate regarding the location of a vehicle that was stolen in the course of the burglary. In the homicide, we feel that the body was transported for a period of time, before it was dumped. The psychic seems to be able to 'sight' a portion of the route traveled by the offender."

Memphis: Ken East, Captain, Homicide Division, said: "We have received general information, and used it as any other information in an investigation."

Nashville: Myra W. Thompson, Sergeant, Planning and Research: "The case was that of a missing child (girl) and the psychic advised the police department that the child had been murdered and also the method; however, could not provide location of the body. Body was eventually discovered."

Omaha: Larry L. Roberts, Homicide Unit Commander, said: "The information, in cases where psychics have contacted us, is usually not confirmed until after the fact."

Portland: Rob H. Aichele, Deputy Chief, said: "Psychics have offered conflicting reports, thus, self-negating each other."

San Diego, James R. Jarvis, Commanding Officer, Homicide Division, said he received "highly speculative information on a possible homicide suspect which proved to be untrue."

San Francisco: Larry R. Gurnett, Deputy Chief of Investigations, said his department has received "suspect descriptions" as well as "victim location."

Seattle: Roy Calvin Skagen, Assistant Chief, said information received has concerned "location of bodies."

Question 5: Do you personally consider information from a psychic more valuable than information received from a regular source?

Of the respondents, 39 said no. *None said yes.* One said it depends on which psychic was used. One said "sometimes." Seven did not answer. Two (Philadelphia and Washington, D.C.) declined to answer.

Several respondents made comments concerning this question:

Austin: Mike Belvin: "I have yet to see any information received from psychics of any value, based on 20 years experience. The information is usually distorted, of no investigative value, and inaccurate. They hamper an investigation and often cause distractions from the main investigation."

Boston: Patrick J. Brady, Detective: "All information received from any source is investigated for its validity."

Cleveland: David P. McNea, Deputy Chief: "Any information offered or brought forth by any so-called psychic would be handled no differently than information obtained from ordinary sources."

Fort Worth: Thomas C. Swan, Homicide Lieutenant: "I have been Homicide Lieutenant for 7 years and know of no time that a psychic has been of any value other than offering false hope to survivors. They surface on sensational cases only. Most fit a mold. They tell you they are 85 percent accurate and are very defensive when you ask them for specifics. It doesn't take long for them to reach the victims' relatives and generate false hope. I would never, no matter what the cost, rely upon a psychic other than to process info the same as we do for everyone else. Where are these psychics when a wino is found murdered in an alley?"

Los Angeles: W. O. Gartland, Commanding Officer, Robbery-Homicide Division: "We have never been able to scientifically validate psychic phenomena, nor have we solved a case as the result of information provided by a purported psychic. This department conducted a study a number of years ago and participated in a series of experiments with parapsychologists involved in a program at the University of California at Los Angeles, which resulted in our stance on psychics."

Omaha: Larry L. Roberts, Homicide Unit Commander: "Psychics often provide us with plausible theories to explore. We have not yet identified a suspect or made an arrest solely on the basis of psychic information. It is simply another investigative tool."

Portland: Rob H. Aichele, Deputy Chief: "Psychic information has been volunteered many times, but has *never* been beneficial to a case."

CONCLUSION

As the results above indicate, there is *not* a prevalent use of psychics among the police departments of our largest cities. Table 2 presents a summary

TABLE 2
Summary of Data

	No. of Cities Responding	"No"	"Yes"
Question 1: "Has your department used or is now presently using psychics?"	48	31 (65%)	17 (35%)

Question 2 (asked of the 17 answering yes to Question 1): "If so, which categories?"

Homicide	15	
Missing Persons	10	
Kidnapping	1	
Sexual Assault	1	
Burglary	1	

	No. of Cities Responding	"No"	"Yes"
Question 3: "Is information from psychics handled differently?"	40	33 (83%)	7 (17.5%)
Question 4 (a): "Was the psychic information more helpful?"	26	26 (100%)	0 (0%)
Question 5: "Is psychic information more valuable?"	41	39 (95%)*	0 (0%)

*One respondent (2.5%) answered, "Sometimes"; and one (2.5%) said, "Depends on which psychic."

of the data with abbreviated questions. One could argue that the psychics pander to and patronize the police but in the end prove to be parasitic. In some instances, as shown by the comments above, they may even hinder effective investigations.

Why then do titles like "Clairvoyant Crime Busters," "Cops Amazed by Crime-busting Psychic," and "Can Psychics See What Detectives Can't?" prevail? The mass media tend to give their audiences what they want. People want to believe there is some mysterious cosmic knowledge into which psychics tap. But, as this investigation reveals, the overwhelming majority of those police who actually do the investigations prefer to work with known tools rather than with unknown ones.

REFERENCES

Alexander, J. 1988. "Cops Amazed by Crime-Busting Psychic." *Weekly World News,* May, p. 45.

Dear, W. 1984. *The Dungeon Master: The Disappearance of James Dallas Egbert III.* New York: Ballantine Books.

Duncan, Lois. 1992. "Can Psychics Solve Crimes?" *Woman's Day,* April 1, pp. 30, 124–30.

Gordon, H. 1987. *ExtraSensory Deception.* Buffalo, N.Y.: Prometheus Books.

Holub, K. 1988. "Sylvia Sells Sooth by the Seer." *West* (Sunday magazine of the *San Jose Mercury News*), July, pp. 4–11.

Lucas, W. 1985. "Police Use of Psychics: A Waste of Resources and Tax Money." *Campus Law Enforcement Journal,* 15:15–21.

Lyons, A., and M. Truzzi. 1991. *The Blue Sense: Psychic Detectives and Crime.* New York: The Mysterious Press.

Morganthau, T., and V. E. Smith. 1980. "Atlanta Goes on a Manhunt." *Newsweek,* December 1, pp. 40, 42.

Ralston, J. 1983. "Can Psychics See What Detectives Can't?" *McCall's,* February, pp. 72–73.

Reiser, M. 1982. *Police Psychology: Collected Papers.* Los Angeles: Lehi Publishing Company.

Stowers, C. 1986. *Careless Whispers: The Lake Waco Murders.* New York: Pocket Books.

Wilson, C. 1987. *The Psychic Detectives.* New York: Berkley Books.

Wolkomir, R., and J. Wolkomir. 1987. "Clairvoyant Crime Busters." *McCall's,* October, pp. 159–64.

Appendix D

Update: Psychics—
Do Police Departments Really Use Them
in Small and Medium-Sized Cities?

Mark W. Durm and Jane Ayers Sweat

ABSTRACT

This study is a follow-up to the original one in which the 50 largest cities in America were surveyed as to their use of psychics. Critics of the first study responded that rural police departments were more apt to use psychics than urban forces. Therefore, the authors conducted this present study in which the police departments of small and medium-sized cities were surveyed.

The results of this present study are even more damaging to the psychics' position. It was found that police departments of cities of this size use psychics even less.

In a recent article in the *Skeptical Inquirer* (Winter 1993, pp. 148–58), the present authors surveyed the police departments of the 50 largest cities in America as to their use of psychics in investigations. The results of that study, as reported in the article, were that there was *not* a prevalent use of psychics among the police departments of America's largest cities. It was stated that psychics "pander to and patronize the police but in the end prove to be parasitic." We, the authors, however, were criticized for not surveying small and medium-sized cities. One critic, Phyllis Galde, writing in *FATE* magazine (1993, pp. 5–6) reported:

> Many more psychics are used in rural than urban areas, which would not show up in this kind of study. Due to the bureaucracy in large-city police departments, the higher ups may not even know what the on-case personnel are doing in their investigations.

Marcello Truzzi, in a letter to the editor of the *Skeptical Inquirer* (1993, pp. 445–46), wrote:

> Even though most previous evidence indicated that psychics have been used more often by rural than by urban police. . . . Sweat and Durm surveyed only urban departments.

Due to these criticisms, we decided to follow up our original study with a survey of small and medium-sized cities.

Using Mark T. Mattson's *Atlas of the 1990 Census* (1992), we sent police departments of the 75 smallest cities listed, ranging in population from 31,092 to 33,181, a letter and questionnaire. Furthermore, the police departments of the 75 medium-sized cities listed, ranging in population from 50,889 to 55,097, were also sent the same letter and questionnaire. Of the 150 cities surveyed, 65 responded, which is 43 percent and is a very good rate when compared to the usual 20 percent return rate of mailed questionnaires.

The questionnaire was the exact same one used in the original study of the 50 largest cities. We chose the original survey instrument even though we received criticisms for its wording (see Letters to the Editor, *Skeptical Inquirer* 17, no. 4 [Summer 1993]: 445–46). It was decided, for the sake of comparison to the original study and because of our belief that the wording was not biased, to use the original questionnaire.

As can be seen from observing the questionnaire, if respondents answered yes to Question 1, they were to answer Questions 2 through 5. If a city had never used psychics, that respondent was only required to answer Question 1, although some answered more than Question 1.

The letter that was sent to the 150 cities was worded in such a way as not to create the impression that we were either proponents or opponents of police use of psychics. The letter is shown below:

FIGURE 1

Questionnaire

Please Circle

yes no 1. In the past has your police department used psychics or does the department presently use them in solving investigations? If yes, please answer questions 2 through 5.

        2. If so, in which of the following categories?

           Homicide   _____

           Missing Persons   _____

           Kidnapping   _____

           Locating Stolen Property   _____

           Other   _____

               Specify _____

yes no 3. Does your police department presently handle information received from a psychic any differently than information from an ordinary source?

yes no 4. a. If your department has used psychics, was the information received more helpful in solving the case than other information received?

           b. What kind of information was it and how was it used?

    _____

    _____

yes no 5. Do you personally consider information from a psychic more valuable than information received from a regular source?

Respondent's Position (Voluntary) _____

Dear Chief:

This is written due to responses of a recently published article entitled "Psychics: Do Police Departments Really Use Them?" in the Winter 1993 issue of an international scholarly journal. In the study, we, the authors, had surveyed the police departments of the 50 largest cities in America.

    We were criticized by some for not surveying middle-sized, and smaller-sized cities. Thus, the reason for your receiving this letter and questionnaire.

Your police department was chosen because the city it protects is considered to be smaller-sized (or middle-sized), according to population, as given in Mark T. Mattson's *Atlas of the 1990 Census,* which lists all cities in America from a population of 31,092 to 7,322,564 which is New York City, the largest metropolis in America.

We would be very appreciative if either you or your designee would complete the survey. It is hoped the results will be publishable. We have included an *optional* "permission to quote" statement at the bottom of the questionnaire.

Again, we would sincerely appreciate your honesty, patience, and time. Please complete the survey and return it in the self-addressed stamped envelope. Thank you.

RESULTS OF SMALL-SIZED CITIES

Of the 75 questionnaires mailed, 32 were completed and returned and three were sent back for insufficient addresses. One could argue that those who failed to respond probably lean more toward an opposing view than a proposing one. It seems if someone were to use or had used psychics, that person would be more than likely to respond. The following are descriptions of those responses.

Question 1: In the past, has your police department used psychics or does the department presently use them in solving investigations?

Of the 32 respondents, 26 answered no, and six answered yes. Therefore, approximately 81 percent of the small cities responding do not use and have never used psychics. Of those 26 responding no to this question, two had comments (all comments in this article are arranged alphabetically by *city*). They are:

Gilroy, California: Vern Gardner wrote, "I would consider using a psychic, if it was a major case that had come to a standstill and the psychic had a good track record. I do have an open mind in this area."
Novi, Michigan: Douglas F. Shaeffer penned, "Any info obtained, from any source, must be independently evaluated and its value assessed."

Three of those responding yes to this question had the following comments:

Longview, Washington: Charles Harper commented that yes, his police department had used them in the past ("The psychics contacted us each time—we did not seek them out") but that they do not presently use them in solving investigations. Harper goes on to write: "The investigator must always keep in mind that a so-called psychic could be a person who is really a witness, offender or third party who has personal knowledge concerning the crime. Therefore, as in all cases witness credibility & their information must be verified & evaluated objectively."

Richland, Washington: David L. Lewis stated that his department had "used once, 13 years ago. Have not used since."

Sherman, Texas: J. D. Miller stated succinctly that he was "against all Psychic Info."

The other three respondents who replied yes had no special comments. The above three comments of those who had used psychics are *definitely not* an endorsement of them.

Question 2: If so, in which of the following categories?

Homicide	_____
Missing Persons	_____
Kidnapping	_____
Locating Stolen Property	_____
Other	_____
Specify	_____

Of those six police departments who had used them, all six listed homicide, three listed missing persons, and two checked kidnapping.

Question 3: Does your police department presently handle information received from a psychic any differently than information from an ordinary source?

Of the six smaller cities which had used psychics, four answered no to this question and the other two said yes.

As for statements, besides David L. Lewis' comment from Richland, Washington, "Have not used since (*in 13 years*)" (emphasis added), Sam S. Bowerman from Parkville, Maryland, wrote, "Basically handled the same, evaluate reliability of information, corroborate all details as they may relate to specific case."

Question 4a: If your department has used psychics, was the information received more helpful in solving the case than other information received?

Of those six having used psychics, all said no to this question. Bowerman of Parkville, Maryland, related that "information was not of significant help." Again, these responses are *not* a good endorsement of the use of psychics.

Question 4b: What kind of information was it and how was it used?

Of those six cities replying who had used psychics, five respondents gave permission to quote. They are as follows:

Longview, Washington: Charles Harper wrote: "In 1985 we had a highly publicized missing child case (which remains unsolved). Several psychics from across the U.S. 'contacted me' wanting to work on the case. Not one of them contributed any information or lead(s) that could be substantiated or followed up on. The motivation and intentions of several alleged psychics was questionable."

Parkview, Maryland: Sam Bowerman stated: "Psychic had description of suspects, location of where victim might be held captive, etc. This Psychic (actually person did not consider self psychic, 'he had visions') *was* very sincere, but information proved of no value."

Richland, Washington: David L. Lewis responded: "General, suspect profile information."

Sherman, Texas: J. D. Miller wrote: "Damness [sic] bunch of wrong information we have ever followed up on. After many hours of time wasted it was thrown away!"

Texarkana, Texas: Duke Schofield penned: "Vague descriptions of suspects and vehicles used in commission of crime. Routinely followed up."

Question 5: Do you personally consider information from a psychic more valuable than information received from a regular source?

Of the six cities who had used psychics, five responded no and the other (David L. Lewis of Richland, Washington) replied: "Don't know." Of the five "no" respondents, the only one to comment was Sam S. Bowerman of Parkville, Maryland. He wrote: "I evaluate the information as it relates to the investigation. The credibility of the source and reliability of their information may be easier to establish than that of a psychic. I consider *all* information *potentially* of value."

Table 1 is a complete listing, item by item, of the smaller-sized cities.

TABLE 1

Responses of Police Departments of Small Cities in America
(Y = Yes, N = No, C = Comment, H = Homicide, K = Kidnapping,
MP = Missing Persons, LSP = Locating Stolen Property,
DK = Do Not Know.)

City	Question 1	Question 2	Question 3	Question 4a	Question 4b	Question 5
Allen Park, Mich.	N	–	–	–	–	–
Auburn, N.Y.	N	–	–	–	–	–
Auburn, Wash.	N	–	–	–	–	–
East Cleveland, Ohio	N	–	N	–	–	N
Danville, Calif.	N	–	–	–	–	–
El Centro, Calif.	N	–	–	–	–	–
Fairborn, Ohio	N	–	N	–	–	–
Garden City, Mich.	N	–	–	–	–	N
Germantown, Tenn.	N	–	–	–	–	–
Gilroy, Calif.	N, C	–	–	–	–	–
Hanover Park, Ill.	N	–	–	–	–	–
Hendersonville, Tenn.	Y	H, MP, K	Y	N	C	N
Longview, Wash.	Y, C	H, MP	N	N	C	N
Manhattan Beach, Calif.	N	–	–	–	–	–
Manitowoc, Wis.	N	–	–	–	–	–
Mankato, Minn.	N	–	N	–	–	N
Marlborough, Mass.	N	–	–	–	–	–
Moorhead, Minn.	N	–	–	–	–	–
North Brunswick, N.J.	N	–	–	–	–	–
North Providence, R.I.	N	–	N	–	–	N
Northbrook, Ill.	N	–	–	–	–	–
Novi, Mich.	N, C	–	N	–	–	N
Parkville, Md.	Y	H, MP	N, C	N	C	N, C
Pekin, Ill.	N	–	N	–	–	N
Richland, Wash.	Y, C	H	N, C	N	C	DK
Sanford, Fla.	N	–	N	N	–	N
Sherman, Tex.	Y	H	N	N	C	N
Sierra Vista, Ark.	N	–	–	–	–	–
Spring, Tex.	N	–	–	–	–	–
Texarkana, Tex.	Y	H, K	N	N	C	N
Waipahu, Hawaii	N	–	–	–	–	–
Williamsport, Penn.	N	–	–	–	–	–

RESULTS OF MEDIUM-SIZED CITIES

Of the 75 medium-sized cities surveyed, 33 cities completed the questionnaire. One was returned for incorrect address and one was also returned unanswered from Santee, California, because it contracts its law enforcement with the Sheriff of San Diego County. Again, one would believe that a proponent of psychics would be more apt to complete the survey than an opponent, but this is speculation on our part.

Question 1: In the past, has your police department used psychics or does the department presently use them in solving investigations?

Of the 33 police departments responding, 24 answered no and nine answered yes. Thus, 73 percent of medium-sized cities responding have never used psychics. None of the nine respondents who had used psychics had any specific comments; however, two of the 24 who had answered no did. They are:

Owensboro, Kentucky: Jack Braden wrote: "I have not used a psychic in any investigation, although I wouldn't refuse any help in solving any crime in our city."

Yuma, Arizona: William D. Robinson offered: "We would not discount the use of psychics on major cases."

Question 2: If so, in which of the following categories?

Homicide	_____
Missing Persons	_____
Kidnapping	_____
Locating Stolen Property	_____
Other	_____
Specify	_____

Seven of the nine cities who had used psychics had used them in homicide cases and there was a total of five instances in the Missing Persons category. None of the other categories was mentioned.

Question 3: Does your police department presently handle information received from a psychic any differently than information from an ordinary source?

Of the nine respondents whose cities had used psychics, six answered no to this question, two answered yes, and one answered "possibly." Of the two who answered yes, no further explanation was given.

Question 4a: If your department has used psychics, was the information received more helpful in solving the case than other information received?

All nine cities who had used psychics answered no to this question! *Again, not a good endorsement of psychics.*

Question 4b: What kind of information was it and how was it used?

Three of those nine respondents gave permission to quote them on this question. They are:

Bellingham, Washington: Duane Schenck offered: "Locating the body in homicide case and also locating missing person."

Redford, Michigan: John L. Crete wrote: "Location of bodies—Description and/or names of perpetrators."

Vineland, New Jersey: Mario R. Brunetta, Jr., penned: "Information concerning perpetrator's description and actions. Information concerning location of body.

Question 5: Do you personally consider information from a psychic more valuable than information received from a regular source?

Of the nine cities answering this question, eight said no. The other respondent, Mario R. Brunetta, Jr., of Vineland, New Jersey, wrote: "This can not be answered by a yes or no. The information is followed up. If it is fruitful it is valuable. You do this in any lead." Table 2 is a complete item by item listing of the medium-sized cities.

CONCLUSION

This present study is even more damaging to the psychics' credibility with police departments than was the original study. Notwithstanding the claims of Galde and Truzzi mentioned earlier, rural police departments use psychics less than large cities. We question and challenge Galde ("Many more psychics are used in rural than urban cities . . .") and Truzzi ("Even though most previous evidence indicates that psychics have been used more often by rural than by urban police . . .") to document their claims.

If one looks at Table 3, which is the summary of both studies, one cannot help but draw the conclusion that psychics are definitely *not* helpful to either urban or rural police departments. In observing the summary results of Question 4a in Table 3, "Was the psychic information more helpful?" all 47 respondents to this question said no! Concerning Question 5 in Table 3, "Is psychic information more valuable?" of the 77 responding 72 said no, one said yes, and four had varying comments. These results are definitely not supportive of the psychics' positions or claims.

As for comments concerning the original study, both Truzzi and Galde

TABLE 2

Responses of Police Departments of Medium-Sized Cities in America
(Y = Yes, N = No, C = Comment, H = Homicide, K = Kidnapping,
MP = Missing Persons, LSP = Locating Stolen Property.)

City	Question 1	Question 2	Question 3	Question 4a	Question 4b	Question 5
Bellingham, Wash.	Y	H, MP	N	N	C	N
Bloomington, Ill.	N	-	N	-	-	N
Bossier City, La.	N	-	-	-	-	-
Bryan, Tex.	N	-	N	-	-	N
Burnsville, Minn.	N	-	N	-	-	N
Camarillo, Calif.	N	-	-	-	-	-
College Station, Tex.	N		-	-	-	-
Coon Rapids, Minn.	N	-	N	N	-	N
Danville, Va.	N	-	N	N	-	N
Edmond, Okla.	Y	H, C	Y	N	C	N
Gastonia, N.C.	N	-	-	-	-	-
Great Falls, Mont.	N	-	N	-	-	N
Irondequoit, N.Y.	Y	H	N	N	C	N
Janesville, Wis.	N	-	N	N	-	N
La Habra, Calif.	N	-	-	-	-	-
Malden, Mass.	N	C	Y	N	C	Y
Midwest City, Okla.	Y, C	H	N	N	C	N
Mount Prospect, Ill.	N	-	N	N	-	N
Owensboro, Ky.	N, C	-	Y	-	-	N
Penn Hills, Penn.	N	-	-	-	-	-
Rapid City, S.D.	N	-	N	-	-	N
Redford, Mich.	Y	H	Y	N	C	N
Roseville, Mich.	N	-	N	-	-	N
St. Charles, Mo.	N	-	N	-	-	N
Troy, N.Y.	Y	MP	N	N	-	N
Victoria, Tex.	Y	MP	N	N	-	N
Vineland, N.J.	Y	H, MP	C	N	C	C
West Bloomfield, Mich.	Y	H, MP	N	N	-	N
West Haven, Conn.	N	-	N	-	-	-
Weymouth, Mass.	N	-	-	-	-	-
Yakima, Wash.	N	-	N	-	-	N
Yorba Linda, Calif.	N	-	-	-	-	-
Yuma, Ariz.	N, C	-	-	-	-	-

write that the admission of 35 percent of police departments of their use of psychics is startling and remarkably extensive—is a misinterpretation. If one reads the comments of those departments, they for the most part make "startling" disclaimers.

One other point, as far the criticisms we received of the first study about the wording of our questionnaire: specifically in that we used the words "more helpful . . ." and "more valuable . . ." instead of "*as* helpful" or "*as* valuable," we remain convinced that the survey is not biased in its wording. We were trying to establish the degree of helpfulness from the psychic and the degree of the value of the information. Does not the

TABLE 3

Summary of Data of Small-Sized, Medium-Sized Cities in America

	No. of Cities Responding	"No"	"Yes"
Question 1: "Has your department used or is now presently using psychics?"	113	81 (72%)	32 (28%)
Question 2: (asked of the 32 answering yes to Question 1): "If so, which categories?"			
Homicide	28		
Missing Persons	18		
Kidnapping	3		
Sexual Assault	1		
Burglary	1		
Question 3: "Is information from psychics handled differently?"	77	64 (83%)*	12 (16%)
Question 4(a): "Was the psychic information more helpful?"	47	47 (100%)	0 (0%)
Question 5: "Is psychic information more valuable?"	77	72 (94%)**	1 (1.3%)

*One respondent wrote "possibly."

**One respondent answered, "Sometimes"; one said, "Depends on which psychic"; one penned, "Don't know"; and one wrote "This cannot be answered by a yes or no. . . ."

use of a comparative word, such as "more," cause the respondent to think in comparative terms? We did this simply to establish the degree of reference and were not trying to elicit negating responses. Furthermore, Webster (ninth edition) defines "more" as: "to a greater or higher degree—often used with an adjective or adverb to form the comparative." Thus, since psychics claim to have extraordinary ("greater" or "higher") powers, the wording "as helpful" or "as valuable" does not seem justified.

The results of this study and the original study stand on their own merit; they need no further justification.

REFERENCES

Galde, P. 1993. "I See By the Papers." *FATE,* April, pp. 5–6.

Mattson, M. T. 1992. *Atlas of the 1990 Census.* New York: Macmillan Publishing Company.

Sweat, J. A., and M. W. Durm. "Psychics: Do Police Departments Really Use Them?" *Skeptical Inquirer* 17, no. 2 (Winter 1993): 148–58.

Truzzi, M. "Letters to the Editor." *Skeptical Inquirer* 17, no. 4 (Summer 1993): 445–46.

Appendix E

Psychic Detectives: A Critical Examination*

Walter F. Rowe

A casual reader of American newspapers and supermarket tabloids would draw the conclusion that American law-enforcement agencies routinely consult "psychics." Such a reader might be excused for wondering how criminals can hope to escape detection in the face of so much paranormal firepower. Digging a little deeper, our reader would even find learned treatises advocating the police use of psychics and recounting the amazing successes of these "psychic detectives." So the case for psychic detectives is conclusively proved? I don't think so.

PSYCHICS VERSUS THE RECORD

In 1989, I collaborated with two graduate students in the Department of Forensic Sciences at George Washington University on a critical examination of the purported achievements of so-called psychic detectives. My colleagues were both members of the U.S. Army Military Police Corps. Captain Eric L. Provost is now executive officer of the U.S. Army Criminal Investigation Laboratory in Camp Zama, Japan. Chief Warrant Officer Jeanette Clark is a U.S. Army Criminal Investigation Division (CID) investigator with many years' experience in criminal investigations. We

*This article is reprinted by permission from *Skeptical Inquirer* 17, no. 2 (Winter 1993): 159–65.

decided to concentrate on psychics who had been recently active in the United States; my colleagues would contact police officials who had supposedly worked with the psychic detectives and solicit their candid appraisal of the contributions the psychics made to their investigations. The psychic detectives chosen for evaluation were selected mainly from the works of Charles R. Farabee (1981) and Whitney S. Hibbard and Raymond W. Worring (1982), along with others whose abilities have been touted in newspapers and popular magazines. In some cases, we were also able to interview the psychic detectives themselves and obtain samples of their press clippings.

Many of the false claims regarding the psychic abilities of Peter Hurkos have been exposed by Piet Hein Hoebens (1985). Hurkos provided American police with information in major cases, such as the Boston Strangler case (which Norma Lee Browning's *The Psychic World of Peter Hurkos* credits Hurkos with solving) and the Sharon Tate murders. In fact, Hurkos did not solve the Boston Strangler case, and the information he provided in the Sharon Tate murders was not merely useless but also hopelessly incorrect. According to Ed Sanders in his book *The Family:*

> Mr. Hurkos crouched down in the bloodstained living room, picking up the vibes. . . . After his void-scan Mr. Hurkos announced that "three men killed Sharon Tate and her four friends and I know who they are. I have identified the killers to the police and told them that these three men must be stopped soon. Otherwise, they will kill again."

The facts are that only three of the victims could reasonably have been called friends of Sharon Tate. The remaining victim was visiting the caretaker and was killed because he happened on the crime in progress. More important, the killers were two women and one man (a third woman acted as lookout). The killers were already in police custody (although not for the Tate murders). Nor was the Sharon Tate murder case Hurkos' only abject failure. According to Detective John Schaeffer of the Chicago Police, whom we had contacted about another psychic detective, Hurkos became unwelcome among the wealthy Chicagoans on whom he "sponged" after he failed to solve a $60,000 burglary committed against his hosts.

Piet Hein Hoebens has also discredited many of the cases allegedly solved by Gerald Croiset in Holland and elsewhere in Europe. We were able to examine one of Croiset's rare American cases. Hibbard and Worring (1982) claim that Croiset successfully located the missing daughter of the chairman of the Political Science Department at the University of Kansas. We contacted Paul Schumaker, the present department chairman, and Earl

Nehring, Schumaker's predecessor. Nehring became chairman in 1972 and had worked in the department for many years prior to that time. Neither Schumaker nor Nehring had heard of any such missing-child case.

Marinus Dykshorn is another Dutch psychic detective. He is credited by Hibbard and Worring with having aided North Carolina State Police in four murder cases. Unfortunately, there is no such organization as the North Carolina State Police. Detective Bill Doubty of the North Carolina *State Bureau of Investigation* (who has been with the bureau for 20 years) has never heard of a psychic named Dykshorn; furthermore, to the best of his knowledge the bureau has never requested the aid of a psychic.

Irene F. Hughes and Beverly C. Jaegers are two other psychic detectives mentioned by Hibbard and Worring. Detective John Schaeffer of the Chicago Police informed us that Hughes was infamous for providing unsolicited information about unsolved crimes and that law-enforcement officers in the Chicago area regarded her information as being without value. Beverly Jaegers has supposedly organized psychic detectives to work on cases throughout the United States. Although Hibbard and Worring give her place of residence as Creve Coeur, Missouri, the Creve Coeur Police Department had never heard of Jaegers and the local telephone directory has no listing for either "Beverly Jaegers" or "B. Jaegers." John Catchings, whose work as a psychic detective I discuss below, informed us that he had once met Jaegers, but had not heard from her in 12 or 15 years. Moreover, she had never approached him to join any organization.

Dorothy Allison is a New Jersey psychic who provided police with information in the Atlanta child-murders. More recently, she was apparently contacted by the Fairfax County Police in the Melissa Brannen abduction. Whether she provided any information to Fairfax police in this instance is not known at this time; however, despite the conviction of Caleb Hughes for Melissa's abduction, Melissa Brannen remains missing. As to Allison's claim to have aided in solving the Atlanta child-murders case, she provided police with 42 different names, none of which was Wayne or Williams. Wayne Williams was apprehended purely as the result of police surveillance of the bridges over the Chattahoochee River, where Williams was disposing of his victims. We did not contact Allison directly; however, Jeanette Clark interviewed Detective Salvatore Lubertazzi, the Nutley, New Jersey, police officer who has worked as Allison's liaison with police for 15 years. He helps police interpret Allison's visions. Lubertazzi added that because Allison works on so many cases she sometimes confuses visions.

John Catchings claims to have located 12 bodies and caused the arrest of 13 people. He claims, however, that his visions are used in conjunction with a commonsense investigation into the circumstances of the case. Law-enforcement officers we contacted felt he had been of significant help in solving cases.

PSYCHICS IN THE DARK

Despite what tabloid writers might have us believe, law-enforcement officials do not always react positively to information provided by psychics. The cases of Brett Cadorette and Steven Paul Linscott illustrate rather hardheaded responses to information volunteered to police by would-be psychics.

Brett Cadorette volunteered to police that he had had psychic visions of the throat slashing and sexual abuse of a Staten Island, New York, woman. He described the victim clutching a clump of hair in her hand (a fact not made public by police spokespersons). Police made Cadorette the prime suspect of their investigations, and he was ultimately convicted of attempted murder.

Steven Linscott, of Oak Park, Illinois, volunteered to police details of a dream he claimed to have had about the death of Karen Anne Phillips, who had been sexually assaulted, beaten, and strangled to death. Police in the course of their investigations routinely questioned Linscott (who lived with his wife in Phillips' apartment house complex). Linscott related to police a dream he had purportedly had on the night of the murder. According to Linscott's dream, the victim had been beaten in a downward fashion, and the victim and the assailant had been spattered with blood. He described the murder scene as the living room (correct) of a two-bedroom apartment (incorrect); he saw a couch in the living room (incorrect). He described the victim as black (incorrect). Linscott was arrested and prosecuted for Phillips' murder. Scientific tests found Linscott's hair to be consistent with that left by the murderer. Serological tests showed that the assailant was either an O secretor (like the victim) or a nonsecretor; Linscott proved to be an AB nonsecretor.

Linscott was convicted; however, his conviction was overturned on the grounds of the prosecutor's prejudicial misrepresentations of the scientific evidence. The Linscott case was resolved on July 27, 1992, when all charges against him were dismissed. DNA profiling of semen found in the victim precluded Linscott's being the perpetrator.

INVESTIGATION OF A D.C. PSYCHIC

The March 15, 1991, *Washington Times* reported that local psychic Ann Gehman had helped an Alexandria, Virginia, family find the body of Festus Harris, who had disappeared while on a visit to friends about a week earlier. The story quoted a family member who said Gehman had had a vision of "a bridge, a garage . . . with lots of traffic." Harris' body was found in a small wooded area in the 1900 block of N. Van Dorn Street near the Ramada Inn. The article further stated:

> Mrs. Gehman is a nationally known psychic who has aided police in a number of high-profile murder cases, including one that led to the conviction of notorious serial killer Ted Bundy in Florida.

I contacted the article's author, Michael Cromwell, at the *Washington Times*' Alexandria bureau. He told me that he was somewhat skeptical of the claims made for Gehman; the background information used in the article was provided by her, and he had made no effort to verify it.

I subsequently interviewed Gehman over the telephone regarding this case. She told me that she had been contacted by Harris' niece and her husband or brother (she did not remember which). At that point Harris had been missing approximately one week, the family had combed the neighborhood without success, and the police had not been able to help. The niece had been referred to Gehman by a co-worker.

When queried about the information she had when consulted by Harris' niece, Gehman stated that she knew that the niece lived in Alexandria; the niece also brought (per Gehman's request) two photographs of her uncle and an article of clothing, a sweatshirt. Gehman stated that she had a feeling of Harris wandering. In her vision she saw a high-rise building and had a sense that Harris had been on the sixth floor. She next saw Harris with a person in uniform and at a telephone booth. She had a sense of a parking lot or garage. Finally, she could see Harris near a bridge and could hear traffic in the background.

Gehman claimed that all of the information in her vision had been confirmed. She further observed that often her visions don't provide her with any information at all.

Gehman said she came from an Amish background and had grown up in Michigan. Formerly, she lived near Orlando, Florida. While living in Florida she had (she claimed) worked on the Ted Bundy case, specifically on the disappearance of Bundy's last victim, Kimberly Leach. Gehman said she had told investigators where to find the victim's body. She said she had described Bundy's appearance and that of his car and had informed investigators that Bundy was using stolen credit cards. One of the investigators she worked with in this case, she asserted, was an FBI agent. Gehman seemed reluctant to discuss other cases, claiming that this information was filed away and not readily accessible. She also could not provide me with newspaper clippings describing her involvement in other cases. I pointed out that other psychic detectives (such as Ginette Matacia) had such "press kits." She laughed and said that she was skeptical of many of the claims of the better-known psychic detectives. She feels that many exaggerate their abilities. At the conclusion of our interview, Gehman said she would contact Harris' niece and see if she would talk with me. (The niece was not named in the article, and Gehman declined to provide me with her telephone number.) Harris' niece has still not contacted me.

The numerous hits in Gehman's vision became less impressive when I visited the site where Harris's body was found. This part of Alexandria has numerous high-rise apartments and parking lots. In fact, on the east side of I-395 high-rises and parking lots alternate for several miles. There are also numerous bridges, some spanning I-395 and others carrying I-395 over streets or streams. As might be expected, I-395 and the neighboring streets carry heavy volumes of traffic. Given the environment in which Harris disappeared, the only features of the vision that turn out to be remarkable are the reference to the sixth floor of the high-rise, the attempted telephone call, and the person in uniform. As I have not been able to interview Harris' niece I have not been able to confirm that these were indeed hits. Given that one of the niece's co-workers is acquainted with Gehman, nonparanormal explanations for these hits come to mind.

Significantly, in her vision Gehman did not see the large red Ramada Inn sign within a few feet of the site where Harris' body was found.

It is possible to evaluate at least some of Gehman's other claims. As for her claim to have worked with an FBI agent in the Ted Bundy case, the FBI does not solicit information from psychics and classifies psychics as unreliable sources. While it may be true that in the Ted Bundy case she provided police with information, her information certainly did not aid in either the apprehension of Bundy or the recovery of the body of Kimberly Leach. Gehman is not mentioned in either Ann Rule's *The Stranger beside Me* or Stephen Michaud and Hugh Aynsworth's *The Only Living Witness,* two detailed accounts of Ted Bundy's criminal career. Bundy was apprehended when a police officer spotted the car he was driving coming out of a restaurant parking lot late one evening. Curious to identify the driver of the car, the officer followed Bundy and radioed in a routine check on the car's license-plate number. When the officer learned that the car was stolen, he gave chase and ultimately subdued Bundy after a struggle.

The recovery of Kimberly Leach's body was the result of good forensic work, not psychic detection. According to Ann Rule:

> When the Dodge van [in which Kimberly had been abducted] was processed, criminalists had taken samples of soil, leaves and bark found inside and caught in its undercarriage. Botanists and soil experts had identified the dirt as coming from somewhere close to a north Florida river.

The discovery of a pile of Winston cigarette butts near the entrance to Suwanee River State Park had focused police attention on the state park and its environs as a possible search area. The ashtray of Bundy's stolen car had also contained Winston cigarettes. A careful ground search of the forests surrounding the park led to the discovery of Kimberly's body under an abandoned shed. The absence of any references in Rule's book to psychics' helping police apprehend Bundy or find his last victim is significant; Rule professes to believe in ESP, and elsewhere in the book relates the (unsuccessful) attempts of psychics to aid police in solving the murders Bundy committed in the Pacific Northwest.

A FINAL NOTE

Lady Wonder has gone down in history as the horse that got Joseph Banks Rhine interested in investigating psychic phenomena. Less commonly known is the fact that the horse was also a psychic detective. In 1952 she was asked to locate a missing boy. As was her wont, she spelled out her answer by touching lettered blocks with her nose. "Pittsfield Water Wheel," she replied to the police chief's query. After the water wheel had been searched without success, the police chief realized (in the words of Bergen Evans) that Lady Wonder had made "an equinopsychical blunder or horsegraphical error." He then made the perfectly obvious correction to "Field and Wilde's water pit," the name of an abandoned quarry near the boy's home. The boy's drowned body was ultimately recovered from the flooded quarry. Unfortunately, this case bears a striking resemblance to most of the cases of purported psychic detection. There was a strong will to believe on the part of police authorities and a fiddling of the evidence to make the psychic's prediction come out right.

A SHORT ANNOTATED BIBLIOGRAPHY

Obviously, a complete bibliography of articles on purported psychic detectives would cover many pages, particularly if all tabloid articles were cited. This list is restricted to writings that purport to be scholarly rather than sensationalized.

Farabee, Charles R. "Contemporary Pyschic Use by Police in America." Master's thesis, University of Southern California at Fresno, 1981. This thesis, written for the Department of Criminal Justice, is chiefly remarkable for accepting as veridical tabloid accounts of psychic detectives. The level of "scholarship" of this author is indicated by his repeating a claim that Julia Grant, the wife of Ulysses S. Grant, had psychic powers and that the reason the Grants did not attend Ford's Theater with President and Mrs. Lincoln was that Mrs. Grant had had a premonition of danger. Farabee's source cited for this claim was noted Civil War historian Bruce Catton. Had Farabee consulted Catton's *Grant Takes Command,* he would have learned that Julia Grant's reluctance to attend the theater with the presidential party stemmed from her presence about a month earlier at one of Mary Lincoln's memorable tantrums; Julia Grant was also concerned because she believed that she had been under surveillance by a strange man most of the day.

Hibbard, Whitney S., and Raymond W. Worring. *Psychic Criminology.* Springfield, Ill.: Charles C. Thomas, 1982. This is similar to the Farabee work mentioned above. The level of scholarship is reflected by references to *New Times, People, Psychic Magazine,* and *Self-Help Update.* Although the publishing house is well known for its catalogue of forensic science and police texts, this work is indistinguishable in quality from pulp potboilers.

Hoebens, Piet Hein. "Reflections on Psychic Sleuths." In *A Skeptic's Handbook of Parapsychology,* ed. by Paul Kurtz. Buffalo, N.Y.: Prometheus Books, 1985. This contains exposures of Peter Hurkos and Gerald Croiset. Readers of the *Skeptical Inquirer* will be familiar with Hoebens's two-part exposé of the shameless promotion of Croiset's "miracles," *Skeptical Inquirer* 6 (1, 2), Fall 1981 and Winter 1981-82.

Lyons, Arthur, and Marcello Truzzi. *The Blue Sense: Psychic Detectives and Crime.* New York: Mysterious Press, 1991. An interesting if ultimately unsuccessful attempt to evaluate objectively the claims of psychic detectives. I am less impressed than the authors with the sincerity of some of the psychics discussed. I do endorse this comment by the authors: "The data are simply inadequate for the refined analysis we need. The major problem is the absence of a proper baseline against which we can judge any claims of success, especially a lack of information about the character and number of both successes and failures by psychic detectives." In the light of this assessment of the state of evidence, the authors' discussion of the legal ramifications of psychic powers seems premature, to say the least.

Marshall, Eliot. "Police Science and Psychics." *Science* 210 (1980) :994-95. This article discusses Dorothy Allison's claims in the Atlanta child-murders case as well as Martin Reiser's research.

Reiser, Martin, et al. "An Evaluation of the Use of Psychics in the Investigation of Major Crimes." *Journal of Police Science and Administration* 7, no. 1 (1979): 18–25.

Reiser, Martin, and N. Klyver. "A Comparison of Psychics, Detectives and Students in the Investigation of Major Crimes." In *Police Psychology: Collected Papers,* ed. by Martin Reiser. Los Angeles: LEHI Publishing, 1982. Reiser's research involved presenting psychic detectives with items of evidence from major cases. The psychics did not score better than detectives or students.

Index